Arabs and Nubians in New Halfa

Arabs and Nubians in New Halfa

A Study of Settlement and Irrigation

Muneera Salem-Murdock

University of Utah Press
Salt Lake City
1989

Library of Congress Cataloging-in-Publication Data

Salem-Murdock, Muneera.
    Arabs and Nubians in New Halfa : a study of settlement &
irrigation / Muneera Salem-Murdock.
        p.   cm.
    Bibliography: p.
    Includes index.
    ISBN 0-87480-310-1
    1. Agriculture — Economic aspects — Sudan — Halfā ' al-Jadīdah.
2. Irrigation — Sudan — Halfā ' al-Jadīdah. 3. Land settlement — Sudan —
Halfā ' al-Jadīdah. 4. Halfā ' al-Jadīdah (Sudan) — Economic
conditions. 5. Arabs — Sudan — Halfā ' al-Jadīdah. 6. Nubians — Sudan —
Halfā ' al-Jadīdah.   I. Title.
HD2123.5.Z9H347   1989
338.1'09629 — dc19   88-23246
                                                                CIP

Contents

LIST OF MAPS

LIST OF TABLES

Foreword

Michael M Horowitz

In his recent discussion of irrigation systems in Africa, Philip Woodhouse (1988:29) notes how unaware water engineers and agronomists are of the socioeconomic organization of the large-scale government-sponsored schemes they plan and manage: "irrigation systems are designed by engineers, operated by agriculturalists, and evaluated by social scientists," ostensibly without reading each others' reports. While these big schemes continue to be the centerpieces of development in many African countries, there is an extraordinary lack of detailed understanding of how they function. As Thayer Scudder (1988:45) tells us, "irrigation in Africa . . . appears to have polarized supporters and critics alike, with the former underestimating problems and the latter underestimating potential." Despite the huge amount of money that has been invested in research and evaluation — more than $50,000,000 in the Senegal Valley alone — such fundamental gaps remain that it has rarely if ever been possible to base development action on a sound foundation of knowledge.

Nowhere is this truer than in the Sudan, whose 1.7 million hectares of irrigated land exceeds the total irrigated land of all the rest of sub-Saharan Africa. Thus, this analysis of the socioeconomy of settlement on the New Halfa Scheme in eastern Sudan is all the more welcome, as a contribution both to Middle Eastern and African ethnology and to rural and agricultural development policy and praxis.

A number of people have studied government-sponsored irrigated farms in the Sudan (Barnett 1977; Sørbø 1985). Muneera Salem-Murdock's examination of individual and household economies complements these studies by detailing the considerable variety of adaptive strategies on the New Halfa Scheme. Aided by her native fluency in Arabic, Salem-Murdock does not so much present the material from

New Halfa as she allows Scheme residents to present themselves. The study achieves an intimacy with the population that is rare in modern anthropology, for the optic is neither that of the inside member of the society, for whom the originality of the situation is often obscured, nor that of the expatriate European or American anthropologist, alien to the subject language and culture. The author grew up in a Middle Eastern environment with cousinly links to the Sudan, a kinship that was acknowledged and embraced by Scheme residents and Corporation officials.

Salem-Murdock emphasizes the case study method and situational and transactive analysis, which remain anthropology's most effective tools for illuminating differentiation within communities. Although almost all Scheme residents are tenants, there is considerable variation among them: they include Arabs, Nubians, and members of other ethnic groups; some have a good deal of formal education, others have a bit, and some have none; they may own land in addition to their tenancies, may have accumulated many tenancies, or may have lost the tenancy they originally received; they live by farming, trading, or raising livestock. Certain aspects of life separate people by gender, by generation, and by social class. Some residents are doing very well on the Scheme, some get by from year to year, and some do very poorly.

Salem-Murdock lets people speak for themselves, without artificially "averaging out the differences" and thereby giving a false picture of homogeneity; she provides us with an understanding of the complexities of agricultural decision making and of the causes of social differentiation and its relevance for economic performance on the New Halfa Scheme today. She reaffirms the critical discovery that an evaluation of the macro-performance of a large-scale development scheme is not simply the aggregate performance of its constituent production units. The fact that the Scheme itself might have failed to achieve production targets or anticipated financial rates-of-return does not necessarily imply that some people, both residents and others within the Scheme's area of influence, have not markedly improved their pre-Scheme standards of living. On the other hand, neither does an attractive macro-level performance necessarily imply that the majority of tenants are benefiting from it.

Muneera Salem-Murdock has persuasively demonstrated the power of participant-observation, of the contribution that field anthropology has to make to the design and implementation, as well as to the evaluation, of relocation projects based on large-scale irrigated production. Her work should help lead to a modification of Woodhouse's observation cited above: irrigation systems should be designed, operated, and evaluated by engineers, agriculturalists, social scientists, and, above all, by the people who will reside on them.

Acknowledgments

Field research for this book and the dissertation that preceded it was supported by a generous grant from the Social Science Research Council, and supplementary grants from the Wenner-Gren Foundation for Anthropological Research and the Institute for Development Anthropology. The writing of the book was facilitated by a two-month sabbatical from the Institute for Development Anthropology. All support received is greatly appreciated.

This book owes a great deal to so many people that I cannot mention them all by name. My first debt is to Dr. Michael Horowitz, my teacher, most beloved friend, colleague, and mentor. He was often hard but thoughtful, very demanding but helpful. The pages that follow bear witness to his generous contributions to my work.

Dr. Thayer Scudder, who is not only an authority on river basin development but also a conscientious and dear friend, has thoroughly read the long and often tedious earlier versions of this book and made valuable comments and suggestions. I thank Vivian Carlip for very careful reading and editing. I also wish to thank Drs. Richard Antoun, Audrey Smedley, and Edward Weisband, all of the State University of New York, Dr. Michael Cernea of the World Bank, and Dr. ʿAbdel Ghaffar Muhamed Ahmed of the University of Khartoum, who invited me to do this study and provided continuous assistance while I was in the field.

I can acknowledge by name only a small sample of all the wonderful people in New Halfa who helped make this study possible. In the New Halfa Agricultural Production Corporation I wish to thank Dr. Sayyid ʿUsman Sid Ahmed and his wife Muneera, Muʿtasim Bayazid and his wife Suʿad, Fahmi as-Sayyigh and his wife Fatma, Ramsees Mikhael and his wife Rita, and ʿUmar Habibullah and his wife Fatma. I also wish to thank all the section and block managers, agricultural inspectors, and field personnel.

I also thank the officers of the New Halfa Farmers' Union, especially Shaikh Ibrahim Ma'ouda, Muhamed al-Hasan 'Atiyatullah, Shaikh Mahmoud at-Tirik, 'Abdel Majid Hasan, Muhamed al-Hardallou, and Ibrahim an-Nour. In New Halfa town I wish to thank Zahra at-Tayyib, the assistant commissioner, and all her colleagues at the Town Council, and Hanim Shawqi and Drs. Leila and Victor Zaki, who made my stay in the area so very pleasant. At the University of Khartoum I wish to thank Drs. Ibrahim al-Hardallou, Sadiq Rashid, Muhamed Hasan Salih, and Muhamed al-Hadi Abu Sin. At the Central Record Office I wish to thank Dr. Muhamed Ibrahim Abu Salim and Mr. Mubarak Sirri 'Umar.

My deepest thanks go to the Shukriya and Halfawis of the study area for their kindness and hospitality, especially 'Abdel Latif Talsam (Beebe) and his wife Asma, who was more than a sister to me and a mother to my daughter Tamara; to my research assistants in Village Eighteen, Khamsa Arab, and Sufiya-j-Jadida; to Shaikh Muhamed Hamad Abu Sin, the former nazir of the Butana; to as-Sadiq wad al-Halal, a beautiful poet; to 'Ali Dakin, his wife Fatma, and their baby daughter Muneera; to Muhamed wad an-Nimir and his wife Sittana, who made her home mine; to al-'Ashshai and his family; and to al-Hadi Abu Sin and Shaikh 'Adlan on the Butana, my honorary father.

My final thanks go to my dear friends Joseph Whitney and Diana Baxter, who provided us with a home away from home during our brief excursions to Khartoum.

Note on Transliteration and Arabic Words

Transliteration of Arabic and Turkish consonants in this book follows the main lines of the system used in the *International Journal of Middle East Studies*, except for omission of the diacritical mark below the line (on h, s, d, t, z). Initial (but not medial and final hamzas have been omitted, as have all diacritical marks to indicate long vowels.

Arabic words are underlined and followed by an English translation the first time they appear in the text. The glossary at the end of the book includes only words that reappear.

1

Introduction

It is 3:30 in the morning in the Nubian village. The heat of the previous day, after stubbornly refusing to leave, finally retreats from an early morning breeze. The only restless creatures in the still night are the insatiable mosquitoes, always hungry for human blood. The village is cloaked with darkness under a beautifully adorned sky. The crowing of impatient roosters, waiting for their early morning feeding, occasionally pierces the stillness, and a few hungry dogs bark.

At 4 the voice of the *imam* (prayer leader) is heard from the mosque, instructing villagers that praying is more rewarding than sleeping. The village starts to wake up. Muna drags herself out of bed reluctantly, since she finally fell asleep only a few hours earlier. Her husband Malik is going to New Halfa market, about seven kilometers away, to unload his first carful of melons, prepared the evening before. Muna walks into the kitchen and places a pot of water on the gas stove for the early morning tea. Malik has a long day ahead of him; he has been working so hard, she thinks. Is it really worth it? she wonders, as she removes from the refrigerator a large container of milk, which their shepherd brought to the house the night before. When the freezer they ordered finally arrives, she will be able to keep a whole slaughtered sheep at home, instead of having to wait daily for Malik's return from the market before she can start food preparation. She thanks God that it is the long rainy season school recess; her daughters will help with the heavy daily chores, and her husband, a teacher as well as a farmer, will not need to rush off to school after having worked continuously for several hours.

In the same Nubian village, Farida and Wasfa are trying to light fires in their courtyards. After long moments of puffing and fanning, the fires are finally lit and large pots of water are placed on to boil.

Their husbands, landless farmers, earn their livings from wage labor, sharecropping, and renting land. Hilmi, Wasfa's husband, washes up in leisurely fashion, puts on a clean *galabiyya* (robe), and walks to the mosque to perform his morning prayer. He meets Hamid, Farida's husband, and the two men exchange village gossip as they walk together to the mosque. Wasfa and her daughters meanwhile put the final touches on a few sacks of vegetables picked from their rented field the evening before, which Hilmi will carry to the New Halfa market. Hilmi comes home, changes into his old galabiyya, drinks a quick glass of sweet tea with milk, and rushes to the village bus stop in order not to miss the truck that will carry him and his load to the market. Hamid returns home and plays with his baby daughter as he drinks his tea. When Farida brings him breakfast, he asks her to leave the children with her mother so that she can stay on the farm and weed.

In an Arab village on the Scheme some twenty-five kilometers distant from New Halfa, Sittana sits in front of her hut. Having prepared her tea on a fire made from wood collected the evening before, she contentedly sips the sweet concoction and thinks of the day ahead. Salim Asad, her husband, sits with her. They listen to the latest gossip related by her brother, who has just arrived from the Butana.[1] A cousin's senior wife spilled a bowl of milk on her co-wife's head, pretending it was an accident. The junior wife, very offended, went back to her father's. On learning what happened, the cousin, who had been away from the camp at the time of the incident, walked into the senior wife's tent and beat her. Without delay, she gathered her things and also ran to her father's. The poor man is alone without a wife to take care of him; neither woman wants to come back. Sittana's brother also brought with him the unwelcome news that the rains have not yet reached Central Butana. The herds are still watered from permanent wells. The grass is gone; animals are dying.

---

[1] The Butana is an area of eastern Sudan defined by the Nile on the west, the Atbara River on the east, ad-Damir on the north, and Qadaref and Fau on the southeast and south and divided into four regions: Western, Central, Eastern, and Suthern Butana (Barbour 1961:215–218). The New Halfa Agricultural Scheme was constructed on Central Butana, on part of the grazing lands of the Shukriya and other eastern Sudan pastoral groups.

Salim Asad is waiting to sow sorghum in his wheat tenancy. He wonders if irrigation water will arrive in the northern part of the Scheme today and he will be able to start cultivating. He and Sittana decide that if the water does not reach them in the next few days, he will sow the seeds in dry ground, hoping that a good rain will fall soon. Sittana thinks of the early days of the Scheme, when water was plentiful and production was good, and wonders why fortune deserted them. They have sold off most of their animals and have invested capital in building their hut, so she resigns herself to the fact that a return to the Butana is very unlikely, as much as she would like to resume pastoral life. Sittana thinks of her son the soldier and hopes he will be able to visit them soon. The few pounds that he usually gives his parents during these visits would surely help.

Fatna sits in front of her hut with other women of the lineage. ᶜAli, her husband, is drinking tea with the men in the lineage guest house. Fatna is expecting a baby. She feels sorry that she has not been able to help ᶜAli in the field lately and will not be able to do so for some time after delivery. Although this is her fifth pregnancy, Fatna is nevertheless apprehensive. Her friends, who share her fears, joke about it. In the guest house, the men wonder what went wrong with the Scheme: why has something with so much promise ended so poorly for so many?

Suᶜad brings a pot of tea to her husband Ibrahim's hut. Since several men are with him, she does not enter but calls a little boy to carry the tray for her. She knows that Ibrahim will stop in his new wife's hut to say good-bye, but she is comforted by the fact that he spent last night with her.[2] Ibrahim is on his way to Kassala to accompany a formal delegation and to pay a social visit to his brother, a new regional minister.

On the Butana, Awad el-Karim and Ahmed stand on top of the last functioning well, laboriously drawing water for their skinny, suffering animals. They look up at the sky momentarily, wondering when that cloud carrying badly needed rain will finally arrive. Meanwhile, Ahmed's son sits in his university office in Khartoum, preparing material for an upcoming conference in Europe.

---

[2] Although ideally a husband should divide his favors equally among his wives, in reality both Shukriya and Halfawi men usually spend a disproportionate amount of time with one of the wives, often the youngest.

THE PROBLEM

This study explores the transformation of an eastern Sudanese society from a basically domestic mode of production, in which agrarian and pastoral products were consumed primarily by the producing households themselves, to a capitalist mode of production, in which the products of the farms and pastures are commodities for exchange. In this process, the elements of production — land, labor, and capital (including livestock) — themselves have increasingly become commodities. The process began before the introduction of the large-scale agricultural development Scheme, although at a much slower pace. It is proceeding now and is clearly not complete, for many elements in the domestic mode of production endure, such as pooling of labor beyond the household itself (under certain circumstances). Yet even this is retreating before a full monetarization of labor.

Within the larger framework of economic transformation, two themes, increasingly debated, are addressed here. The first is the issue of rural development — in this case, the differential impacts on local populations of large-scale, capital-intensive irrigated agricultural development projects (e.g., Adegboro 1983; Barnett 1977; Dey 1980; Heinritz 1980; Pearson 1980; Sørbø 1977a, 1977b, 1985). The second theme, which has become a major concern of many social scientists (e.g., Barlett 1977, 1980, 1982; Chibnik 1980; Deere and de Janvry 1979; Ortiz 1979; Wood 1981), is agricultural decision making.

The people are Nubian/Halfawi farmers and Shukriya/Arab herders who have been brought together on the New Halfa Agricultural Scheme in eastern Sudan. In 1959, Egypt and the Sudan concluded a treaty on water use, replacing an agreement of 1929. Under the terms of the new agreement, which provided for construction of the Aswan High Dam in Egypt and the consequent flooding of the Wadi Halfa region, the Sudan's annual offtake of Nile waters was increased from 4×10^9 cubic meters to $18.5 \times 10^9 \text{m}^3$. With Egyptian financial help, the Sudanese drew on this new resource by damming the highly seasonal Atbara River, a Nile tributary, and establishing the New Halfa Agricultural Scheme. The lands brought under irrigation were planted in cotton and groundnuts to increase export earnings, and in wheat and sugar to reduce dependence on imports.

The flooding of Wadi Halfa forced the evacuation of some 50,000 Sudanese, most of them Nubians, and the New Halfa Scheme was envisaged for their resettlement. Yet, as is so often the case where people are forced to relocate, the land chosen for their settlement was not without prior claimants. The western banks of the Atbara River constituted part of the traditional grazing lands of the Shukriya, an Arabic-speaking tribe of pastoral herders. Given the ideology of the times that regarded the sedentarization of "nomads" as a progressive act (Abou-Zeid 1959; Amiran and Ben-Arieh 1963; Asad, Cunnison, and Hill 1966; Awad 1954; Musham 1959; UNESCO 1959), and the need to provide some compensation to people deprived of their dry season pasture and rainfed *wadi* (riverbed) lands, incorporation of the Shukriya and other pastoralists into the Scheme seemed a natural event.

AGRICULTURAL DECISION MAKING

The ineffectiveness of "normative" or "jural" models of social structure in dealing with nonunilineal descent groups, nondescent kin groups, and other groups and networks prompted many anthropologists to search for a more dynamic model to explain group composition and formation (Leach 1961). Keesing (1967) advocated an actor-oriented decision model that explained norms as the aggregate of decisions, defined by a "range of culturally acceptable alternative courses of action in [a given] situation" (1967:2), by many different individuals who form kin units and groups and who are primarily interested in self-promotion. Anthropologists used decision-making models to account for social change (Barth 1967), household economics (Barlett 1977; Ortiz 1967, 1973), and litigation (Quinn 1973). From an initial satisfaction with the ability of the model to describe the process of decision making, some anthropologists sought to explore its predictive value (Horowitz 1967).

Recently, the models have been used in studying the impact of farmers' decisions and choices on agricultural production and rural development (Barlett 1980, 1982). Starting from the premise that small agricultural producers are neither irrational nor tradition bound (Barlett 1980:3), and going beyond the substantivist-formalist controversy of the 1950s and 1960s (Dalton 1961; Leclair and Schneider 1968; Polanyi 1957), researchers have explored various aspects of agricultural decision making: how decisions are made; what influences them; and what impact they have on the decisions of others and on the larger economic and social arena.

The agricultural decision-making component of this study does not dramatically depart from the work of other researchers. It follows an actor-oriented analysis that stresses individual differentiation within a common framework of socioeconomic institutions (Barlett 1982). Although many factors—household composition, natural environment, national and international prices—are germane, access to resources is the most crucial factor, determining success and failure and shaping the labor strategies of New Halfa tenants and inhabitants. Contrary to a once popular view that rural populations in developing countries are uniformly poor, a large degree of social differentiation exists among agricultural and rural households. Differential access to land and wealth greatly influences the kind of production and exchange decisions that are made.

On the New Halfa Scheme people are differentiated in many ways. They are differentiated ethnically, between largely Nubian-speaking Halfawis and Arabic-speaking Shukriya (in addition to some Hadandawa or Beja, Arabic-speaking Rashaida, Khawalda, and others). They are differentiated by economic class—affluent farmers and traders who control large numbers of tenancies and freehold lands, small-scale producers on single tenancies, and landless laborers—and by occupation—farmers, herders, and skilled, semiskilled, and unskilled laborers. They are differentiated by region and religion, with Arabs, Nubians, and Hadandawa from the Muslim north (again internally divided between western Sudanese from Kordofan and Darfur and eastern Sudanese) and Dinka and Nuer from the south. They are differentiated between Sudanese nationals and foreigners, including Muslim West Africans (generally labeled Fallata), and largely non-Muslim Eritreans, refugees from Ethiopia.

Ethnic differentiation is manifest not only in speech and dress, but also in conflicts expressed in ethnic terms. Unlike the Halfawis, who were resettled in planned villages and in the town of New Halfa and were granted freehold lands to compensate for the land they lost in Wadi Halfa, the Shukriya received neither. The lack of planned villages and attendant social services for the Arabs and the fact that freehold lands were granted only to Halfawis are points of friction between the Halfawis and the Shukriya. The Halfawi villages are surrounded by their tenancies, facilitating easy movement between homes and fields. The Shukriya villages and tenancies are dispersed throughout the Scheme, often in areas where no villages are located, making it difficult for the farmers to travel to and from their fields.[3] The Shukriya also have to bear a percentage — sometimes as high as 60 percent — of the costs of the social services that they wish to bring to their villages, whereas the same services were accorded to the Halfawis free. For the Halfawis, no benefits yet received can compensate for their lost homes in Wadi Halfa. The Shukriya, however, see only the Halfawis' benefits, not their losses.

RURAL DEVELOPMENT: LARGE-SCALE
IRRIGATED DEVELOPMENT SCHEMES

Large-scale agricultural development schemes associated with the construction of high dams have received considerable attention (Adegboro 1983; Baldwin 1957; Barnett 1975, 1977; Blench 1987; Cernea 1988; Chambers 1969; Fahim 1981; Hance 1958; Hoyle 1977; Little 1965; Moxon 1969; Pearson 1980; Reining 1966; Scudder 1973, 1975, 1976, 1981, 1988; Scudder and Colson 1979, 1981; Sørbø 1977a, 1977b, 1985; Yousif 1985). Most studies, whether strongly positive (Hance 1958) or largely negative (Chambers 1969; Reining 1966), tend to view agricultural schemes in terms of their relative achievement of overall objectives and their aggregate effects on local populations. Describing the impact of the Gezira Scheme on the local pastoral nomads in the Sudan, Hance writes:

> Before the scheme was begun the semi-pastoral population of the area lived a traditional life, still enslaved by the requirements of a capricious climate. . . . The rainfall permitted the planting of drought-tolerant grain, but at least two years in five produced poor crops. . . . The livestock in these days were mainly goats, which browsed on the sparse thorn-bush of the plain. Water for man and beast had to be hauled night and day from 120-foot-deep, hand-dug wells.
> Today about one million acres, or one-fifth of the area, have been brought into the Scheme and about half of them are irrigated each year. Cotton is the economic mainstay of the operation but there is also an assured production of food and fodder. *A highly organized, highly productive irrigation system has replaced a low-productive, precarious*

---

[3] The Corporation is trying to correct this mistake. Tenancy transfer applications are seriously considered by the block section managers and are almost always granted if two tenants from different parts of the Scheme agree to exchange their tenancies.

semi-pastoralism. The ability to support people has been enormously increased. (1958:22; emphasis added)

Hance believes that the Gezira has been a success not only in terms of overall productivity, but also by improving the income of tenant farmers:

> The standard of living of 29,000 tenant families has been raised from one of poverty and uncertainty to a level that compares very favourably with that of other peasants in Africa and the Middle East. . . . There is security of tenure. The Tenants Reserve Fund and the allowance of ample space for subsistence and fodder crops insure that any unusual reduction in cash returns will not unduly reduce standards of health and nutrition. (1958:37)

Barnett (1975, 1977), on the other hand, who looked at the Gezira almost two decades later, does not share Hance's optimistic assessments of its benefits for the tenant farmer. On the contrary, seeing the Gezira as an instrument of British mercantile capitalism in a colonial context, he argues that the Scheme existed in order to provide the raw material—cotton—for the British textile industry and, therefore, was managed by the Sudan Plantations Syndicate in such a way as to extract the maximum value from the tenants and to provide them with little return beyond that needed for physical reproduction and maintenance of labor.

Although the contract between the Syndicate and the tenants was portrayed as a partnership, it was clearly asymmetrical. The Syndicate, the author of the contract, accorded itself the right to take whatever action it deemed necessary to safeguard the crops, without the consent of the tenants. This included charging against the tenants' share of profits all crop expenses incurred. The Syndicate, on the other hand, accorded itself considerable freedom of action. Although it was to supply water for the crops, the tenants had no right to claim compensation from the Syndicate if, for whatever reason, the water supply was interrupted.

> Indeed the underlying unequal nature of this contract of supposed "partnership" is epitomized in the final paragraph, which clearly stated: "The English copy of the Tenancy Agreement shall . . . form the official contract. The Arabic translation thereof is merely for the information of the tenants." The tenant's role in the Gezira Scheme was defined in terms of English legal categories and in the English language. He had many obligations, but few rights. But above all he now became a

legal person defined in terms of a legal system originating in a capitalist, European society. (Barnett 1975:195)

Barnett thus views the Gezira Scheme as a component of the capitalist world system. The development that others claimed to see on the Scheme was to him an illusion. What the Scheme succeeded in producing was a transformation of the existing society into an underclass for the support of the capitalist exploiters in the colonial metropole, and the double creation of relations of dependence: the tenant vis-à-vis the administration (Scheme management) and the Sudan vis-à-vis the industrial capitalist countries of the north. Barnett has contributed a case study to dependency theory, best known through the writings of A. Gunder Frank (1969) and the French neo-Marxist anthropologists, like Godelier (1978) and Meillassoux (1978).

Despite its attractiveness as an explanatory model, dependency theory is limited in attempting to come to terms with empirical social relationships at the local level. The great differentiation that exists among the tenants on the New Halfa Scheme can be captured only by looking at individuals in relationship to other individuals and households. Relationships should be viewed in terms of the organization of production. What kinds of relationships exist among the producers? Who is working for whom? Who has control over the produce, and how is it distributed? What resources are invoked? In this study of the New Halfa Scheme, the focus is precisely at that local level, for I am concerned not only with the fact that some tenants seem to do well while most others do poorly, but also with identifying these tenants and discovering why they have been able to do better than others.

The New Halfa Scheme has received a good deal of attention from social scientists (Abdalla 1970; Abubaker 1979; Ajouba 1979; Blanckenberg and Hubert 1969; Dafalla 1975; Ebrahim 1983; Fahim 1972, 1981; Heinritz 1978, 1982; Hoyle 1977; Sørbø 1973, 1977a, 1977b, 1985). Heinritz's earlier work (1978) is largely sociogeographic, with an emphasis on the spatial distribution of Scheme inhabitants, including labor migrants. The increased engagement of Halfawis in nonagricultural occupations—and the continued reluctance of the nomads to settle or to change their economy, which centers around animals—resulted in the immigration of agricultural workers into the area. Heinritz views the full integration of migrants into the project as an economic necessity. His later work (1982) deals directly with western Sudanese migration into the area.

Fahim (1972, 1981), whose major contribution is to Egyptian Nubian studies, focuses his attention on the general impact of the Scheme on the relocatees. Starting with Scudder's (1973:71) multi-dimensional stress syndrome, which accompanies relocation in the first years of transition and has the effect of creating dependency of the relocatees on the government or the sponsoring agency, Fahim points out that this dependency might be minimized if, at the initial stage, the government spells out the role of the people themselves. This, Fahim concludes, will have the effect of promoting feelings of shared responsibility and local initiative.

Abdalla (1970) and Dafalla (1975) provide summarized historical renditions of the Halfawi movement to the Scheme. Ebrahim (1983) describes New Halfa in the context of irrigated projects in the Sudan. Despite the many agricultural problems that tenants face, he observes, nomads who settled on the Scheme have undoubtedly benefited from the combination of herding and farming and from the new access to schools, clean water, and medical units. Ajouba (1979) describes the incorporation of the Khashm el-Girba regional economy into a changing national and world economy and the impact of that incorporation on the local population. Abubaker (1979) describes participation on the Scheme from an almost exclusively institutional viewpoint. Hoyle (1977) notes the failure of the government to settle nomads and attributes that failure to economic conditions on the Scheme, which led 60 to 70 percent of tenant nomads to rely heavily on livestock raising as a major source of income.

Gunnar Sørbø's (1977a, 1977b, 1985) description and analysis of pastoral adaptation on the New Halfa Scheme has contributed to our understanding of irrigated development schemes, not only in New Halfa, but in other parts of the Sudan and perhaps in semiarid areas everywhere. Sørbø is most concerned with the issue of tenant absenteeism and off-Scheme interests. He argues that, contrary to the popular official view that the nomads are irrationally attached to their animals and Halfawis prefer salaried jobs over agriculture, Halfawi and Arab off-Scheme interests make sound economic sense if we consider them in the context of the overall economic situation on the Scheme. With low cotton returns, the spread of weeds, fuel shortages, and so on, tenants often have no choice but to engage in those off-Scheme activities to assure the survival of their families. For the Shukriya, Sørbø states, animals represent a more profitable and secure source of income than tenancy, which is thus regarded as a supplementary source of income rather than an alternative one. Sørbø also suggests that in appraising the achievements of the Scheme we must consider not only its economic performance but also its impact on the region. In his view, the Scheme has affected the region adversely.

Sørbø's contributions, especially the relevant notion of on- and off-Scheme interests, are significant, but I depart from his position in two major areas: his portrayal of the Shukriya and his conclusion regarding the adverse effect of the Scheme on the regional economy.[4]

The Shukriya

Sørbø's portrayal of the Shukriya is flawed in several ways. He presents them as a homogeneous group, all of whom have been affected by the Scheme in a similar fashion. He generalizes the importance of livestock raising in Shukriya tenants' household economy, as he compares income generated from the tenancy with that generated from herding, and concludes that Shukriya tenants' annual incomes come mainly from herding, with tenancy cultivation playing a minor role and supplying households with merely supplementary income. This view understates the great disparities that exist among the Shukriya in livestock ownership and in the number of individually controlled

---

[4] A Sørbø revised his position, although without much elaboration, in 1985, in *Tenants and Nomads in Eastern Sudan*. Regarding the first point he writes:

> As has been correctly observed by Salem-Murdock, my earlier portrayal of the Shukriya tends to present them "as if they are a homogeneous group all of whom have been affected by the Scheme in a similar fashion" (1984:16). In fact, some Shukriya own large numbers of animals while others have very few or none at all. And while most Shukriya households on the Scheme are one-tenancy holders, some are landless and others control a large number of tenancies. (1985:96)

Regarding the second point, Sørbø observes:

> In view of the serious problems that affect the various participants on the New Halfa Scheme, some readers may find it surprising that a substantial number of individuals and households have in fact been able to benefit from settling in the Scheme area. It could even be argued that a negative evaluation of the New Halfa Scheme is not firmly grounded granted that the Scheme is supporting a very large number of nonfarm households and many different businesses (Salem-Murdock 1984:22), and granted that it has largely achieved a number of the goals associated with its establishment, such as the effectiveness of settlement as well as various political aims. (1985:21)

tenancies. Some Shukriya own large numbers of animals, while others have very few or none at all. The latter clearly do not earn more from herding than from Scheme cultivation. While most Scheme Shukriya are one-tenancy holders or have no holdings, a few control a large number of tenancies. These large holders make considerable profits from Scheme cultivation. Those with one tenancy or with no tenancy at all merely survive from year to year. Some do have animals on the Butana, but there are many whose animal holdings consist of only a few goats and others with no animals at all. These stock-poor people derive little if any income from herding.

Sórbó's generalization (1977b:138) regarding the "social relations of production" among the Shukriya may also be questioned. Discussing the division of labor, he states (1977b:138) that "a distinction can be made among masculine and feminine labor processes, the division being maintained by notions of shame that exclude adult women from activities involving livestock, particularly milking." Although the sexual division of labor as described by Sórbó is the ideal model, application of the model to the Shukriya must be qualified because of such variables as labor availability, nature of work, distance from home, age, economic status, and kinship affiliation (Salem-Murdock 1979:48–52). The Shukriya are far from being homogeneous. They are segmented politically, socioeconomically, lineally, and by gender, and the impact of the Scheme on a particular household, the resources it possesses, the types of incentives and constraints its members might encounter, and the labor strategies they adopt are directly linked to this segmentation.

The Shukriya elite, particularly lineages associated with the traditional rulers, seem to have garnered much profit from their involvement with the Scheme; the gap between them and the poorer members of the group has in fact greatly widened in consequence. Members of the elite have been able to accumulate tenancies and have thereby been able to maintain and even expand their livestock holdings through access to Scheme lands for postharvest dry-season grazing. Thus, while the Scheme has contracted grazing lands available to the Shukriya in general by removing from public access the rich alluvial pastures along the western bank of the Atbara River, holders of aggregated tenancies bring their animals on the Scheme after the Butana open pastures are exhausted.

Although elite Shukriya men appear to have profited from their involvement in the Scheme, its specific economic benefit to elite women is less clear. On the other hand, there is no reason to believe that they lost ground due to its introduction. Elite women traditionally were severely restricted in their public activities and were put under tremendous pressure to adhere to Islamic ideals of female modesty and segregation. Household slaves relieved high-status women of domestic tasks—even today one meets elderly women who never learned how to brew coffee. In the tent, slave girls cooked, cleaned, and washed. While in principle women could inherit land and animals, among the elite there was a decided tendency for them to decline these legacies in favor of sons and brothers.

Despite very little change in their economic status, these women deem themselves socially better off on the Scheme. Although periodically many elite women speak nostalgically of the Butana and the relatively free movement there, they appreciate the services the Scheme offers. Compared to what Halfawis receive, these seem very minor; compared to what the elite Shukriya knew on the Butana, they are a substantial improvement. Women seem most to appreciate education for their children, especially for boys, easy access to water (usually from the irrigation canals but sometimes from standing pipes), clinics, and the relative proximity to markets.

Income levels of elite Shukriya families seem to have risen substantially with their involvement on the Scheme—from their point of view, the Scheme is a success. For the nonelite, however, the story is less satisfactory. A single tenancy of 15 feddan (1 feddan = 1.04 acres = 0.42 hectares) does not yield enough to support a household on its own. Combined with other activities, like stock raising or sorghum cultivation off the Scheme or agricultural or nonagricultural wage labor on the Scheme, a tenancy can provide enough supplementary income to be attractive. But for a household with few resources of capital and land, a proper mix of labor is essential for success. Households without sufficient resources and without sufficient labor are clearly at a great disadvantage on the Scheme. The question, however, is: were they not perhaps also at a disadvantage before the Scheme?

Among nonelite women, the impact of the Scheme is also mixed. Women whose husbands left pastoralism for a small tenancy may be the biggest losers. On the Butana, such women were economically active and had clear rights in animals and wadi lands for sorghum cultivation. Many of the women who followed their husbands to these irrigated lands have lost the independence they once had in their right to own and allocate the benefits of animals and land; in consequence, the socioeconomic position of men has risen in relation to that of women along with changes in the complementary gender-based roles that existed in the pastoral environment. With those changes in women's roles and position, one would expect them to have a strong resentment toward the Scheme and a desire to resume pastoral life.

Contrary to my expectations and to the conclusions of many women researchers concerning the status of rural women in male-focused development projects (e.g., Boserup 1970; Staudt 1982), Shukriya women whose husbands were able to make a living on the Scheme almost invariably stated that they were much better off on the Scheme than they were before and, although they occasionally spoke nostalgically of the Butana, expressed little desire to go back. Such an unexpected response so contradicted everything I had read about women and development that I often found myself questioning the women, asking if they really meant what they said. It took me time to hear what they were saying and much longer to digest it. The women are very aware of the discriminatory allocation of tenancies. Many would like to have their own tenancies, but they recognize that tenancy distribution and their exclusion from it is part of the social environment with which they have to deal. Women say that the Scheme offered them and their families opportunities that they never had before. "On the Butana we often threw out [gave away] surplus milk; here we can sell it." Women often cited the different goods and services they could sell on the Scheme — goods that had been given away without compensation on the Butana — and proudly showed off the household goods they had purchased with their own money.

In addition to wider economic opportunities, women often speak of Scheme conveniences, in the form of easy access to water, health services, shops, and education. My negative assessment of the efficiency and quality of these services does not deny their favorable local standing. For the first time in their lives, many women had the opportunity not only to send their children to school, but to attend literacy classes themselves. Although the standards and regularity of these classes leave a lot to be desired, every woman I spoke to, irrespective of her economic situation and of whether she herself attended the classes or not, spoke in favor of them. Those who did not attend attributed it to the objections of husbands, fathers, and brothers.

The New Halfa Scheme in a Regional Context

Sørbø (1977b:133–134) observes, "when appraising the achievements of the Khashm el Girba project, it will be necessary not only to consider the economic performance of the Scheme itself but also its impact on the surrounding region," and concludes that the Scheme "has restricted opportunities for growth in the Butana region and adversely affected the regional eco-system." Unfortunately, he does not elaborate on this beyond suggesting (1977b:134) that the reason for the Scheme's failure in a regional context is the government's policy, "which has almost exclusively been aimed at expansion of irrigation agriculture and the production of export crops. That the economic potential of the Scheme has not yet been fully utilized, will also be blamed on the lack of an encompassing strategy of development covering all sectors of economic activity." Yet Sørbø does not indicate that the generation of nonfarm as well as farm employment is an important consideration in Scheme evaluation. Scudder (1981:179), who has conducted a global evaluation of resettlement, suggests that the generally negative assessment of these large-scale schemes might be less persuasive if nonfarm employment were included in the evaluation.

Evaluated in terms of its agricultural objectives alone, the New Halfa Scheme is disappointing in its failure to achieve stated national, regional, Scheme, or single-tenancy-holder objectives. The Scheme— which did not achieve its stated production goal of six big qantar of cotton per feddan even at the beginning,[5] when the land was more fertile, water more available, weeds less widespread, and equipment new—is moving further and further away from attaining that goal. This is evidenced by the launching of a largely World Bank–financed, multimillion-dollar rehabilitation project, and by the recommendations of the feasibility studies to decrease cotton and groundnut area, eliminate wheat, and incorporate livestock and sorghum in Scheme production. However, if we look at the Scheme in terms of diversification of income sources and generation of nonfarm employment, a different conclusion might emerge. The Scheme is supporting a very large number of nonfarm households and many different businesses, some of which are very small village shops. The town of New Halfa has a sugar factory, flour mills, and groundnut strippers, not to men-

---

[5] Small qantar = 100 lbs.; big qantar = 315 lbs.

tion various small enterprises in the industrial area, and hundreds of large and small shops, bakeries, and vegetable stalls. On this basis, a negative evaluation becomes much less firmly grounded.

This is far from stating that large-scale, capital-intensive irrigated development schemes are the most appropriate vehicles for regional development, or that schemes in general function to reduce the wide gap between the rich and the poor by raising the latter's standards of living. On the contrary, one of the major impacts of the New Halfa Scheme has been to increase social, political, and economic differentiation in the area, greatly widening the gap that already existed between the rich and the poor. As several researchers have stated (e.g., Hoyle 1977; Sørbø 1977a, 1977b), the Scheme does not even offer the tenants a stable though low income. Income generated from the cultivation of one tenancy, especially in the last several years, is likely to be well below income derived from herding and sorghum cultivation for those who have access to wadi lands and animals. However, if we combine the different incomes generated by a household as a result of the diversification provided by the Scheme, we are likely to note a considerable increase in total income for most tenant households. To be able to exploit the various opportunities, however, one minimally needs to be strong and healthy and to have access to household labor.

RESEARCH METHODS

The field research upon which this book is based was conducted in the Sudan from September to December 1978 and from June 1980 to December 1981. The preliminary research was supported by invitational travel from the United States Agency for International Development in Khartoum, and the later research by the Social Science Research Council, the Wenner-Gren Foundation for Anthropological Research, State University of New York at Binghamton, and the Institute for Development Anthropology. A subsequent visit to northern Sudan was made in July–August 1987 on behalf of the World Bank.

A base of operations was established in Village Eighteen, a Halfawi village about seven kilometers from New Halfa, the administrative and market center of the New Halfa Agricultural Scheme. This village was selected because of its close proximity to the town where the New Halfa Agricultural Production Corporation (NHAPC) administration and the Farmers' Union are based, and where major political, economic, and ethnic transactions take place. I divided my time among Village Eighteen, three other Scheme villages — two of which were Arab — and the Butana.

Travel among the various sites was facilitated by a Land Rover provided jointly by the Institute for Development Anthropology and the Wenner-Gren Foundation for Anthropological Research (which was donated at the termination of research to the Development Studies and Research Centre of the University of Khartoum); by the kindness of the New Halfa District and Town Council authorities, who, despite often severe fuel shortages, ensured its availability; by the agricultural manager of the NHAPC, who accompanied me on my first tours, as a guide and to introduce me to the block and section agricultural inspectors; and by the hospitality of Shukriya and Halfawi households in research sites, who did not require advance warning to share their dwellings, food, often very scarce water supply, and their lives, and who provided continuous and enthusiastic support and unrelenting patience as the research progressed.

Through participant observation, I was able to take part in both special and mundane Shukriya and Halfawi household activities ranging from food preparation, child rearing, cultivation, animal herding, and marketing, to weddings, childbirth, funerals, circumcision, and the *zar*, a spirit possession cult among Halfawi women. An intensive case-study method combined with life histories was also employed. In each of the study sites, two to six households were examined in depth. With the aid of research assistants, these households received more concentrated attention than others. Various techniques were used, including participant observation, formal and informal discussions with villagers about the designated households' activities, and in-depth life-history interviews with household heads. The point was to determine how individuals and households with different opportunity profiles reacted to the Scheme — who gained and who lost.

Household surveys in the research sites were carried out to expand the understanding achieved through participant observation and intensive case studies. As many households as possible were surveyed at each site. In Village Eighteen, 100 percent of the households were surveyed; in Village Fifteen, only about 10 percent. It is difficult to determine the percentage of households surveyed in the Arab villages and on the Butana, since residence there is intermittent and households come and go. The surveys (in Arab villages) covered more than 50 percent of the households then present. Many of these households retain pastoral links and do not remain in the village throughout the year. The surveys in Halfawi villages were conducted by three research assistants from Village Eighteen in addition to myself. In other sites I was assisted by elementary school and kindergarten teachers who volunteered their time. Interviews were conducted in Arabic except that an interpreter was employed for some of the older Nubian women whose Arabic is poor.

Information on the history of the Shukriya on the Butana and the Halfawis in Wadi Halfa was gathered through archival research at the Central Records Office in Khartoum and other library research, in addition to conversations with key informants. Shaikh Muhamed Hamad Abu Sin, the former *nazir* (highest political rank in the Native Administration) of the Butana, and as-Sadiq wad al-Halal, a Shukriya poet, provided invaluable information regarding the initial Shukriya reaction to the Scheme.

The New Halfa Agricultural Production Corporation, the Farmers' Union, and the New Halfa District Council made their records available to me, and these were important supplements to field materials. A German consulting corporation, Agrar, prepared two reports that were shared with me by the NHAPC, and these provided information—although not always precise—on population, ethnic composition of villages, amount of land under cultivation and amount in different crops, social services, and livestock numbers and composition. Agrar also provided some excellent maps.

2

The New Halfa Agricultural Development Scheme: A Background

INTRODUCTION

The New Halfa Agricultural Development Scheme is situated along the Atbara River, a tributary of the Nile, in the semiarid Butana plain, in Kassala Province in eastern Sudan, about eighty kilometers west of Kassala and four hundred kilometers east of Khartoum (maps 1 and 2).[1] The Scheme is ninety-six kilometers long and between twenty and thirty-five kilometers wide, covering a total area of about 500,000 feddan; it has an estimated population of 300,000 persons, including about 41,000 semipermanent wage laborers and 200,000 farmers of Nubian/Halfawi and pastoral nomadic origin, distributed among 22,000 tenancies of 15 feddan each. Halfawi tenants live in twenty-five planned villages with an array of social services, including pumped water and electricity in some of the villages. The pastoral nomads, most of whom are Shukriya Arabs, live in about fifty-seven unplanned, emergent, and pre-Scheme villages with few services (map 3).[2]

The town of New Halfa is the commercial, political, administrative, and industrial heart of the Scheme. The government provides most of the employment in the town through the New Halfa Agricultural Production Corporation (NHAPC, the parastatal organiza-

---

[1] The information in this section is based on the Agrar reports of 1978 and 1980, and on personal communications with the New Halfa Agricultural Production Corporation staff.

[2] According to Mr. Ibrahim Maᶜouda, president of the Farmers' Union, all Halfawi villages were electrified by 1988. Only six of the Arab villages were in the last stages of preparation to receive electricity by the same date.

tion in charge of Scheme administration), the New Halfa district and town councils, educational and health services, and the police. NHAPC, however, is the largest single employer in the town, with a total staff of 3,106 people as opposed to 2,000 employed by the other government services combined (Agrar 1978, I, annex 8).

Although the major responsibility for operating the Scheme lies with NHAPC, which is a subsidiary of the Ministry of Agriculture, this responsibility is shared with several other ministries.[3] NHAPC directs all agricultural aspects of the Scheme, including the distribution of water from minor canals into the fields. The Ministry of Irrigation and Hydro-Electric Power is in charge of all other water activities, excluding the minor canals, and of canal maintenance through its subsidiary, the Earth Moving Corporation. Hydropower generation at the Khashm el-Girba dam lies within the domain of the Ministry of Energy and Mining, through the Public Water and Electricity Corporation, while the Ministry of Industry is in charge of the Scheme's sugar estate and factory (Agrar 1978, I:10). The complexity of Scheme administration creates conflicts between the different ministries — especially between the ministries of Irrigation and Agriculture — over the use of water.

SETTLEMENT ON THE SCHEME

From its inauguration in 1964/1965 to 1968/1969, the New Halfa Scheme went through five phases, during which a total of 447,000 feddan were brought under cultivation: 330,000 feddan were divided into tenancies or *hawashat* of 15 feddan each;[4] 41,000 were reserved for the sugar estate, 24,000 for freehold lands, 19,000 for reserved area, 2,500 for afforestation, and 1,000 for a research station; 29,500 feddan were occupied by roads and other infrastructures. The Scheme was settled by Nubian/Halfawis, by Shukriya and other pastoral Arabs,

---

[3] Until 25 January 1980, NHAPC was a subsidiary of the Public Agricultural Production Corporation (PAPC), which was responsible for all agricultural schemes in the Sudan. On that date, President Nimeiri signed the Establishment Order of the New Halfa Agricultural Production Corporation "with autonomous status in perpetuity with its own seal; it may be empowered to sue as plaintiff and be sued as defendant" (Agrar 1980, II, annex 7, appendix 1).

[4] The term *hawasha* (pl. *hawashat*) refers to the 15-feddan tenancies allocated to Scheme tenants; to each of the three 5-feddan subdivisions within a tenancy; and to a 5-feddan plot of freehold land.

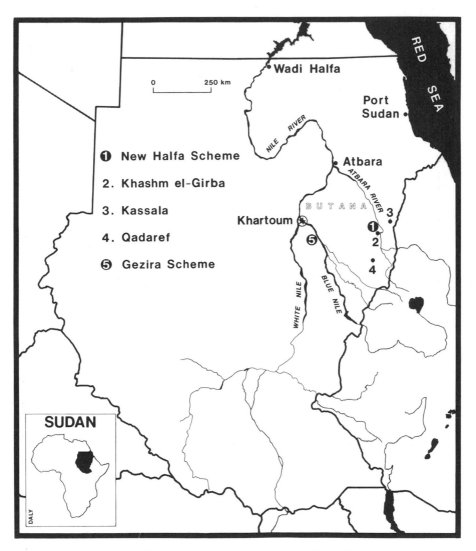

Map 1   The Democratic Republic of the Sudan

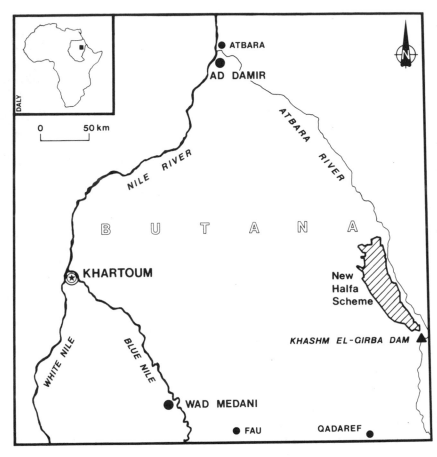

Map 2   Eastern Sudan

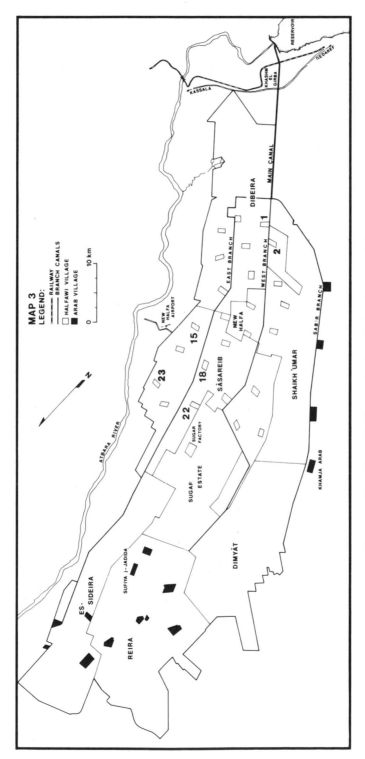

Map 3 The New Halfa Agricultural Production Scheme

and by Beja tribes, among whom the Hadandawa are the best known. It was also gradually entered by migrant labor populations from western and southern Sudan, and later by Eritrean refugees.

The Nubian/Halfawis

The word *Halfawi* is derived from Halfa and Wadi Halfa. The suffix *i* in Arabic designates an adjective meaning "belonging to; coming from; being part of." A Halfawi is a person who comes from Wadi Halfa, in the same manner that a *Sudani* is someone who comes from the Sudan, a *Nubi* from Nubia, and a *Shukri* from the Shukriya. *Halfawi* is often used loosely as synonymous with *Nubi* or *Nubian*, although it is not always a correct usage. While the word *Nubi* has ethnic and linguistic connotations, the word *Halfawi* refers only to a geographic attribute. Hence, although all Nubians are Halfawis, at least in origin, not all Halfawis are Nubians. In addition to Nubians, several ethnic groups lived in Wadi Halfa; some of them, such as the Kunouz and the Basalwa, had lived there for generations.[5] The Wadi Halfa District covered an area of 18,690 square kilometers, extending from 22 to 24 degrees latitude. The inhabited area, however, was restricted to two long strips along the banks of the Nile composed of twenty-seven villages and Halfa market.

The decision to amend the 1929 Nile Waters Agreement between Egypt and the Sudan to allow for the construction of the Aswan High Dam in Egypt, with the consequent flooding of the Wadi Halfa region and the displacement of about 50,000 Sudanese Nubians, was announced in a communiqué simultaneously broadcast by Sudanese and Egyptian radio stations on 10 November 1959. The announcement was quickly followed by a presidential visit to Wadi Halfa to appease angry and disconcerted local populations. The president delivered a speech praising the people and promising them fair compensation and a resettlement place of their choice:

> I declare that I undertake to provide you with good livelihood and fair and equitable compensation for all your property which will be lost, and that every one of you can be assured of the preservation of his

[5] Although the Kunouz are known as Nubians by outsiders, within the Nubian community itself, at least in the Sudan, they are distinguished from the "real" Nubians. Kunouz often spoke of themselves as Nubians when alone, but among "real" Nubians they identified themselves as Kunouz.

rights. . . . *As for the selection of your new home, I promise to accept your choice of place, wherever you want to go, in any part of the Sudan, and that none of you will be forced to go anywhere against his will.* (Dafalla 1975:92; emphasis added)

Before departure, he promised to give due consideration to a petition presented to him requesting that resettlement should be based on sound economic, social, and health understandings, that all property should be moved along with the settlers, that they should be allowed to participate in site selection, that they should be given a monopoly over industrial development in their new home area, and that they should be exempted from all taxes during the period of evacuation and resettlement (Dafalla 1975:92–93).

The president's speech sheds important light on compulsory relocation. With the excitement the government's decision generated in Wadi Halfa and in the Sudan as a whole, the president, in good faith perhaps, promised the Halfawis a place of their choice. However, not only were the settlers unable to choose a place of their liking, they were not even granted their first or second choices among six proposed resettlement sites. This is not surprising, since in compulsory relocation the choice of places from which people are removed and in which they are resettled is usually based on concerns that are external to the people involved. As we shall see, the government had long before committed itself to the construction of a dam on the Atbara River at Khashm el-Girba.

A five-member Commission for the Resettlement of Wadi Halfa People was composed of undersecretaries of the ministries of Agriculture, Irrigation and Works, Finance and Economics, and the Interior, in addition to the Nubian governor of Kassala Province, who was appointed chairman in February 1960 (Dafalla 1975:104). The Commission selected six sites for the people's consideration: Wadi el-Khawi, in the Dongola District, south of Wadi Halfa; an area northwest of the Gezira Scheme; Wad el-Haddad, at the southern end of the Gezira, near Sennar; el-Kadaru, at the northern reach of Khartoum Province; the Managil extension west of the Gezira; and Khashm el-Girba in Kassala Province. A local committee to act as a liaison between the people and the Commission was appointed. Arguments among the Halfawis about where to go grew so severe that subcommittees representing different neighborhoods and villages and pushing for different sites emerged (Dafalla 1975:109–110). Finally, a vote was taken and the majority of the Halfawis chose the area northwest of the Gezira Scheme.

On 10 October, rumors that the government had already chosen Khashm el-Girba for the resettlement reached Wadi Halfa. In December, the Nubian chairman of the Commission was removed. The local committee protested the decision and the government responded by dismantling it.

The first group of relocatees departed Wadi Halfa on 6 January 1964, and the last on 20 September 1964. Tenancy, freehold lands, and housing distribution were based on property ownership in Wadi Halfa. Those with houses in Wadi Halfa received a house and a 15-feddan tenancy, and those who owned land were granted twice the amount in freehold lands on the Scheme. In 1978, the Halfawi population on the Scheme was estimated at 6,966 tenants, making a total of almost 68,000 people (Agrar 1978, I, annex 8).

The Shukriya and Other Arabs

A lack of proper surveys among the Arabs and other pastoral nomads who occupied the Butana left Scheme allocation entirely in the hands of the Native Administration, which distributed the tenancies through a hierarchy of positions of *shaikh khat*, *umda*, and local *shaikh*. Since fewer tenancies were available at each level than the number of potentially eligible tenants, some had to be excluded; the decision was made by applying traditional values that favor kinsmen and followers over opponents and strangers:

> Thus the benefits of Scheme participation through the allocation of tenancies were largely absorbed by the elite Shukriya themselves, and within the elite to those families who were closely allied, by ties of kinship and politics, to the chiefs of the Native Administration. . . .
>
> The concentration of tenancies in elite hands was facilitated by the reluctance and suspicion with which the Scheme was viewed by the pastoralists. Faced with the choice of herding and cultivating rainfed sorghum or settling permanently on the Scheme, many decided to stay with familiar routines. By the time some of these changed their minds, and sought to participate, no more tenancies were available. (Salem-Murdock 1979:20–21)

The number of Shukriya tenants is recorded at 6,915, with an estimated total population of 67,412 (Agrar 1978, I, annex 8). Considering the great mobility of most Shukriya, these figures should be regarded with caution. However, the Shukriya are dominant in over thirty Scheme villages, some of which they share with the Lahawiyeen and other groups.

Other prominent Arab tribes on the Scheme are the Lahawiyeen, the Ahamda, the Rashaida (also known as the Zibeidiya), and the Kawahla, in addition to some Ja'aliyeen, Bataheen, and Khawalda. Agrar estimates the number of Lahawiyeen tenancies at 2,358 and their population at 22,990 (1978, I, annex 8). The Lahawiyeen have been, for generations, closely associated by kinship or marriage with the Shukriya. On the Scheme, they concentrate in thirteen villages in the south and southwestern parts. The Corporation records the presence of 1,061 Ahamda, 631 Rashaida, and 615 Kawahla tenancies on the Scheme. Both the Ahamda and the Kawahla have had long associations with the Shukriya on the Butana. The Rashaida, on the other hand, are new in the area as well as in the Sudan. They claim to have come from Saudi Arabia less than 200 years ago and are readily distinguishable from the other Arabs in the area in features, clothes, and dialect. Their Arabic is much closer to dialects spoken in Saudi Arabia and the Gulf States than to the Arabic of the Sudan. The Rashaida migrated to the Scheme from Kassala and the Red Sea provinces. They are scattered among many Arab villages and often camp in close proximity to Halfawi ones. Two villages in the northern part of the Scheme, Rashaida North and Rashaida South, are dominantly Rashaida.

The Beja

The Corporation records 2,393 Beja tenants on the Scheme. The Beja are divided into several groups, the most numerous and prominent of which are the Hadandawa. The others are Beni Amir, Amrar, and Bishariyeen. Like the Rashaida, the Beja are not native to the area but migrated from Kassala and the Red Sea provinces. The Corporation considers the Beja the most unsettled group of the Scheme's pastoral population since, unlike most other groups, the majority have no permanent villages of their own and many live on the tenancies themselves during the cultivation season, after which they return to Kassala. Some Beja work as seasonal laborers for the sugar factory or hire themselves out as shepherds and agricultural laborers, especially for the Halfawis, or reside around the town of New Halfa and sell milk to its inhabitants.

Migrant Labor and Refugee Camps

Like other agricultural schemes in the Sudan, New Halfa has attracted a large migrant labor population that works on the tenancies and on the government-owned sugar estate and factory. Most of the migrants come from western Sudan, especially Fur and Zaghawa, and work as farm laborers and sharecroppers. The southern Sudanese, including Dinka and Nuer, largely concentrate in the sugar estate, where they are employed as cane cutters and sugar factory workers. There are also small groups of migrants of West African origin, generically known as Fallata, whose men hire themselves out as shepherds and whose women often work as maids or washerwomen. The Scheme has about twenty labor camps (Agrar 1978, I, annex 8), most of them identified with persons of a certain ethnic group, from a specific area, often carrying the name of the hometown, area, or tribe. Several Eritrean refugee camps have emerged on the Scheme in the last few years, especially around the town of New Halfa. Many Eritrean men have found employment as agricultural laborers and waiters in urban coffee shops, and some women as domestic servants.

ADMINISTRATIVE AND IRRIGATION STRUCTURE ON THE SCHEME

Administratively, the Scheme is divided into six sections: five are subdivided into three blocks each, the sixth into four. Each block is administered by an inspector, an assistant inspector, and several agriculturalists. Block inspectors report to their section managers, who in turn report to the general agricultural manager of the Scheme in New Halfa. Reporting is accomplished through formal and informal visits by the agricultural manager to the various divisions and subdivisions; scheduled and unscheduled meetings between the agricultural manager and one, several, or all block inspectors and section managers; and correspondence and written reports.

The Khashm el-Girba dam rises 55 meters high with an 80-kilometer reservoir, with an original storage capacity of 1.3 billion cubic meters. Due to sedimentation, however, this capacity had been reduced some 40 percent to 0.775 billion cubic meters by 1977 (Agrar 1980, I:13).

The idea of building a dam to irrigate the fertile soils on the western bank of the Atbara River, a tributary of the Nile that rises in the Ethiopian highland, preceded the construction of the Aswan

High Dam and the relocation of the Halfawis. The idea was initiated in 1956 by the minister of irrigation and was incorporated in the government's ten-year plan (Dafalla 1975:139). The necessity of resettling the Halfawis made construction of the dam a top priority and the project was allocated 1.62 billion cubic meters annually of the Sudan's share of the Nile waters.

Irrigation and Water Distribution

Water travels from the reservoir to the Scheme through a 26-kilometer main canal. Three branch canals, totaling 245 kilometers, carry water on the Scheme to smaller secondary ("major") and tertiary ("minor") canals, the latter two comprising a network of more than 1,450 kilometers, forming the core of the irrigation system. From the minor canals to a *nimra* (a field composed of 18 tenancies in Arab areas and 36 tenancies in Halfawi areas), water travels through a network of quaternary and even smaller field canals and ditches.

Although water supply is the responsibility of the Ministry of Irrigation, NHAPC estimates daily water requirements of the Scheme. This follows a certain hierarchy: field inspectors submit to their block inspector requisitions that estimate water-level requirements for the quaternary canals; block inspectors then calculate water needs for the whole block, separately for each crop, and submit them to the assistant divisional engineer, with a copy to their section manager. Water is requested and allocated according to irrigation subdivisions, partitions that do not always correspond with the administrative divisions of the Scheme (Salem-Murdock 1984:48–50).

It is interesting to note the lack of tenant involvement in water distribution and canal maintenance on the Scheme through water users' associations. Despite the positive experience of irrigation schemes in other parts of the world (e.g. south and southeast Asia), in which tenant water users' associations play prominent managerial roles in allocating that scarce resource (Coward 1976, 1979, 1980, 1984), no such associations were encouraged to emerge at New Halfa or on other Sudanese schemes. Allocation of water is the prerogative solely of Corporation and other government personnel, although some affluent farmers, as we shall see later, are able informally to influence the judgments of these professionals to their personal benefit.

OVERALL PROFITABILITY OF SCHEME CROPS

Like many such schemes throughout the former colonial world, the New Halfa Agricultural Scheme has not had a very successful record.

Production and income are low; absenteeism is high; there are repeated shortages of vehicles and fuel; pests and weeds invade the fields, requiring tremendous labor and financial efforts to remove them; needed seeds, fertilizers, and pesticides rarely arrive on time; poor storage facilities cause deterioration and losses; the distribution of irrigation water is frequently faulty, causing waterlogging of some fields and desiccation of others; and, over time, sedimentation in the reservoir has resulted in reduced capacity to store water.

The New Halfa Scheme was established for the rotational cultivation of cotton, groundnuts, and wheat and for the production of sugarcane on estate lands. Cotton and groundnuts were produced for sale on the international market, while wheat, the main staple of the Halfawi settlers, was produced for local consumption, with the surplus to be marketed elsewhere in the Sudan. The interests of two-thirds of the tenants, the Shukriya and other pastoral groups, whose prime staple was not wheat but sorghum, were conspicuously ignored in the official crop decisions; animal husbandry, their main occupation, was also excluded from the Scheme.

Cotton

Arab and Halfawi tenants, whose interests in relation to animal husbandry and cereal cultivation are often in conflict, share opposition to cotton, whose production costs almost invariably exceed returns. Tenants have periodically agitated for the reduction or even the elimination of cotton from the rotation. Cultivation begins in June, starting with prewatering to allow the residual weeds to germinate, ploughing to get rid of the weeds, and sowing. Ideally, sowing should be completed by August, with September, October, and November dedicated to weeding. Harvesting should begin in December and be completed by the middle of February, but due to low production returns and competing demands for labor from more remunerative activities, the cotton harvest often continues until the end of March or the beginning of April. Because these months coincide with the worst of the dry season, when pasture on the Butana becomes scarce and of low nutritional quality, the cotton fields are especially vulnerable to animal incursion, and the Corporation has had to resort to the Sudanese army in attempts to keep livestock away from the crop, and to primary school students who are transported to the fields on Corporation vehicles to assist in harvesting.

The status of cotton in the eyes of tenants is also influenced by the relations of production between the tenants and NHAPC regarding the crop. All the major agricultural decisions about cotton are made, and all inputs other than labor are provided, by the Corporation. The tenant is reduced to a provider of human energy only. In the beginning of the Scheme, all cotton expenses, including land preparation, provision of inputs, sowing, harvesting, and marketing, were charged against a joint account agreement between the tenants and the Corporation (table 2.1). The total cost of production was deducted from gross revenues and the remainder was divided equally between the Corporation and the tenants, after a 2 percent deduction for land tax. Tenants' shares were taxed an additional 2 percent for a tenant reserve fund. By the end of the 1972/1973 season, tenants' accumulated total cotton debt to NHAPC was £S606,489, while NHAPC's accumulated debt to tenants was £S140,598 (Farmers' Union files).

In addition to the joint account, NHAPC kept individual accounts of expenses that did not fall under the joint account system, including all the cash advances made to tenants and the amount of cotton produced on each tenancy. All loans pertaining to other crops were also charged against this individual account.

As cotton revenues declined and expenses rose, farmers started to complain about the joint account system, which, they felt, taxed efficient tenants too heavily by having them absorb the expenses of inefficient ones. In 1975/1976, the old joint account system was abandoned and two new accounts were adopted: a general joint account, where the Corporation and all tenants share general expenses equally, and an individual joint account, where the Corporation and those tenants for whom special services have been performed are responsible for the costs.

The third set of records is the individual account, which includes the cost of inputs and services over and above expenses recorded under general/joint and individual/joint accounts, such as the cost of all agricultural operations that the Corporation conducts on behalf of the tenant, from weeding and watering to hiring wage labor for cotton picking. At the end of a season, one-half of the expenses of the general/joint and individual/joint accounts and all of the individual account expenses are deducted from a tenant's cotton earnings. When revenues are lower than total costs, the tenant is in debt to the Corporation. This operation takes about two years to com-

TABLE 2.1
Cotton Earnings in £S according to Old Joint Account

	1971/72	1972/73	1973/74	1974/75
Gross earnings	6,634,386	4,468,294	11,422,481	8,197,718
Gross expenditure	3,716,152	2,897,599	4,170,033	5,244,084
Net earnings	2,918,234	1,570,695	7,252,448	2,953,634
−2% land tax	58,365	31,414	145,049	59,073
Net after deduction	2,859,869	1,539,281	7,107,399	2,894,561
NHAPC share	1,429,935	769,641	3,553,699	1,447,280
Tenant share	1,429,935	769,641	3,553,699	1,447,280
−2% res. fund	28,599	15,393	71,074	28,946
Tenant net share	1,401,336	754,248	3,482,625	1,418,334
Total prod. big qantar[a]	?	285,580	432,508	437,975
Tenant £S share/qantar	?	3	8	3

Compiled from Farmers' Union files. All references to Corporation, Farmers' Union, or Sudan Agricultural Bank files have been translated from Arabic by the author.
[a] 1 big qantar = 315 lbs.

plete, since the Corporation has to wait until the cotton is processed and marketed before the tenant's earnings can be calculated.

Table 2.2 shows the increase in the cost of cotton production from 1975/1976 to 1980/1981. The cost of production per feddan increased every year until 1980/1981, when the total cost of production declined because insecticide was unavailable that season.

Table 2.3 tabulates information on cultivated area and on average yield for cotton from 1964/1965 to 1980/1981. We notice the tremendous increase in the area cultivated between 1964/1965 and 1969/1970, reflecting the gradual incorporation of Arab tenants on the Scheme; a slower rate of increase between 1969/1970—the final phase of Scheme settlement—and 1973/1974; and a gradual decline thereafter to about half the area cultivated in 1973/1974 by 1980/1981. This decline in cultivated area reflects either the Corporation's decisions concerning unsuitability of certain tenancies for cultivation or machinery and fuel shortages. Average production per feddan started at 3.50 big qantar per feddan, rose to an average of about 4.60 between 1967/1968 and 1971/1972, and declined to 2.62 in 1972/1973. Although it increased again in 1973/1974 and 1974/1975, tenants' shares declined from £S8 in 1973/1974 to £S3 in 1974/1975 (see table 2.1). Production per feddan declined sporadically, reaching its lowest in 1979/1980. This was due to a com-

TABLE 2.2
Cost of Cotton Production in £S per 5-Feddan Tenancies

Season	Production	Spraying	Total
1975/76	190	240	430
1976/77	221	286	507
1977/78	259	301	560
1978/79	259	305	564
1979/80	312	368	680
1980/81	422	72	494

Compiled from Farmers' Union files.

TABLE 2.3
Cotton Cultivation in Feddan and Average Production, 1964/65–1980/81

Season	Area Cultivated/Feddan	Average Big Qantar/Feddan
1964/65	15,365	3.50
1965/66	32,965	2.50
1966/67	53,375	3.60
1967/68	70,755	4.90
1968/69	91,605	4.68
1969/70	102,475	4.80
1970/71	107,385	4.52
1971/72	108,025	4.11
1972/73	109,000	2.62
1973/74	109,151	3.88
1974/75	108,960	4.02
1975/76	81,290	1.77
1976/77	109,105	3.70
1977/78	99,120	4.10
1978/79	85,560	2.02
1979/80	61,845	0.91
1980/81	55,210	2.00

Compiled from NHAPC files.

bination of water and insecticide shortages, spread of weeds, and constant animal incursion on tenancies.

Tenants' debts to the Corporation are widespread. These debts are calculated annually when tenants, usually Arabs, apply to transfer their tenancies from one area of the Scheme to another, to be closer to their villages, after informally having arranged for an exchange with another tenant. In this case, debts carried by both tenancies are calculated so that tenants may carry debts of the old tenancies to the new ones. Accumulated debts among seventy-two tenants who had applied for tenancy transfer in the Abu Najma block, between 1976 and 1980, were £S7,944 (Abu Najma block files).

Recognizing the serious difficulties facing the Scheme, the Project Planning Unit of the Ministry of Planning initiated, with financing from the World Bank, a two-phase New Halfa Rehabilitation Project feasibility study contracted to Agrar und Hydrotechnik, a German consulting firm. Phase I, conducted between January and May 1978 by a 26-member team, covered a range of topics from soils, irrigation and drainage, and agricultural production, to sociology, livestock, forestry, and health (Agrar 1978, I). Agrar's task was to review the Scheme and recommend both the immediate inputs that were essential to improve the Scheme's short-run productivity and future studies to be undertaken in a later phase. An important conclusion of the research team was:

> As a project the Scheme's economics are only just satisfactory, outputs only marginally covering inputs. The economics at farmer level are unsatisfactory: for cotton the average tenant has actually made a small loss in recent years, a loss which would have been even greater apart from a hidden subsidy to the tenant by the Corporation, in the form of low mechanization costs; the position is equally unsatisfactory for wheat, and it is only from groundnuts that a satisfactory farmgate level return is obtained. (Agrar 1978, I:22)

The study recommended a number of immediate inputs, including 151 tractors and equipment, spare parts, fuel and storage, and workshop improvement. It also identified twenty main constraints, including reservoir siltation, poor water management practices, agricultural machinery, spare parts, fuel, both skilled and unskilled labor shortages, and health problems, and recommended fifteen studies to be undertaken in phase II, only nine of which were actually carried out.

Based on Agrar's phase I studies, in addition to proposals that were developed independently by the World Bank, a number of donor organizations, including the International Development Association (IDA), the International Fund for Agricultural Development (IFAD), and the African Development Bank (ADB), provided the government of the Sudan, in April 1980, with a US$65 million loan to implement a rehabilitation project in New Halfa, commencing with the phase II feasibility studies carried out by Agrar.

The new Agrar studies, which aimed at identifying "the necessary support measures for the successful implementation of the initial rehabilitation programme under Reduced Water Supply (RWS) . . . and Full Water Supply (FWS) which would be provided by an Upper Atbara Reservoir from 1986 onwards" (Agrar 1980, II:n.p.), were completed in August 1980. The results dealt with short-term support measures under RWS conditions, an animal husbandry feasibility study under both RWS and FWS conditions, and long-term measures considered necessary for consolidating the Scheme, assuming the construction of a new dam.

The Agrar studies calculated the 1979/1980 irrigation efficiency on the Scheme at 37 percent. This efficiency was predicted to increase to 48 percent during an initial five years of rehabilitation due to the introduction of short-term support measures. The situation of declining water supply would continue thereafter, however, and the only hope lay in the construction of a new dam at a cost of £S230 million, which Agrar felt could be borne by the additional net benefit realized under a full water supply situation. Under the then-current reduced water supply situation, the studies recommended discontinuing the cultivation of wheat and replacing it with rainfed sorghum for human and animal consumption. They further recommended the immediate reduction of the area in cotton and groundnuts by 40 percent. Groundnuts would be phased out entirely by the year 2009 and cotton reduced to only 7,600 feddan by the year 2010. Agrar predicted that 1986 would mark the beginning of renewed decline of production on the Scheme (assuming that the short-term measures were implemented in time) with a crisis like that of 1981 recurring in 1988/1989.

The studies further recommended the incorporation of livestock under both reduced and full water supply conditions. The proposed livestock models involved the introduction of artificial insemination, animal stalls, and feed lots with a capacity for 2,000 fattened animals (Salem-Murdock 1987).

Wheat

Tables 2.4–2.6 give an indication of the high cost of production of wheat, a crop highly esteemed by the Halfawis, for whom it is the main staple, and by the Shukriya and other Arabs, who regard it as a profitable alternative cash crop.

TABLE 2.4
Average Cost of Production of Wheat, 1975/76–1980/81

	1975/76	1976/77	1977/78	1978/79	1979/80	1980/81
Ridging	3.06	3.28	4.04	5.05	6.36	7.77
Canal maintenance	3.42	4.73	6.08	6.52	5.25	9.72
Prewatering	0.71	0.84	1.00	1.16	1.23	1.75
Soil leveling	6.04	6.32	8.12	9.91	10.86	15.30
Sowing	3.63	4.14	5.06	5.97	6.50	8.73
Basin maintenance	3.56	4.03	4.87	5.97	7.09	11.24
Fertilizer	24.75	38.77	42.38	44.14	59.30	72.20
Patching[a]	2.34	2.19	3.22	4.00	–	3.70
8 waterings[b]	4.25	5.64	6.40	7.09	8.66	11.21
Weeding	4.42	6.22	7.69	10.41	8.00	19.46
2 sprayings	10.00	10.00	10.00	10.00	17.50	24.58
Harvesting	17.50	17.50	20.00	25.00	–	34.50
Seeds	19.08	21.63	26.77	28.67	60.00	53.70
Sacks[c]	5.71	6.41	6.84	8.49	–	15.04
Labor[d]	2.63	3.65	3.84	4.49	–	6.50
Weighing	4.64	5.22	5.32	6.17	–	10.23
Total	115.74	140.57	161.63	183.04	190.75[e]	305.63

Adapted from the NHAPC files. Cost is calculated in terms of 5-feddan tenancies.
[a]Patching refers to reseeding areas where seeds did not germinate.
[b]This figure refers to the cost of labor and is not a water fee.
[c]This is based on the assumption that new sacks are used and the average production per tenancy is 20 sacks.
[d]This refers to labor expenses after harvest; all labor figures assume that tenants hire all or most of the labor. In fact, many tenants rely almost totally on themselves and household labor.
[e]The 1979/80 figures do not include the cost of patching, harvesting, cost of sacks, and so forth, which are nevertheless collected from tenants upon harvest.

TABLE 2.5
Tenants' Reliance on Wage Labor in a Halfawi Village

		Number
Noncultivators		25
Totally reliant on wage labor		12
Regularly provide all inputs	5	
Usually provide all inputs	7	
Considerably reliant on wage labor		8
Considerably reliant on household labor		15
Total		60

TABLE 2.6
Cultivated Areas of Wheat and Average Production
in Metric Tons per 5-Feddan Tenancy

Season	Area (Feddan)	Average Production/Metric Ton
1964/65	3,250	2.25
1965/66	35,500	2.00
1966/67	58,871	2.50
1967/68	83,771	1.95
1968/69	105,061	2.40
1969/70	120,121	1.75
1970/71	111,280	2.60
1971/72	117,588	2.05
1972/73	62,608	3.00
1973/74	120,158	1.40
1974/75	120,608	3.00
1975/76	91,340	1.40
1976/77	78,435	1.30
1977/78	72,240	1.60
1978/79	42,222	0.95
1979/80	34,225	1.50
1980/81	48,865	1.20

Adapted from NHAPC files.

Table 2.4 shows the increase in the cost of production from about £S116 in 1975/1976 to about £S306 in 1980/1981. The figures should be regarded with caution since they are based on the assumption that all labor is hired and all inputs are provided according to NHAPC recommendations. This is not usually the case. Those who rely totally on hired labor are usually either nonfarmer tenants, tenants with access to several tenancies that require more labor than can be provided by the household, or affluent tenants who can afford labor costs. The last two attributes often go hand in hand. Full-time one-tenancy farmers try to depend as much as possible on household labor to perform agricultural work. However, while the out-of-pocket costs for labor might be zero for the latter group, there is an opportunity cost.

Among sixty tenancy-owning household heads in the Halfawi Village Eighteen (table 2.5), twenty-five did not practice cultivation. Their tenancies were under the control of the village agricultural cooperative, providing neither labor nor inputs, and received only two sacks of wheat a year. Among the thirty-five others, twelve relied totally on wage labor. Ten of those relied on occupations other than agriculture as the major source of income; each of the others was a farmer with a large number of tenancies. For the remaining twenty-three tenants, eight performed as much of the agricultural work as possible but had to rely considerably on wage labor since they practiced other occupations as well; the other fifteen were full-time farmers who depended mainly on their own and family labor. Among these tenants only five (the same number as those totally reliant on wage labor) said that they regularly provided all necessary inputs for wheat cultivation; seven said that they provided necessary inputs most of the time. The remainder said that the inputs and labor they provide vary from year to year. Table 2.6 demonstrates the generally low starting yields and further decline in wheat production over the years, with some fluctuation.

As evident in various reports and minutes of meetings, the high cost of production of wheat and its low yields have been major concerns of NHAPC from the very beginning (Salem-Murdock 1984:93–98). NHAPC viewed the problem as largely technical, however—water shortages, unavailability of seeds, and agricultural machinery scarcity—with the implication that if the technical problems were corrected, production rates and financial returns to the tenants would increase. The tenant himself is not even discussed unless the Corporation is concerned with how to make him pay back his debts or how to convince him to sell his surplus wheat to the Corporation, to guarantee seed availability the following season.

Groundnuts

Groundnuts, the third crop in the rotation, also show the high cost of production and low returns. Table 2.7 shows the rise of the cost of production from 1975/1976 to 1980/1981. The table is based on the assumption that all agricultural operations are performed as recommended and all inputs utilized and that the average production is 120 sacks for a 5-feddan tenancy. Neither assumption is always valid. Because of the rising cost of production, which almost doubled between 1975/1976 and 1980/1981 if harvesting was done by machine and more than doubled if it was done by hand, many tenants cannot afford to follow the Corporation's recommendations regarding groundnut cultivation to the letter. Tenants often reduce the intensity of land preparation, perform most of the work themselves, or leave a number of tasks uncompleted. This in effect reduces both

TABLE 2.7
Average Cost of Groundnut Production in £S per 5-Feddan Tenancy
Based on Average Production of 120 Sacks, 1975/76–1980/81

	1975/76	1976/77	1977/78	1978/79	1979/80	1980/81
Weeding	4.9	6.5	7.6	6.3	6.2	8.3
Dry ridging	3.3	4.1	4.7	5.7	6.8	8.7
Canal main- tenance	4.3	5.7	6.4	6.1	7.7	8.5
Prewatering	—	0.9	1.0	1.1	1.2	1.2
Weed ploughing	3.4	4.3	5.9	5.7	6.6	8.3
Dry ridging	3.7	4.3	5.0	5.7	6.8	9.3
Seeds	17.9	18.8	20.2	21.6	25.0	30.7
Sowing	4.5	5.3	6.3	6.2	8.5	10.3
First watering	1.0	1.0	1.4	1.1	1.4	1.5
Patching	1.9	1.9	3.1	2.3	2.8	3.4
First weeding	11.5	16.9	20.5	16.6	25.4	31.4
Second watering	0.8	0.8	0.9	0.9	1.0	—
Second weeding	14.8	17.0	19.2	14.6	23.4	30.0
Green ridging	3.7	5.5	5.0	4.5	6.2	—
Third watering	0.8	0.8	0.8	0.9	1.0	—
Third weeding	10.8	11.8	13.6	10.8	17.6	20.6
Other waterings	2.3	2.3	2.5	2.9	3.0	5.6
Machine pulling	12.0	12.0	12.0	14.4	—	20.0
Hand pulling	14.5	16.4	21.0	20.0	30.0	36.2
Gathering	7.0	7.1	8.6	10.6	12.5	17.0
Machine shelling	35.0	35.4	45.0	50.0	55.0	56.0
Hand shelling	35.0	38.5	47.5	60.0	70.0	65.3
Washing	7.3	8.4	10.2	8.0	11.2	15.7
Sacks	19.6	28.8	35.1	35.6	44.1	55.8
Filling & sowing	4.7	6.6	6.6	6.3	5.5	9.1
Market transport	18.2	21.7	22.8	25.5	26.0	33.2
Weighing	17.3	20.0	23.4	26.5	27.0	26.6
Total (hand)	213.2	254.9	299.3	305.5	376.9	436.7
(machine)	210.7	247.4	287.8	289.9	361.9	411.2

Compiled from NHAPC files.

the cost and the volume of production. Table 2.8 shows that average actual production on the Scheme between 1964/1965 and 1980/1981 never reached the ideal 120 qantar per 5-feddan tenancy (the closest was an average of 107 for 5 feddan in 1966/1977), and that in most years production was actually far below the desired figure. Table 2.9 shows the official and, when available, market prices of groundnuts and the average returns in Sudanese pounds from 1972/1973 to 1980/1981. The market price increase in 1980/1981 was unprece-

TABLE 2.8
Cultivated Groundnut Area and Average Production in Qantar per Feddan

Season	Area/Feddan	Qantar/Feddan
1964/65	700	11.11
1965/66	3,000	4.44
1966/67	5,700	21.33
1967/68	4,455	10.22
1968/69	2,315	7.55
1969/70	34,545	10.22
1970/71	25,450	11.33
1971/72	12,905	11.55
1972/73	40,000	15.55
1973/74	45,335	14.88
1974/75	68,000	17.77
1975/76	53,800	7.11
1976/77	38,315	16.66
1977/78	60,340	21.11
1978/79	31,310	11.33
1979/80	20,417	17.67
1980/81	35,005	15.06

Compiled from NHAPC accounts.

TABLE 2.9
Groundnut Prices per Qantar and Average Return in £S

Season	Prices		Average Return per 5-Feddan Tenancy	
	Official	Market	Official	Market
1972/73	1.60		128.28	
1973/74	1.85		137.64	
1974/75	1.75		155.48	
1975/76	3.30		117.31	
1976/77	3.30		274.89	
1977/78	3.30		348.31	
1978/79	3.85		218.10	
1979/80	4.40	4.30–4.60	388.74	393.15
1980/81	5.30	10.00–22.00	399.09	1204.80

Compiled from NHAPC files and personal communication.

dented, reflecting the great groundnut shortage on the international market that year. The high cost of production and low returns are reflected in area cultivated in groundnuts each year (table 2.10), which never exceeded 62 percent of the proposed area through 1980/1981, and which was as low as 3 percent in 1968/1969. In the seventeen years between 1964/1965 and 1980/1981, the average area cultivated was about 30 percent of the proposed area.

The size of the cultivated area is not always as responsive to price increases as we would expect. This does not stem from tenants' reluctance to take the risk or from their setting a great value on leisure. The high cost of production, in the absence of easy and sufficient credit, prohibits many tenants from cultivating groundnuts despite expectations of high returns. The tenants who are most likely to expand cultivation in response to price increases are those with more than one tenancy, who opted in the past either not to cultivate altogether or to restrict cultivation to one or two tenancies, since the crop is considered both capital- and labor-intensive. When prices are low, these tenants often find it more remunerative to invest capital and labor—whether personal, household, or hired—in other crops and economic activities that are either less demanding of scarce labor resources or more rewarding. When prices rise to the extent of covering the cost of production and yielding benefits that compare favorably with those of other economic activities, the area in groundnuts increases.

Scheme tenants, both Nubian and Arab, who were questioned about their intentions to cultivate groundnuts in 1981/1982 responded as summarized in table 2.11. We should note that the degree of control the fourteen tenants in group 2 have over the second tenancy is minimal, resulting from an arrangement made with an absentee holder, usually close kin, where the resident tenant is acting more as an agent than as a holder. The table illustrates the small variation between single- (or effectively single) and multiple-tenancy holders concerning their intentions to cultivate groundnuts. The variation is substantial, however, when it comes to the realization of intentions, as we see in table 2.12. Despite the potential for price responsiveness that exists among the fifty-two tenants, other variables, especially size of holding, interfere when it comes to actual cultivation.

The great discrepancy between intended and actual behavior among small tenants and the very small discrepancy among big ones

TABLE 2.10
Groundnut Cultivation vs. Proposed Area in Feddan

Season	Proposed	Cultivated	Percentage Cultivated
1964/65	32,500	700	2
1965/66	35,000	3,000	9
1966/67	58,875	5,700	10
1967/68	83,773	4,455	5
1968/69	91,650	2,315	3
1969/70	102,500	34,545	34
1970/71	110,000	25,450	23
1971/72	110,000	12,905	12
1972/73	110,000	40,000	36
1973/74	110,000	45,335	41
1974/75	110,000	68,000	62
1975/76	110,000	53,800	49
1976/77	110,000	38,315	35
1977/78	110,000	60,340	55
1978/79	110,000	31,310	28
1979/80	110,000	20,417	19
1980/81	110,000	35,005	32

Compiled from NHAPC files.

TABLE 2.11
Intention to Grow Groundnuts among 52 Tenants

	No. of Tenants	No. of Tenancies per Tenant	Total No. of Tenancies	Intended to Cultivate	Percentage
Group 1	27	1	27	23	85
Group 2	14	2	28	23	82
Group 3	5	4	20	20	100
Group 4	6	5 +	69	62	90

show the impact of large holdings and, in turn, of wealth on the ability to plan. (On the basis of participant observation, I have found a positive correlation between size of holding and wealth levels.) Although approximately the same general information concerning conditions of cultivation is available to all groups of tenants, affluent tenants base their plans on a realistic assessment of the cost of production, sources and availability of credit, and so on. Small tenants

TABLE 2.12
Area Cultivated in Groundnuts 1981/82 among 52 Tenants

Tenants	Tenancies per Tenant	Total No. of Tenancies	No. Cultivating Groundnuts	% of Total Tenancies	% of Area[a]
27	1	27	8	30	35
14	2	28	9	32	39
5	4	20	19	95	95
6	5 +	69	62	90	100

Compiled from NHAPC files.
[a]Percentage of area intended for groundnut cultivation.

base their plans on the hope that credit might become available. The most important reason tenants in the first two groups gave for not cultivating was unavailability of credit or difficulty in securing it. In groups 3 and 4, on the other hand, the most important reasons for not cultivating a particular tenancy were unsuitability of land, spread of weeds, or competing demands.

Sorghum

Sorghum or *dura* is the staple food of the Shukriya and the other pastoral nomadic groups on the Scheme. Large-scale cultivation of sorghum on the Scheme was first permitted in 1980/1981. Many reasons have been cited for the legalization of sorghum: it has been grown illegally on the Scheme for years; for more than half of the Scheme tenants, sorghum rather than wheat is the preferred dietary staple; tenants have been asking for a long time to be allowed to grow it; a large number of tenants are absent from the Scheme during the rainy season, which coincides with the sorghum growing season on the Butana—the legalization of sorghum might persuade them to remain during this season.

What persuaded NHAPC, however, was that incorporation of sorghum within the Scheme rotation was one of the recommendations of the Agrar feasibility studies for Scheme rehabilitation. The studies predicted that unless a new dam was built to counter the decline in water supply due to reservoir siltation, the area cultivated in groundnuts and cotton would be sharply reduced. The studies therefore recommended the exclusion of wheat cultivation, with its high water demands, from 1981 on, and the introduction in its place of special varieties of rainfed sorghum, for both human and livestock consumption.

The sorghum varieties such as Umbinein, chosen by the agricultural experts to replace local varieties for on-Scheme cultivation (because these varieties were successful in a controlled situation), have proven to be far more susceptible to disease than the local ones, however. In the NHAPC weekly agricultural report of 22 September 1980 we read: "Stemborer disease incidence is very high, especially among the Umbinein and Maylo varieties more than the local ones." The 13 January 1981 report says: "Harvest is almost over and the average production is five to seven sacks per feddan, especially in the Umbinein variety."

Despite the legalization of sorghum cultivation and its consideration as a necessary component of Scheme rehabilitation, the Corporation and others continue to hold numerous prejudices against it. Although tenants do not always follow regulations—principally because of unavailability of seeds—restrictions on the varieties to be grown still apply. Tenants who are planning to grow sorghum have to communicate their intentions to their block inspectors in advance. They are often the victims of Irrigation Department–induced water shortages, since the Department still feels that irrigation of sorghum is illegitimate despite the recent legalization.

ANIMALS ON THE SCHEME

Despite the government's attempts to encourage Arabs to settle and its hope that the alternative source of income that the Scheme provides will encourage them to give up "nomadism" and become sedentary farmers, Arab tenants remain as interested in raising animals as they ever were (Hoyle 1977; Salem-Murdock 1979; Sørbø 1977a, 1977b). Moreover, Nubians, who were severe critics of the presence of Arab animals on the Scheme, are themselves increasingly turning to animal raising, and a number of them are doing it on a very large scale.

The Corporation regards Arab animal raising, on and off the Scheme, as a nuisance at best. Animals cause crop damage while on the Scheme, and tenants abandon their tenancies when agricultural demands are at their peak to look after them when they are off the Scheme. According to Hoyle (1977:126), absenteeism on the Scheme is slightly over 50 percent for most of the year.

The Corporation sometimes attributes its "failure" to settle the pastoral nomads to their irrational attachment to animals and love of movement (Idriss 1978). Movement, they say, is the nomad's nature; it is in his blood. Yet herding is a rational adaptation to the ecologic conditions of the Butana. The pastoralist is proud of his or her animals and takes real joy in seeing the herd grow, but that pride and joy serve to support sound economic behavior. A single tenancy in itself does not generate enough income to maintain a family. It may be important as a supplementary source of income, however, not only for the cash it generates but also because it provides the pastoralist with grazing in the extremely harsh dry season. But to both exploit the tenancy and raise livestock, a household must have the proper mix of labor resources. The fact that pastoralists combine herding and irrigated cultivation is evidence of their rationality rather than the reverse:

> The strength and durability of the herdsman's adaptation to the arid Sahelian environment is found in multiple resource exploitation (Salzman 1972). That is, instead of concentrating efforts and investments on a single economic activity, the Sahelian pastoralist distributes his activities across a spectrum of ecological niches. He thus hedges his bets, assuring himself and his family of a reasonable level of living in all but the most rainfall deficient years, a level which supports an exceptionally large number of persons in an environment which seems to have no alternative uses. (Brokensha, Horowitz, and Scudder 1977:23)

Arab tenants' absence from the Scheme because of off-Scheme animal husbandry and rainfed sorghum cultivation represent only one dimension of the problem as perceived by the Corporation. The other dimension is the presence of illegal animals on the Scheme, which threaten — very often successfully — to cause considerable crop damage. In an attempt to protect crops from animals, regulations such as the Local Order for the Organization of the Presence of Animals on the Scheme were introduced in the early years, but with poor results (Salem-Murdock 1984:179–181). Although animals are still regarded as a nuisance, the rationality of the Arab decision is not as often questioned. An early indication of a possible change of mind, if not heart, came in a 1976 letter from a staff member to the agricultural manager (NHAPC n.d.). Although the tone of the letter vis-à-vis animal presence on the Scheme remains negative, it proposes the introduction of a fodder crop in the rotation.

The New Halfa Rehabilitation Project, sponsored mainly by the World Bank, goes a step further and recommends a close integration of animals in the Scheme rotation, with a major switch in crop emphasis from export to fodder crops. The Bank's recommendations, based on the multidimensional studies conducted by Agrar, stem not from a sudden desire to address itself to tenants' needs and preferences, but from a realization that, under the current situation of continuous reduction in irrigation water supplies, the Scheme will soon be unable to support the current crops (Salem-Murdock 1984, 1987). Although the idea of livestock integration in the Scheme is commendable, the five models of livestock-producing tenants that Agrar proposes are far removed from the realities of livestock raising in the area (for a detailed discussion of the five models see Salem-Murdock 1987:347–348).

3

Elements of Production

INTRODUCTION

Large-scale, capital-intensive agricultural development schemes like New Halfa discourage individual initiative and local participation in management. Conceived, designed, and implemented from above, the schemes are top-heavy with administrative personnel who—along with local, regional, and national government bureaucracies and, indeed, experts provided by bilateral and multilateral donor organizations—seek to reduce tenants to passivity in eliminating all traces of preexisting production systems. The poor economic performance of many of these schemes is at least in part attributable to the exclusion of local participation and the denial of considerable talent and expertise found among the farmers.

That the schemes survive at all may, ironically, be due to their inability fully to frustrate decision making at the level of the tenant farm. The New Halfa Agricultural Production Corporation lacks the ability to assure that all its regulations are followed to the letter; in the niche opened by managerial inefficiency, tenant farmers elaborate strategies that facilitate household survival. For example, although a tenant has to grow at least some cotton to qualify for land, the amount of time and effort that he invests, despite government disapproval and threats, and the manner in which he allocates his time and resources among the various legal crops and other agricultural and nonagricultural activities on and off the Scheme, even if not entirely within the law, are left to his own discretion.

The available options differ from tenant to tenant, depending on control over the factors of production, on the socioeconomic and political environment, and on the tenant's specific position within this environment. Tenants use various methods to expand control over production. To acquire labor, for example, a tenant may use his own time, assuming that he is healthy and that there are no equally competing demands; he may also use the labor of wife and children if available; a Shukriya tenant may be able to call a *nafir*, a work party based on exchange labor; or an individual may hire labor if it is available and if he is able to pay for it. Land may be inherited or it may be assigned to an individual on a long- or short-term basis by a local leader, by the government in the person of the Corporation, by a family member, or by other individuals or groups. Land may also be bought, rented, or sharecropped. Capital may be acquired by selling one's own labor, the product of labor, land, or livestock.

PRODUCTION SPHERES ON THE NEW HALFA SCHEME

The organization of production on the New Halfa Scheme portrays the articulation of capitalist and domestic modes of production (Foster-Carter 1978; Long 1977; Meillassoux 1972, 1978, 1981). Cotton, groundnuts, wheat, vegetables, and fruits involve largely capitalist modes of production, despite the presence of such noncapitalist elements as labor sharing among kinsmen; sorghum and livestock rearing largely follow noncapitalist modes of production, despite the increased commoditization of labor. The existence of noncapitalist modes of production, rather than hindering capitalist expansion, functions to support it by facilitating the reproduction of tenant households that provide low-cost labor to the Corporation. This relationship between the two modes of production is evident in the case of the many one-tenancy holders whose low tenancy incomes are supplemented by pre-Scheme types of economic activities like livestock rearing and sorghum cultivation. Scheme officials often blame tenant absenteeism and off-Scheme economic activities as major causes of low on-Scheme production. But most tenants would not be able to produce on the Scheme at all if Scheme cultivation was not a complementary but an alternative source of income.

Given the articulation of capitalist and noncapitalist modes of production on the Scheme, and the dependency relationship of the tenants vis-à-vis the world economy, what strategies can tenants employ to make the system more rewarding? In examining this question, it is useful to view production processes of the different crops, not as parts of the same or different modes of production, but as distinct, though not mutually exclusive, production spheres.

Sphere as used here does not follow the definitions of Bohannan (1955) and Barth (1967), but refers to a set of interrelated activities involving the production, distribution, consumption, and commercialization of specific cultigens, including livestock. Tenants often exploit more than one of the spheres; those who are able exploit several. In terms of their market articulation, the spheres can be plotted along a local-international continuum, with sorghum at one end and cotton at the other. As is true of the spheres themselves, their market articulations are not mutually exclusive. Sorghum, which is largely consumed internally, often by the producing households, finds its way to local, regional, national, and even overseas markets. Cotton, which is produced mainly for international export, is also marketed nationally for local industries and sometimes used, albeit illegally, as animal feed.

Cotton

A main feature of the cotton sphere is the fact that two essential means of production — land and capital — are government-owned. Labor, the third means of production, is provided by the tenants, who, in return, are promised an equal share of profits according to a joint account system. Theoretically, the crop is owned jointly by the government, as represented by NHAPC, and the tenants; they share expenses and divide profits. In reality, the farmer acts more as a wage laborer than as a manager of his tenancies, since decisions from start to finish are supposed to be made by the Corporation.

Although tenants seldom include the value of their labor when they calculate profit, they are more often than not losers in this enterprise. This loss results mainly from the fact that cotton yields have been very low and prices are dictated by a world market system of which the Sudanese government is as much a victim as the tenants themselves. Another reason for the poor returns from cotton production is that, because of the structure of cotton marketing, the tenant is the first to lose when the prices drop and the last to gain when they rise. Before the tenant receives any part of the profit, the government deducts production costs, including the expenses of transportation paid to local traders who add a good margin of profit in billing for their services.

Cotton marketing on the Scheme is an NHAPC monopsony. The crop is collected in individual tenancies, brought either to the collection centers within each block or to section collection stations, and then transported to New Halfa for ginning. From there, it is shipped either to Khartoum for distribution to local industries or to Port Sudan for export.

In most years, tenants end the season in debt to the Corporation. The government also often loses in this operation—not only must it bear the high production costs and low returns, but it must effectively absorb the debts of the very large number of tenants who end the season owing the Corporation money they are unable to repay.

Groundnuts

As a cash crop intended mainly for international export, groundnut production differs in many respects from cotton production. Although the tenancy, at least for the term of occupation, is generally regarded as the tenant's own, the area under cotton cultivation is treated as totally the government's, with various tenants being responsible for different pieces of it. The government decides whether or not to cultivate a cotton field on the basis of criteria that do not include the individual tenant's situation. Government policy regarding groundnut cultivation is different, however. It is largely up to the tenant to cultivate or not in a particular season, and it is also up to him to pay the cost of production and to reap the benefits—if there are any. In a sense, the tenant enjoys a degree of freedom he does not have with cotton. Since it is not the Corporation's responsibility to offer loans or advances or to provide inputs, the tenant is also left with the responsibility of generating capital to cover the cost of production, by borrowing from relatives, selling livestock, or applying for an agricultural loan from the Sudan Agricultural Bank.

Groundnut marketing also follows a somewhat different route from cotton marketing. Groundnuts are produced and marketed by the tenant, who pays the total cost and keeps the total profit. Although the tenant can supposedly do with the crop as he pleases, some market regulations were introduced in 1973, presumably to protect the tenant from greedy traders. Accordingly, groundnuts can be marketed only in the Crop Market in New Halfa and only according to government-set minimum prices. Thus, ideally, the whole groundnut crop should move from the various tenancies throughout the Scheme to the town of New Halfa for marketing, and from there to other areas of the Sudan, mainly Khartoum, or, like cotton, to Port Sudan for export.

In fact, this is not always the case. Merchants often go illegally to villages and buy groundnuts directly from the tenants at low farm-gate prices. Many tenants prefer to sell their crop in this manner since it relieves them of the cost of transportation to the Crop Market in New Halfa. It also protects those who owe money to the Sudan Agricultural Bank from having to pay their debts and from paying local taxes. Merchants are agreeable to this arrangement, because it enables them to buy groundnuts at very advantageous prices. The amount of groundnuts exchanged in this manner is unknown but is thought to be substantial. Although some of the groundnuts so purchased subsequently utilize the Crop Market, most move directly from the farms to Khartoum, Port Sudan, and other areas of the Sudan.

In the New Halfa Crop Market, a few local traders, representing large merchants from Khartoum, dominate trade and control prices. Until 1981, international export of groundnuts from Port Sudan was monopolized by the Oil Seeds Company, a parastatal corporation owned in large part by a wealthy merchant. In that year, open competition was introduced in theory, but in fact the market continued to be controlled as before. The effective monopsony discriminates against the myriad of small producers who are unable to organize effectively in a way that would beneficially influence farm or local market-gate prices.

Wheat

The wheat crop is the property of the tenant; he has to finance it, often with Corporation assistance, and can keep all profit. The Corporation collects *all* debts relating to wheat directly upon harvest. Furthermore, as with groundnuts, there are some government regulations concerning wheat marketing. Wheat that is not directly consumed by the producing tenant household is sold to the flour mill cooperative in New Halfa, at official prices, which are usually lower than the market ones. It is illegal to store wheat in excess of anticipated household requirements—although many do so—or to export it outside the area, although this is often done with the full knowledge if not the approval of the Corporation and the local government. Tenants often smuggle wheat to the Northern District because of higher prices. Some officials attribute smuggling to the fact that even government-set wheat prices are not uniform throughout the Sudan.

Tenants who benefit most from the different illegal economic transactions that take place in wheat marketing are those who are in charge of large numbers of tenancies, since they are the ones who have the resources to produce large quantities of wheat; have their own transportation, thus making undercover transport outside the area easier; and have connections throughout the system to get out of trouble, if necessary.

Small tenants are usually the hardest hit, not only because they are most likely to sell their wheat at the official low prices, but also because of the Corporation's insistence on day-of-harvest repayment, in cash or in kind, of *all* wheat-related agricultural loans advanced to the tenants in the form of agricultural inputs or plowing and harvesting. Since poorer tenants are not likely to have the necessary cash on hand, they tend to repay their debts in kind. This means that their wheat is sold to the Corporation at prices lower than those offered on the free market. The discrepancy between what tenants get from the Corporation and what they can get on the market increases with the time they wait before selling the wheat. Those with greater resources can outwait poorer tenants.

Another important exploiting factor is the merchant who makes private arrangements with the tenants, offering them cash to repay their debts. These merchants purchase the wheat at a slightly higher price than offered by the Corporation, but not nearly as high as the price the merchants get when they sell the wheat at a later date— possibly back to the tenants themselves.

Sorghum

Sorghum, legalized since the 1981/1982 season, is the only crop within the Scheme rotation that does not have to be transported to New Halfa for marketing. The farmers can do whatever they like with it. However, this leeway might change as sorghum becomes more and more integrated in Scheme activities.

The fact that the state does not get involved in sorghum production, distribution, and consumption does not free this crop from other modes of exploitation. The *sheil* system, where the crop is sold to a local merchant at very low prices while it stands in the field, is very common, especially outside the Scheme boundaries. Sorghum is mainly consumed by producing households or exchanged locally without the involvement of market institutions, at least in the first stage of distribution.

Fruits and Vegetables

Fruits and vegetables are grown only on freehold lands, owned by some Nubian tenants. This is thus a strategy unavailable to non-Nubians and to Nubians who do not own freehold land, except where such a person arranges to rent a piece of freehold land, either for cash or for a share of the crop. Some of the vegetables, melons, and watermelons are marketed in the villages of the producers themselves, but the bulk moves to New Halfa or is transported elsewhere, depending on demand, transport availability, and cost. A very few orchard-owning tenants grow fruits such as lemons, grapefruits, oranges, guavas, and mangoes on a commercial basis. Such fruits are almost never marketed in the villages of origin but are transported to New Halfa, Khartoum, Qadaref, or Port Sudan.

Livestock

Livestock rearing is a very important strategy that many Scheme tenants — including the Nubians, for whom it has become a prominent activity since their arrival on the Scheme — adopt when feasible. Although the permitted number of animals on the Scheme is only two units (one cow and two sheep or goats) per household, this limit has never been strictly enforced, and people who have freehold lands may keep as many animals as they wish.

The majority of the tenants keep animals to supplement their agricultural income with milk, clarified butter, and, on rare occasions, meat. Animals, especially small ones, are often sold to buy sorghum and other necessary food items or to support agricultural activities. Animals from the Scheme and the Butana are also marketed locally or in other parts of the Sudan. (There are about fourteen butchers in the town of New Halfa alone, and some of the villages on the Scheme have their own periodic butchers.)

PRODUCTION RESOURCES

A variety of resources are relevant to production in choosing particular labor strategies to achieve particular goals: material, such as land, livestock, and money; sociopolitical, such as kinship, tribal and ethnic affiliation, education, political and social position, and *ma'rifa* and *wasta* (connection). These resources are not mutually exclusive: they complement and reinforce each other.

Land: Freehold and Tenancy

Land is available in two forms on the Scheme: freehold and tenancy. Ethnic affiliation influences whether a tenant owns freehold land — only Nubians were granted such plots in the original distribution (twice the size of farmland lost in Wadi Halfa). Although ownership of freehold land is very restricted, access to it is much more flexible. Owners of freehold lands may cultivate, rent, sharecrop, lend, sell the lands, or leave them uncultivated. Since many of the Nubian freehold landowners are either absentee or, if they live on the Scheme, employed in nonfarm occupations (such as working for the Corporation or the local government or teaching), many of their plots are regularly available for renting, sharecropping, or lending to other family members without compensation. This gives tenants who own small parcels of freehold lands the opportunity to enlarge their holdings and allows those who do not own any land to cultivate crops that are not part of the regular Scheme rotation of cotton, groundnuts, and wheat or sorghum.

In principle, there is nothing to prevent a Nubian landowner from renting or selling a freehold plot to a member of some other ethnic group. There appear to be no cases of Arabs working freehold lands, however. This ethnic exclusiveness may be due in part to social pressure on the Nubians to maintain control over freehold lands as an ethnic prerogative and in part to the remoteness of these plots from Arab villages.

Not all Scheme farmers hold tenancies. Of the seventy-seven households interviewed between October 1980 and June 1981 in the Shukriya village of Sufiya-j-Jadida, fifteen held no tenancies. Yet all but one of these fifteen household heads identified themselves as farmers. A similar distribution obtains in other Scheme villages, both Arab and Halfawi. Although the principle "one household/one tenancy" was supposed to guide the distribution of holdings, many individuals were able to assume control over more than a single tenancy, and a few were able to gain control over a substantial number. Among Arabs, several very prominent local leaders have been able to get a number of tenancies directly assigned to them. In Sufiya-j-Jadida, three members of the founding elite extended household have been assigned more than one tenancy each.

The more common means of accumulating tenancies is to obtain effective control without actually having the title reassigned from the original holder. Among both Halfawis and Arabs, although more commonly with the latter, the situation often results from the existence of absentee or nonfarming tenancy holders who assign effective control over the land to brothers, cousins, and other relatives. This movement of tenancies among close kin was facilitated for the Arabs, since the initial distribution of tenancies was frequently made to a number of individuals of the same household, thus enabling a few persons to control many holdings.

Livestock

The formal attitude of Scheme management toward livestock raising is one of hostility: animals are seen as competitors for space and for the attention of tenants. Yet many, perhaps most, tenants invest time and capital in varying degrees in livestock rearing. Three broad approaches can be discerned. First are those households for whom livestock approaches agriculture in contributing to overall revenues from productive activities—the two components of production are integrated for mutual support. Cattle, sheep, and goats may be sold to provide the cash needed for such agricultural operations as land preparation, sowing, and harvesting. Agricultural surplus may then be used to replace animals sold earlier or to increase the herd. This heavy emphasis on livestock rearing is characteristic mainly of tenants of pastoral origins who allocate household labor across the year to allow both crop production on the Scheme and grazing on the Butana.

The second category of livestock rearing is the polar opposite of the first: households that keep just a few small ruminants to provide milk and occasionally meat for domestic consumption. Most of the animal-owning Halfawis keep only a small number of sheep and goats, but there are also former pastoral households that have dropped out of animal husbandry through a vicious circle of having to sell more stock to support farming than they were able to purchase from agricultural returns.

The third category, including both pastoralists and Halfawis, is composed of people who maintain large numbers of animals for investment. Their herds sometimes number in the hundreds, and they are heavily involved in marketing live animals, meat, and milk. These animals are normally consigned to professional shepherds who graze them on the Butana during the cropping seasons and then move them onto the Scheme during the brief fallow period at the end of the dry season. Investment in livestock has attracted traders, big farmers, and government officials, who purchase animals cheaply in the dry season, then fatten and sell them at much more attractive prices several months later.

Money, Hospitality, and Influence

Scheme residents operate in an economy that has become increasingly monetized. Money has been a significant component of transactions for a long time on the Butana, clearly predating the establishment of the New Halfa Agricultural Scheme and playing an important role even in precolonial days. But the presence of the Scheme and the incorporation of its products into the world economy have led to the rapid commoditization of land and labor.

While precapitalist formations continue to operate among pastoral peoples off the Scheme (for whom labor is rarely calibrated in monetary terms, and access to pasture is broadly available to members of the ethnic group and subgroup habitually associated with a specific range), labor is more and more often exchanged for cash on the Scheme, even among persons related by ties of kinship (although still rare within the household or productive unit itself). Persons with money are able to hire labor at certain critical points during the agricultural cycle, and the increased production from this labor usually more than compensates for its costs. Those without funds and without sufficient labor resources within the domestic unit frequently find themselves in a descending spiral of lowered production, yielding small cash returns and rendering it more difficult to obtain additional labor. Such persons, after selling off their livestock, often lose effective control over their tenancies and end up as wage laborers themselves.

Money is also used to obtain agricultural inputs in a timely way, to purchase or hire tractors, to buy fertilizer, to rent additional lands, and to get improved seeds. Money is required to support a child through the educational system with the hope that he or she will obtain a remunerative position with the government or in the private sector. Money is used conspicuously, to confirm or display social status.

Conspicuous public display is especially characteristic of the Halfawis, whose houses are often a true indication of their financial standing. Unlike the Arab and Beja-speaking pastoralists settled on the Scheme, who built their houses and villages of traditional materials, Halfawi settlers were provided with cement houses set in high, cement-walled compounds, laid out along a gridwork of streets in planned villages. Every one of the twenty-five Halfawi villages on the Scheme provides running water to individual compounds, schools, and health units; by the end of 1981, six of the villages had electricity. Halfawi villagers with sufficient funds often invest in improving their houses, enlarging them, installing expensive, highly decorated iron gates, screening porches against the constant invasion of insects, and purchasing electric refrigerators, electric fans, bottled-gas stoves and ovens, and furniture.

Halfawis, especially those with productive freehold lands, are in general more affluent than even "wealthy" Arabs on the Scheme and are able to express their wealth by purchasing personally owned vehicles. For example, in the Halfawi Village Eighteen, which contained 198 households by the end of 1981, there were 14 privately owned vehicles, not including agricultural equipment. On the other hand, none of the 267 households in the Arab village Sufiya-j-Jadida owned either a vehicle or a tractor. Of course, most Halfawis, like most Arabs, own neither.

Money facilitates consummation of relationships expressing two fundamental Sudanese values: *husn dhiyafa* (hospitality) and *karam* (generosity). Although these values are related, the people clearly distinguish between them and recognize that one may be hospitable without necessarily being generous. Husn dhiyafa is offered in one's home; although very much admired, it does not reach the value of generosity, which involves the whole community. They say that although not all hospitable people are generous, all generous people are by definition hospitable.

To offer either, one needs resources to dispense. To be hospitable only to those who are your superiors, or to those who are in a position to benefit you, is not truly husn dhiyafa. For example, people frequently compared two of the wealthiest men in a Halfawi village. Although one man's house was the most modern, with such clear indicators of wealth as modern furniture, fans, an air conditioner, a videotape machine, and a color television—and although he owned two private vehicles, a tractor, a fruit orchard, animals, tenancies, and freehold lots—he was constantly criticized for being inhospitable, miserly, unsocial, and selfish. "Yes," the villagers would say, "he does entertain his business associates, the men from Khartoum

and Qadaref, but his house is not open" — meaning it is not unequiv-
ocally open to all villagers. Then they would inventory his selfishness.
Throughout the years, they had never tasted a piece of fruit from his
orchard. He had never given any of them a ride anywhere; he would
drive by in his empty car, passing villagers awaiting the bus, but he
would never consider picking up any of them.

The other wealthy man, on the other hand, was praised for being
both hospitable and generous. Although his hospitality most often
was extended to Corporation officials and to a few educated, well-to-
do village men who frequented his house and were always offered
food and drink, villagers said of him, "His hand is open; his house is
open. God is generous to him and he does not mind sharing with
others." The man's house was indeed open. Guests frequented his
house practically every evening. They often stayed up eating, drinking, and discussing various issues until the early morning hours.
Additionally, every year, he gave away part of his wheat harvest to
poor relatives and villagers and loaned small amounts of money,
interest-free, to those in need. Even relatives who had a slight grudge
against him for having controlled their lands for so many years would
always qualify their statements by saying, "but he is good and would
never send you away empty-handed."

Hospitality is a virtue much admired in the Sudan, but it is not
its own reward. For those who can afford it, hospitality is an essential
component of building influence. It brings ma'rifa and wasta (connections), and thereby administrative and political access. On the
Scheme, critical inputs, including water, are often in short supply;
any advantage in their allocation may strongly benefit the recipient.

One of the wealthy Halfawi settlers responded to my questions
about the rumor that some tenants bribe water guards (*ghafir*) to
increase their share of irrigation water. He confirmed the rumor, but
added that only those who were "stupid" would resort to such a
strategy. "I would never do such a thing," he said. "What can a
ghafir do? He does not control that much. When I have a problem
with [the lack of] water, I go to the chief engineer himself. You saw
how I had been running around like a chicken with its head cut off
in the last few days because of water shortages. I knocked at the chief
engineer's door in the very early morning hours and woke him up to
have him give me a letter to the ghafir to turn the water on for my
tenancies." I said he must agree that the majority of tenants are not
in a position to go knocking at the chief engineer's door at any time,

let alone very early in the morning—one must know a person fairly well before one can do such a thing. "I agree," he said, "but there is no one in this town [meaning important persons in New Halfa] who has not eaten a meal at my house. I know all those people. You see how they come to my house all the time. They are all friends of mine."

Kinship and Tribal and Ethnic Affiliation

A recurrent theme of this book is ethnic identity, which plays so prominent a role in differentiating groups on the New Halfa Scheme. The major division between tenants is drawn along ethnic lines, between Halfawis and Arabs. Yet the terms refer to somewhat different kinds of realities. *Halfawi* is a spatial term, encompassing all the peoples who had to be relocated from Wadi Halfa, including Nubians, who form the majority, Mahas, Ja°afra, and others. *Arab* is an occupational or ecologic specialization term, referring to the pastoral nomadic occupants of the Butana, who were settled on the Scheme in partial compensation for lost pasture and to satisfy an ideological preference for sedentary over pastoral people. Thus, both the Arabic-speaking Shukriya and the Beja-speaking Hadandawa are "Arabs" from the perspective of the Corporation, of the Halfawis, and, indeed, of many former pastoralists themselves.

Halfawis and Arabs monopolize the tenancies on the Scheme (many of them also provide wage labor), and the Halfawis control all the freehold lands. But a number of other ethnic groups, who constitute an agricultural proletariat, provide wage labor on the tenancies at certain critical times during the cultivation cycle and on the government-owned sugar estate. Some of them also find agro-industrial employment in the sugar factory and the flour mill.

The Corporation uses the term *Sudanese* to refer to several ethnic groups whose origins are Sudanese, but who did not obtain rights to tenancies. Most of these come from the western Sudan, especially the Fur, and from the southern Sudan, mainly Dinka and Nuer. The Fur are fellow Muslims who, once they learn or improve their Arabic, tend to slip into the dominant Arab and Halfawi groups as sharecroppers. The southern Sudanese are distinguishable, not only by religion, since very few are Muslim, and by their at best imperfect command of Arabic, but also by their dark skin color and especially by their extreme height.

The term *Fallata* refers generally to persons of western Sudanese
origins, whose roots are in countries west of Lake Chad, such as
Niger, Nigeria, and Burkina Faso. Many, but not all, of the Fallata
are Hausa-speaking and came to the Sudan—or their parents or grand-
parents did—on their way to or from Mecca, since the great overland
hadj (pilgrimage) route connects Kano, Zinder, and Kanem with
Darfur, Kordofan, and Khartoum.

Finally, there are the Eritreans, refugees from the ethno-political
warfare in neighboring Ethiopia. Most of the Eritreans do not live on
the Scheme itself but in specially designated refugee camps, such as
those in Kassala and in Khashm el-Girba. Corporation trucks visit
these camps during peak labor demand times and hire men by the
day for work in the fields and factories.

The Arabs have looked unenthusiastically at each new group of
immigrants. Describing the entrance of strangers into the Butana,
the poet as-Sadiq wad al-Halal wrote:

> qaatli rkeiba ᶜaan-il-umma haadhi kthurha
> id-dinka-w-nweir khassar dhughumti kdurha.
> [the Butana said to me,
> "Watch how many these people are.
> The Dinka and the Nuer have violated me."]

Kinship and tribal and ethnic affiliation played important roles
in the tenancy distribution process described earlier. Whereas resettled Halfawis had the right to a tenancy and a house, and some of
them received freehold lands, none of the pastoral tenants received
either a house or freehold land in compensation for their diminished
grazing and rainfed farmlands. Since pastoral lands had not been
individually registered, the government felt it did not owe the herders any compensation other than allowing them to settle and farm
on the Scheme.

Tenancy allocation to Shukriya and other pastoralists took place
over a four-year period. Allocation of tenancies for pastoralists was
assigned to the Native Adminstration with the recommendation that
a "first-come, first-served" principle should be observed. Since the
number of potentially eligible households was higher than available
tenancies, some had to be excluded. The process by which certain
families were selected for inclusion in the Scheme and others left out
involved the application of locally understood values. The modern
European/North American world looks with disfavor on using fam-

ily and friendship ties in distributing social benefits, and nepotism has strong negative connotations. But among the Shukriya and many other Middle Eastern groups, providing benefits for kinsmen and supporters is expected and—although sometimes reluctantly—accepted. Favoring a stranger over a relative would be viewed as repudiation of one's family obligations; favoring a political opponent or neutral over a political supporter would be sheer madness. Not using the power to allocate tenancies to generate new ties and supporters, as well as to reinforce existing ones, would be interpreted as foolishness. Thus, the benefits of Scheme participation among the Shukriya through the allocation of tenancies were largely absorbed by the elite, and within the elite by those families who were closely allied, by ties of kinship and politics, to the chiefs of the Native Administration. Since, in principle, the rule of "one man/one tenancy" had to be served, tenancies were assigned to children, to persons who were absent, and in some cases to the dead (Salem-Murdock 1979:21). Before giving examples of tenancy accumulation among the elite, it is useful to summarize Shukriya history and tribal structure.

The Shukriya today number between 300,000 and 500,000—no accurate count of the pastoral populations yet exists. The majority of the *nusab* (genealogy experts) classify the Shukriya as Juhayna Arabs, thus coming from Qahtan (MacMichael 1967:250). Hasan (1973:158) traces their origin to a Bashir bin Dhubyan. The Shukriya themselves insist that they are Adnani Arabs descended from Shakir bin Ibrahim bin Own, a descendant of Ja'far bin Abi Talib, an uncle of the Prophet, thus connecting themselves to the Prophet himself.[1]

Shakir, the Shukriya say, entered the Sudan around the fourteenth century, coming across the Red Sea from Arabia with his brother Bashir, the ancestor of the Bawadira and the Um Badiriya. Shakir had seven sons, including three sets of twins: Miheid and Riteim, the ancestors of the Miheidat and the Rutamat; Ifeis and Fiteis, the ancestors of the Afasa and the Fteisat; and Hasan

---

[1] The Arabs are divided into two major groups: *al-Arab al-Ariba* or Arabian Arabs, and *al-Arab al-musta'riba*, or Arabized Arabs; the first group is Yemenite (southern), descended from Qahtan, and the second group is Hijazi and Najdi (northern), descended from Adnan (Hitti 1960:31-32). Since the Prophet's family, Quraysh, is from Adnan, many Arab tribes assert an Adnani origin.

an-Nayim and Hamad an-Nazzaz, the ancestors of the Nawayma and the Nazzaween. The seventh son was Zeidan.

The historical memory of the Shukriya goes back to Sha'id-Din bin Tuweim, reported to have lived in the early seventeenth century (Crowford 1951:86). His tomb, along with that of his wife, Bayaki *bit el mek* (the king's daughter) can be seen near Jebel Qeili, at the northwest edge of Central Butana (MacMichael 1967:251). The Shukriya do not appear to have played a very important role during the seventeenth and eighteenth centuries. They were portrayed in their traditions as having occupied a somewhat humble position on the Butana compared with their kinsmen, the Bawadira and the Um Badiriya, and with their traditional enemies the Rikabiyeen (Hillelson 1920:42). It was in the period of Awad el-Karim Abu 'Ali and his sons that the Shukriya acquired mastery of the Butana, after the Battle of Mandara against the Funj about 1779 (MacMichael 1967:251). Awad el-Karim Abu 'Ali was succeeded by his grandson, Awad el-Karim Abu Sin, as chief of the Shukriya; he was named Abu Sin (literally, the father of tooth) because he had a blackened front tooth (Hillelson 1920:55). The Abu Sin family remains among the most prominent Shukriya to this day.

The greatest of the Shukriya shaikhs was Ahmed bin Awad el-Karim Abu Sin (1790?–1890?), who witnessed the Turko-Egyptian conquest of the Sudan. After their conquest, the Turks sought the support of the influential shaikhs of the Sudan; Shaikh Ahmed became one of their most trusted allies (MacMichael 1967:252). He was rewarded with the title *bey* and given large grants of land east of the Blue Nile (Hillelson 1920:60). He was also named governor of Khartoum and remained in office for ten years (Holt 1976:9). During this period, under the leadership of his son Awad el-Karim, the Shukriya became the official lords of the Butana and held "a general overlordship over all the nomads of the Blue Nile, the Gezira and the 'Atbara, and tithes were paid to the Abu Sin family on the crops of nearly every *wadi* in the ancient land of Meroe" (MacMichael 1967:252). Sir Samuel Baker, who visited the Butana in 1861, recounts his meeting with Shaikh Ahmed Bey Abu Sin:

> He was the most magnificent specimen of an Arab that I had ever seen. Although upwards of eighty years of age, he was as erect as a lance, and did not appear more than between fifty and sixty; he was of Herculean stature, about six feet three inches high, with immensely broad shoulders and chest. . . . As a desert patriarch he was superb, the

very perfection of all that imagination could paint, if we could personify Abraham at the head of his people. (1868:132)

During the Mahdia (1881–1889), the position of the Shukriya became somewhat ambiguous. They were never totally trusted by the khalifa, the Mahdi's successor, since they never gave him more than partial support; they even helped to provision Kassala during the Ansar's (the Mahdi's followers) siege, which began in November 1883 and lasted twenty months (Holt 1958:147). Shaikh Awad el-Karim Ahmed Abu Sin, the chief of the tribe, remained loyal to the Egyptians. When the khalifa asked him to bring his tribe to Umdurman to show support, the shaikh declined. In retaliation, the khalifa summoned him to Umdurman and put him in prison, where he died in 1886. The Shukriya were deprived of the camels and horses that were the foundation of their wealth. The disaster culminated in a great famine that ravaged the Sudan in 1888 (Holt 1958:152). Father Joseph Ohrwalder reports of the famine: "The great Shukrieh [*sic*] tribe had eaten almost all their camels, and its numbers dwindled from forty thousand to four thousand souls" (Wingate n.d.:34).

With the Anglo-Egyptian conquest, Shaikh Muhamed Awad el-Karim was appointed the nazir of the Shukriya and remained in office until his death in 1902. He was succeeded by his brother Abdallah. In 1912, the British appointed Abdallah's son, Awad el-Karim, as the *wakil nazir* (deputy) with the understanding that he would succeed his father as nazir. Shaikh Abdallah died in 1923 and was succeeded by this son, who held office until 1943. Upon his death, there was a dispute among the Abu Sin family over the nazirate. Muhamed, the son of Hamad and the grandson of the first nazir, Muhamed Awad el-Karim, argued that the nazirate should be returned to the first nazir's direct line, especially since the third nazir, Awad el-Karim, had no descendants. Muhamed, another son of the second nazir Abdallah and the third nazir Awad el-Karim's younger brother, argued that he should follow his father and brother. The British resolved the problem by dividing the nazirate in two: the Rufaʿa nazirate, headed by Shaikh Muhamed Abdallah Abu Sin, who was followed by Shaikh Muhamed Ahmed Hilmi Abu Sin, and the Qadaref nazirate, headed by Shaikh Muhamed Hamad Abu Sin. In 1972, the Sudanese government did away with the Native Administration and replaced it with locally elected rural councils.

Let us go back to tenancy accumulation on the Scheme. In the Sufiya block, which is entirely Arab, one of the nineteen blocks on the Scheme, 1,102 tenancies are recorded in the 1975/1976 tenants' cotton account. The tenancies are divided among five villages: Sufiya-j-Jadida, Qeili-j-Jadida, al-Amlat, al-Haraza, and Tambai, the last a new Hadandawa (Beja) settlement. The major ethnic groups represented in the villages are Shukriya, Hadandawa, Dleigab, Zibeidiya, and Ahamda.

The village of Sufiya-j-Jadida can serve as an example. According to a 1981/1982 sugar distribution list, 267 households were recorded as eligible for sugar allocation.[2] Among those households, 129 were listed as Shukriya, 37 as Shammasha (formerly Shukriya dependents), 61 as Hadandawa, and 40 as "others" (a Corporation agricultural inspector, a few teachers, a health worker, and a few policemen, in addition to some pastoral/nomadic households who came to the village periodically for short periods of time, to graze their flocks). Since the 40 "other" households did not own any tenancies and lived in the village for purposes other than cultivation, the effective population of the village is 227 households, with the ethnic and tribal composition shown in table 3.1.

Although the Sinnab represented only 19 percent of the effective number of households in the village, the percentage of their tenancy holdings was higher (there are about 230 tenancies in the village). Among 77 households interviewed from among the 227, tenancy ownership was as shown in table 3.2. Only one Sinnab head of household among the 16 interviewed did not possess a tenancy, as opposed to 9 of the 41 other Shukriya household heads interviewed. The one Sinnab nonowner was a young man, about 25 years old, and was not a descendant of Ahmed Bey Abu Sin. Three Sinnabs were the only tenants interviewed who had a direct holding of more than one tenancy each.

Two of the interviewed Sinnab household heads who owned more than a tenancy each were brothers. The older one, a politically influential Butana elder during tenancy distribution, had three tenancies, all registered under his own name without any attempt at concealment. The younger brother, who occupied a political position during the same period and still carried the title, had effective control over nine tenancies, two of which were in his own name, four in the

---

[2] Because of shortages, sugar is usually supplied by the government and distributed at official prices among village/town households according to size.

TABLE 3.1
Ethnic and Tribal Composition in Sufiya-j-Jadida

Ethnic Group			Households	
			Number	Percent
Shukriya Lineages			129	57
	Number	Percent		
Sinnab	42	19		
Dreishab	48	21		
Nourab	12	5		
Hassanab	7	3		
Others	20	9		
Shammasha			37	16
Hadandawa			61	27
			227	100

TABLE 3.2
Tenancy Ownership among 77 Households in Sufiya-j-Jadida

Ethnic Groups	Number of Households Interviewed in Village		Number of Tenancies Held		
			None	One	Several
Shukriya	57	129	10	44	3
Sinnab	16	42	1	12	3
Dreishab	25	48	7	18	—
Nourab	4	12	—	4	—
Hassanab	4	7	—	4	—
Others	8	20	2	6	—
Shammasha	10	37	3	7	—
Hadandawa	10	61	2	8	—

names of brothers (three of whom lived in other parts of the Sudan and one who lived on the Butana, attending family herds), two in the names of his sons (one of whom lived outside the Sudan and the other in Khartoum), and one in the name of a nephew, a small boy. He also had some control over an unknown number of other tenancies that belonged to cousins and other kinfolk. This man relied totally on hired labor to work his fields.

Education

Scheme tenants are very aware of education and regard it as valuable in itself, as a resource and as an investment. The term *daris* or *mit^calim* (educated) is applied to people at different levels of schooling. A person with any kind of formal education who can read and write with some efficiency might be called daris. A different term, *jami^ci* (university educated), is used to refer to education above the high school level, even if the person does not hold a college degree.

Education is esteemed by most Scheme inhabitants, tenants and nontenants alike, although the level aspired to differs among individuals. Most people would like their children, especially boys, to be able minimally to read and write. They perceive these skills to be very important in the Scheme context, where government announcements and regulations are always in a written form. Tenants who cannot read the status of their cotton account, for example, find it very frustrating and, in the presence of more-educated people, embarrassing. A tenant will often apologize for not being able to read or write but will immediately add that his son is attending school and can do both. Arab tenants often blame what they perceive as their inferior position on the Scheme, relative to that of the Halfawis, on the fact that the latter are better educated; Halfawi men can read and write and can talk knowledgeably to the Corporation staff. The Halfawis do not disagree. Many Arab leaders feel it is often easier for Halfawi leaders to communicate agricultural policies to villagers because their people are in a position to understand and are thereby more receptive. Also, the very high percentage of educated people in Halfawi villages compensates for the presence of a few illiterates, since the latter always have someone around to read and explain announcements.

Educated tenants who are at least high school graduates have a great advantage over the rest, *ceteris paribus*. Throughout most of the agricultural operations on the Scheme, such as ploughing, sowing, fertilizing, spraying, watering, and receiving credit, tenants have to come in contact with agricultural staff of the Corporation whenever they have complaints, to deal with formal notices, and so on. It is much easier for a tenant with some education to communicate with the different agricultural officers, since there is an initial receptivity that is often lacking when the tenant is illiterate. The more junior the officer, the more important this becomes.

One July, I accompanied the Higher Irrigation Committee, which consisted of the Ministry of Irrigation's chief engineer, the agricultural director of the Corporation, and the secretary-general of the Farmers' Union, on a tour of several days throughout the Scheme to investigate water shortage problems, especially in the northern parts. As we were leaving a branch agricultural office, we were intercepted by some Arab tenants, all illiterate, who made fierce criticisms of the inspectors and agricultural extension workers in their block. They said the inspectors treated them as they would not even treat a dog (not a favored pet in most Middle Eastern countries). They were often ordered out of the offices and were threatened with forcible removal if they did not leave voluntarily. The mistreatment of illiterate tenants by inspectors and agriculturalists is a complaint that I have often heard in all Arab areas of the Scheme.

Another point is that most tenants educated at the high school or equivalent level hold positions in addition to farming. As teachers, health workers, and Corporation employees, they can deal with agricultural officers on more equal terms.

Education also gives some tenants the opportunity for social interaction with Corporation officials. It is not uncommon for a high school teacher/tenant, for example, regularly to invite and be invited to the homes of senior Corporation officials. They become friends who eat and drink together. Although these are primarily social gatherings, agricultural matters are always discussed. Such tenants and their associates tend to be the first to know when needed inputs arrive, what their availability is, and the best times to obtain them.

Political/Social Positions

Political and social access depends on the presence of such already noted resources as tribal and kinship affiliation, wealth, and education. People with the right kinship and tribal ties, wealth, and/or education are far better placed to obtain key political positions than those who do not have these advantages. The importance of tribal affiliation and kinship ties is underscored among the Arabs, where political representation is concentrated in a few families. The initial composition of the regional government in eastern Sudan, introduced in 1981, provides an excellent example. Among the five appointed regional ministers, two were from the Hadandawa and one was a Shukriya. One of the Hadandawa ministers was the son of a former nazir and belonged to one of their most powerful families. The Shukriya minister was from the elite Sinnab lineage. Another minister was a Nubian from one of the Scheme villages. Since many of the local decisions are tied to regional and central offices, knowing people at the regional and central levels is very important.

Ma^crifa and Wasta (Connections)

Ma^crifa and wasta play important roles in socioeconomic and political interaction in many societies. It is always useful to know someone in a key position or someone who is willing to intervene on your behalf. A man who has ma^crifa (knows people) is admired and looked up to. Ma^crifa, in this sense, does not apply to just anybody, however, but only to those who are in a position to offer help when you need it. It is good to have *ma^carif* (connections), but invoking them normally requires other attributes, such as kinship ties, wealth, and/or education. People you can reach in times of need and disturb in the middle of the night, for example, have to be more than mere acquaintances. The relationship is cultivated in advance by offerings of hospitality, and hospitality presumes control over adequate resources. To be able to retain these relationships and have them grow and flourish requires that such hospitality be regular and continuous. This is a very costly enterprise, one in which most tenants cannot engage.

AGRICULTURAL INPUTS, WATER, AND CREDIT

Introduction

The establishment of a highly centralized, mechanized, irrigated development scheme in an area in which production had centered around small-scale, subsistence-oriented livestock raising and rainfed sorghum cultivation led to a broad range of social, economic, and political transformations. Individual producers were transformed from relatively autonomous managers of land, livestock, labor, and water to tenants dependent on the parastatal corporation for the provision of the major elements of production and for the commercialization of significant portions of their crops. The dependency situation at New Halfa is exacerbated by the continuous deterioration of machinery, shortages of fuel and spare parts, declining fertility of the soil, erratic provisioning of improved seeds (especially for wheat), and siltation of the reservoir with consequent progressively declining amounts of irrigation water. As the availability of timely provisioned inputs deteriorates, there is an inevitable competition for those that remain. Seeds, traction, and water that may be on hand are not equitably or randomly distributed. Instead, access has been accumulating in the hands of an elite of prosperous tenants who have been able to expand their holdings at the expense of those who have had to give them up. The process by which agricultural inputs gravitate to affluent farmers can be seen in the cases of heavy machinery for preparing land and harvesting wheat, improved seeds, fertilizers, insecticides, herbicides, water, and credit. Less easy to demonstrate, but surely as crucial to the success of the agricultural operation, is access to information, which similarly has been accumulating among the elite.

Agricultural Inputs

Tenants are commonly faced with the problem of agricultural input shortages at the early stage of land preparation. All three crops (cotton, groundnuts, and wheat; now also sorghum) require a complex series of land preparation. Fields are prewatered to encourage early growth of weeds. The land is then plowed to get rid of the weeds; depending on the condition of the soil, several ploughings might be required. Dry and green ridging (rebuilding inner field ridges before sowing and again when plants are very young) follows ploughing. Canals need to be cleared to facilitate irrigation, and ridges that border tenancies have to be heightened to prevent irrigation water from flooding the roads. Heavy machinery has to be in good operating condition, and fuel and spare parts should be available, along with people trained to operate and repair these machines. Machine operators, surprisingly, are not in short supply. Land preparation, however, which is supposed to follow a certain timetable, is often far behind schedule, with consequent delays in sowing and harvesting.

Shortages of improved seeds are most prevalent for wheat. The following letter from tenants in an Arab block (from Farmers' Union files), addressed to the Corporation manager and dated 11 September 1973, refers to this situation:

> Good greetings:
> We 137 farmers of *tur^{c}a* Seven [area of canal No. 7] in Block Five inform you of our critical need . . . for wheat seeds. . . .
> As the inspector of Section Two knows very well, we are hardworking farmers [on] tenancies [that] are our only source of livelihood. . . . We have suffered two severe years, especially from water shortages, especially for the wheat crop . . . . Add to this the fact that we have cultivated [we were allowed to cultivate] only half of the area of our tenancies last year, which led to low production, which, in turn, led to our lack of seeds this year. . . . This year's spreading drought is not unknown to you. . . .

There is no indication that this request for seeds was honored. Shortages and untimely arrival of harvesters are difficulties that tenants often face. The problem of fertilizer is often one of cost rather than of unavailability. The Corporation recommends a certain amount of fertilizer to be applied to each crop. However, for crops other than cotton, the tenant is free to use his own discretion. For cotton, the Corporation decides how much is to be used and distributes that amount to the tenants. Since for most tenants the cotton crop is not cost effective, many try when they can to hide some of the fertilizer for use on other crops or for sale on the black market. Many tenants cannot afford to apply the recommended amount of fertilizer to their wheat crop; in years when the cost increases, fewer are able to do so.

Fertilizers can also be obtained from the Sudan Agricultural Bank. In 1981/1982, it sold fertilizer at £S8.00 per sack as opposed to the Corporation price of £S11.80. This was possible because it was the previous year's, purchased at earlier prices. Since there is usually not enough to satisfy everybody's needs, deals like that are normally reserved for those whom the Bank manager refers to as "preferred customers," those who are capable of repaying their debts on time and who have been dealing with the Bank faithfully, and on a regular basis, for years. "They are dependent on us and most of them have large numbers of tenancies. We cannot fail them. You know, it is like some sort of an informal, unwritten contract. We supply them with fertilizers according to their needs and the number of their tenancies. We cannot address ourselves to the needs of others until we satisfy theirs" (personal communication). From the Agricultural Bank's viewpoint, this is good business. For the majority of the tenants, however, the poor always have to pay more for the same (or inferior) goods.

Water

Several factors contribute to severe water problems on the Scheme. One has to do with the division of responsibility between the ministries of Agriculture and Irrigation regarding water distribution and their often discrepant priorities. A second has to do with the reservoir situation. A third involves the mechanics of water distribution on the Scheme and a certain amount of corruption, especially at the most junior levels.

The Ministry of Irrigation is responsible for water distribution from the dam to the minor canals and also for canal maintenance

(Salem-Murdock 1984:44-47). The Ministry of Agriculture, represented by the Corporation, is responsible for distributing water from the minor canals into the tenant fields and for estimating daily water requirements of different Scheme crops.

Estimated water needs are allocated to four irrigation subdivisions on the Scheme. It is up to the Engineering Department, however, to decide whether to give a certain subdivision all or part of its estimated needs, depending on water availability in the reservoir and the Department's own estimation of water priorities. For example, although sorghum production was finally legalized in 1980/1981, and the Corporation acknowledges the crop's legitimate need for water, the Engineering Department does not always share that view. From its perspective, sorghum is a pest. Department officials feel that irrigation water was originally conceived for a three-crop rotation, two in the rainy season, and one—wheat—in the dry season. The legalization of sorghum increased the rainy season's irrigable crops to three, overtaxing the already diminishing capacity of the reservoir. They also feel that irrigation is too costly to waste on food crops that can grow in a rainfed area.

Subdivisions are thus often allocated less water than the tenants feel they need. We see this expressed by the Butana poet as-Sadiq wad al-Halal. The tenancy and the tenant are having an argument. The man scolds the land for not being productive. The tenancy responds: "bitbee^cu-s-samaad wil-lowm tissow mqaablini / nas ar-rai baraahum bil-^catash harqini" (You sell the fertilizer and then put the blame on me / The irrigation people alone have burnt me down with thirst).

The reservoir siltation problem is so serious that the World Bank— in collaboration with the International Development Associations, the International Fund for Agricultural Development, and the African Development Bank—has launched a $65-million project to rehabilitate the Scheme. Among the recommendations of a detailed feasibility study carried out by Agrar was either construction of a new dam upstream from the present site to counteract the continuous siltation of Khashm el-Girba, or gradual transformation of the Scheme from agricultural to livestock production.

One problem with the mechanics of water distribution stems from the fact that, for reasons already mentioned, less water is available for distribution than is needed. Therefore, if some people are to get their full water requirements, others have to receive less or no water at all. This scarcity invites corruption. At high levels, it is discreet and performed with style, without outright bribery. Arrangements are made within a context of hospitality, socialization, and entertainment: doing a good friend a little favor. It would be unbecoming for a water engineer to allow hundreds of cultivated feddan that belong to a man who wined and dined him to wither for lack of water.

Corruption at the lower level is on a much smaller scale, but apparently widespread. Although no tenant ever admits to having bribed a water guard, such allegations are often heard against those whose fields seem unreasonably productive. Some tenants confided that the reason they themselves did not bribe the guards was simply a lack of funds. The issue of bribing water guards was raised during a trip with the agricultural manager. The manager saw the problem as twofold. First, although water guards were granted about one-fifth of a feddan for private use as vegetable gardens, some were cultivating from 2 to 5 feddan each. These guards tended to neglect their work in favor of their gardens. Second, it was reported to him that many received bribes from farmers. The manager felt the problem was more common among Halfawis than among Arabs, since, according to reports that reached him, it took place more often on freehold lands than on government tenancies. He told agriculturalists and inspectors that the fault was more theirs than the guards'—had they been careful about water distribution, it would not have happened. He said that if they did not watch the guards carefully and protect the farmers from them, the strong farmers "will eat the weak."

Another problem area in water distribution is poor management and coordination. Often some tenancies are waterlogged, while others are desiccated.

Credit

In addition to credit exchanged among family members and relatives and that offered by well-to-do tenants to dependents and sharecroppers, sources of credit on the New Halfa Scheme can be broadly divided into five categories: running accounts at local stores; the sheil system; loans offered by NHAPC in the form of cash advances for the cotton crop; loans offered by NHAPC in the form of inputs and services for the wheat crop; and loans offered by the New Halfa branch of the Sudan Agricultural Bank, mainly for groundnuts, fruits, and vegetables, and for other small- and medium-scale enterprises.

Store Accounts. This is a very common source of credit that is independent of the Scheme. Villagers tend to buy all their needs from a particular shop that extends them credit, and they pay back on a monthly, seasonal, or annual basis, depending on the source of their income. Shopkeepers do not charge any interest for extending credit. The only advantage seems to be tying customers to a particular store, since it is very unbecoming for a customer to desert the store that offered him credit in times of need in favor of another one that might offer better prices when he has the cash in hand. In addition, the customer would thereby risk the discontinuation of his credit at that particular store. Shopkeepers, generally speaking, do not lend cash to their customers, except for very small amounts in times of dire necessity. Again, interest is usually not charged on these debts.

Among the three shopkeepers in Village Eighteen, all provided food and other goods to customers on credit. I never heard a customer complain that the shopkeeper fiddled with his account or a shopkeeper complain that a customer was not repaying his debts. In North Kordofan, Reeves and Frankenberger (1981:37-38) report that shopkeepers do make interest-bearing cash loans to their customers: "The rate varies between 25% and 50% depending on the length of time before repayment. Two months is considered the maximum limit of time for repayment." I found no such cases on the Scheme or in New Halfa.

The Sheil System. Sheil is payment for a crop in advance of harvest. Farmers frequently need cash, especially in the preharvest months, when their own consumption stocks of grain may be exhausted and they are forced to purchase cereals in the market. Their own crop is then mortgaged against the loan, and the merchant or shopkeeper to whom they are in debt claims the agreed-upon quantity of grain at harvest. According to Reeves and Frankenberger (1981:37–38), "profit margins of 100 percent are not unheard of in these cases." The need for cash and its prompt availability from the merchant persuade the farmer to mortgage his crop for a price far lower than he would receive were he able to market the harvest himself. But his cash needs may be so pressing that he enters into a sheil loan, despite its obvious economic disadvantage.

On the New Halfa Scheme, Halfawis appear to enter into sheil relationships rarely, if ever. None of the tenants or shopkeepers in Village Eighteen acknowledged its existence within the village, and some denied ever having heard of it. Others professed that some of the large merchants in the town of New Halfa extended credit on a sheil basis, but said that none of the tenants whom they knew availed themselves of it.

There is some sentiment that sheil may be illegal, and villagers may have thought it wiser to dissociate themselves from it. On the other hand, in Arab villages on the Scheme, most tenants questioned acknowledged both the existence of the system and their involvement in its practice. The bulk of the exchanges involved sorghum, although increasingly groundnuts were entering the system. In one of the Arab villages, a farmer explained the sheil system as follows: "Suppose I need £S100 for this or that. It might be for agricultural reasons or to meet a certain obligation, such as performing one's duty for a wedding or a funeral. I come to a shopkeeper and say to him, 'I need £S100 and for that amount *bashayyilak* [I will let you have; literally, carry] my sorghum, in such and such wadi, and for such and such amount per *ardab*' [weight measure: 2 sacks of wheat or 366 lbs.]. At harvest time, I go to the shopkeeper and say to him, 'Come and *sheel al-ᶜish bitaaᶜak* [take away your sorghum].' This happens with both sorghum and groundnuts."

I asked my informant why the farmer would follow the sheil system when he knew very well it went against his own interest. Why not borrow money instead? "You see, the problem with borrowing money is that the shopkeeper would not want to lend you money without interest. With interest, it is considered *ribaa* and is forbidden by Islam. The sheil is considered an economic exchange. The only difference between it and other exchanges is that you get the price early and deliver the merchandise late." The tenant continued,

> The sheil is like a contract and happens in front of witnesses; if, at harvest time, the farmer refuses to give the merchant his sorghum, the judge will side with the merchant, if there were witnesses. The farmer cannot say to the merchant, "You lent me £S100 and here is your money." The judge will say to him, "*inta shayyaltu ᶜeishak* [You sold him your sorghum on a sheil basis]." There were cases where the judge sided with the farmer, but that was only if the merchant failed to produce witnesses. But even that is hard to do. You see, the people of the village will start making the farmer the target of their jokes. He could not go out in the streets without being shamed. Men, women, and children would laugh at him. It will reach the point where the farmer can stand it no longer and will go to the merchant begging him to take the sorghum.

Tenants sometimes resort to the sheil system to support such agricultural operations as weeding groundnuts. According to informants,

> People who do not have enough money will have to borrow by sheil, borrow from a bank, or do the weeding themselves. The problem with the Agricultural Bank is that you cannot get a loan unless you deposit a security. A merchant has to guarantee you. Many merchants refuse to do that unless the farmer promises to sell them his crop. A farmer who has a family does not need to resort to sheil. Only the ones with just a wife or only small children. What happened last season with many farmers is that they utilized the sheil for their groundnut crop on the basis of £S2–2.5 per sack. At harvest time the price of groundnuts rose to £S16–21 per sack. The farmers tried to get out of their sheil obligations, but were cornered by the merchants. At the end, the merchants agreed to pay the farmers £S5–6 per sack instead of the agreed upon amount of £S2–2.5.

Despite farmers' acceptance of sheil as given, they do regard it as exploitive. Tenants who resort to sheil as a source of credit rather than to the Agricultural Bank do so not because they favor sheil, but because they realize that the Bank's loan requirements are often beyond their means.

Corporation Loans: Cash Advances for Cotton. Cash advances ideally are available to all tenants who cultivate cotton in a particular year. In the 1981/1982 season, the amount of the advance was £S87.50, divided as follows:

Sowing—£S15. For sowing cotton seeds, patching the soil and filling in holes, dividing a tenancy into terraces, and thinning the cotton seedlings.

First weeding—£S20. Besides weeding, this cash advance covered the construction of a structure to protect picked cotton.

Second weeding—£S17.5. Tenants were expected to do two weedings for this amount.

Third weeding—£S15. Tenants were expected to do a "fourth" weeding—in fact a fifth, assuming they weeded twice at "second weeding." At the end of this stage, if the Corporation was satisfied with the tenant's performance, he received an additional £S10. Another £S10 was offered at the end to tenants who picked well, thus bringing the total cash received to £S87.5.

It is worth noting that a tenancy that the Corporation views as worth cultivating will be farmed, whether or not the tenant himself thinks it worthwhile. The Corporation hires labor for any of the agricultural work that the tenant does not perform himself and records the cost against his individual account. When performed by hired labor, the jobs always cost considerably more than the amount of cash advance the Corporation offers the tenants for doing the same job. For example, in 1981/1982, when the Corporation offered between £S15 and £S20 for weeding, hired laborers charged between £S30 and £S50.

Cash advances are deducted upon harvest from the tenant's share of profits, if there are any. If at any stage the Corporation decides that the crop is not worth pursuing, the payment of the cash advance stops. Besides being insufficient and divided over many stages, cash advances are frequently late. To receive small amounts of money, tenants often have to make several trips to the block office and wait there for long hours, subjecting themselves to humiliation from agriculturalists and inspectors who regard them as ignorant. As-Sadiq wad al-Halal portrays this situation in the form of an argument between a herder and a tenant farmer. The herder says to the farmer: "it taabi͑-s-sarf mow mhaddideenlak yowm / w-͑ummaal-il-qutun taab͑aak shateema-w-lowm" (You are always after the cash advances but they have not set a date for you / The cotton laborers are meanwhile following you with their curses). Then the herder addresses the cotton: "miskeen il-muzaari͑ zarzarouh-l-͑ummaal / is-salafiyya maabithillu w-mardoum maal" (Poor is the farmer, the laborers are cornering him / The cash advance will not solve his problems, he will stay in debt).

Corporation Loans: Inputs and Services for the Wheat Crop. As with the cotton crop, tenants are eligible for wheat advances. These are not in the form of cash, however, but in services (land preparation, canal clearing, sowing, harvesting) and in material inputs (fertilizers, insecticides, and sacks). Tenants are required to reimburse the cost of these services and inputs promptly after harvest. If the tenant does not have sufficient cash to repay these costs, the Corporation appropriates a portion of the wheat harvest, based on an "official" price that is substantially lower than what the tenant might obtain on the open market.

If the loan is paid off in wheat, the tenant is allowed to retain a maximum of three sacks per tenancy. Those whose harvest is insufficient to liquidate the debt have to carry it over to the following year.

Indebted tenants may find themselves excluded from the distribution of improved seeds whenever the supply is inadequate to cover all demands. In 1977, tenants with unliquidated debts were left out of seed distribution; curiously, in what seemed to be the first equity-based decision in a long time, the Corporation also decided to exclude those whose net cotton revenues exceeded £S100 per tenancy, under the assumption that the affluent could afford to purchase wheat seeds on the open market. As it turned out, the decision was short-lived, and elite tenants with connections were able to get Corporation seeds after all.

Sudan Agricultural Bank Loans. The New Halfa branch of the Sudan Agricultural Bank, which opened in 1965, started by financing the groundnut crop. Farmers who received loans had to mortgage their crop to the Bank. The Bank collected the debt with interest as soon as the crop was sold. The Corporation acted as tenants' guarantor. With a joint-account system operating in reference to the cotton crop, the Corporation was able, in case a tenant's groundnut crop failed, to reimburse the Bank with money taken out of the cotton account and register the debt against a tenant's individual account.

As the returns from cotton started going from bad to worse, this proved to be unprofitable for the Corporation. Loans were offered to tenants with Corporation backing between 1970/1971 and 1979/1980, except for two seasons, 1975/1976 and 1978/1979, when the Corporation refused to guarantee the loans. The Bank then required tenants to mortgage property other than government tenancies in order to qualify for loans. Effectively, this limited lending to Halfawis with freehold lands, already an affluent minority on the Scheme. The amount of loan offered in the 1975/1976 season was £S45. The Corporation did not guarantee tenant groundnut loans in 1980/1981 or 1981/1982.

The schedule in table 3.3 shows the amount of money loaned, the number of tenants receiving the loans, and the area covered for the groundnut crop for four consecutive years.The amount of loans available for the groundnut crop for the 1981/1982 season was £S60 per feddan. Tenants who were cultivating 5 feddan or less had to guarantee repayment by depositing a personal check in the amount of the dispersed loan with the Bank. For larger areas, a tenant had to be able to guarantee repayment by mortgaging personal property.

TABLE 3.3
Sudan Agricultural Bank Groundnut Loans, 1977/78–1980/81

Season	Number of Tenants	Area in Feddan	Loans in £S
1977/78	4,444	22,220	200,000
1978/79	5	140	2,020
1979/80	2,000	100,000	150,000
1980/81	6	180	3,712

Sudan Agricultural Bank, New Halfa Branch 1980:8.

The Bank also finances wheat, although on a much smaller scale, largely for Halfawi tenants. As with groundnut loans, wheat loans are limited to those who can guarantee repayment by depositing a personal check for the amount with the Bank. Table 3.4 shows the amount of money loaned for the wheat crop for three consecutive seasons.

Besides groundnuts and wheat, the Bank also finances red onions, white onions, tomatoes, hot peppers, eggplants, okra, sweet potatoes, and squash. The amounts of loans given out for onions and for other vegetables for three consecutive seasons are shown in table 3.5.

The Bank tries to ensure debt collection by controlling two factors: the persons to whom loans are issued and the purposes. The requirement that tenants leave with the Bank a signed check for the amount borrowed, to be cashed in case of tenant default, discriminates against tenants who not only do not have accounts, but to whom the whole banking system is foreign. From the Bank's point of view, securing loans with collateral for small farmers and for those unknown to management is a very sound strategy. According to personal communications with Bank officials, the collateral requirement is often waived when they are dealing with well-known — which implies more affluent — farmers. The manager said: "Most of our loans are made against guaranteed checks. But we cannot [meaning, it is not done] enforce this requirement when we are dealing with well-known farmers; someone like [so and so], for example. I cannot ask him to prove that he has enough money in the Bank before issuing him a loan. It is not becoming. I trust his word. I know he will repay. His reputation is too important to him to default on a loan" (personal communication). The amount of loans offered by crop in £S per feddan for the 1981/1982 season is indicated in table 3.6.

TABLE 3.4
Sudan Agricultural Bank Wheat Loans, 1978/79–1980/81

Season	Area in Feddan	Loans in £S
1978/79	915	4,837
1979/80	720	6,928
1980/81	2,500	42,740

Sudan Agricultural Bank, New Halfa Branch 1980:8.

TABLE 3.5
Sudan Agricultural Bank Vegetable Loans, 1978/79–1980/81

| | Onions | | Vegetables | |
Season	Area in Feddan	Loans in £S	Area in Feddan	Loans in £S
1978/79	269	7,899	219	13,589
1979/80	199	8,300	300	16,441
1980/81	80	4,533	224	8,081

Sudan Agricultural Bank, New Halfa Branch 1980:9.

TABLE 3.6
Sudan Agricultural Bank Vegetable Loans by Crop, 1981/82

Crop	Average Amount of Loan per Feddan in £S
Groundnuts	60.00
Red onions	73.50
White onions	62.50
Wheat	34.60
Tomatoes	64.00
Hot peppers	71.00
Eggplant	49.75
Sweet potatoes	64.50
Squash	40.50
Okra	46.00

Compiled from Farmers' Union files.

The Bank issued 650 loans for the 1981/1982 season for the groundnut crop, all against guaranteed checks. The checks do not need to be from the tenant himself. They are usually issued by notables. The manager explained: "If we know the person, we allow him

TABLE 3.7
Disaggregated 1981/82 Groundnut Loans

Stage of Cultivation	Amount of Loan per Feddan in £S
Heavy disc ploughing	7.5
Ploughing	7.0
Building terraces	3.5
Seeds	5.0
First weeding	6.0
Second weeding	5.0
Third weeding	4.0
Patching	2.0
Pulling/washing/shelling	20.0
Total	60.0 x 5 = 300

Compiled from Farmers' Union files.

to guarantee, with one check, up to fifteen persons; we hold the uncashed checks here for safekeeping. Each loan is for a maximum of £S300; they are to be repaid with an interest of up to £S32 per £S300, by April 30, 1982. The interest varies between 7 and 9 percent, depending on time of repayment. So a merchant who guarantees fifteen tenants has to deposit with the Bank a check for £S15 times 32; only the amount of interest." Why only the amount of interest in the case of big merchants guaranteeing farmers? "We cannot expect a merchant to deposit with the Bank the full amount for a large number of loans. He would go out of business. Since those people are known to the community and have reputations to protect we feel that receiving only the amount of interest from them is sufficient."

Tenants seldom receive £S300 in one sum, however; rather, the loan is divided according to the different stages of cultivation. For the 1981/1982 season, the £S300 loan was divided, per feddan, as indicated in table 3.7. The banker continued, "A farmer may ask for all or some of the amount. We make sure that he has planted before giving him the next installment, for weeding, for example. This season, about 80 percent of groundnut loans were issued to Arab tenants, mostly Shukriya, since Halfawis were not much interested in groundnut cultivation this year, although last year's prices were very high" (personal communication).

In addition to short-term loans issued on a single-crop, seasonal basis, the Bank offers medium-term loans. Short-term loans are issued

TABLE 3.8

Harvester Loans in £S, 1968–1971 and 1973

Year	No. Loans	Amount	Interest	Total for Bank
1968	1	5,810	1,046	6,856
1969	1	2,500	355	2,855
1970	1	5,000	1,118	6,118
1971	1	3,750	793	4,543
1973	1	5,000	872	5,872
Total	5	22,060	4,184	26,244
Debt collection: 100 percent				

Sudan Agricultural Bank, New Halfa Branch 1980:11.

TABLE 3.9

Tractor/Attachment Loans in £S, 1966–1972 and 1974–1978

Year	Number	Amount	Interest	Total	Repaid	Percentage Repaid
1966	1	1,428	306	1,734	1,734	100
1967	6	11,813	2,957	14,770	14,770	100
1968	2	4,329	1,756	6,085	6,085	100
1969	4	6,578	1,696	8,274	8,274	100
1970	1	2,800	626	3,426	3,426	100
1971	2	3,570	951	4,521	4,521	100
1972	8	18,401	4,805	23,206	23,206	100
1974	5	9,561	2,585	12,146	12,146	100
1975	20	47,100	10,742	57,842	54,154	94
1976	1	1,750	330	2,080	2,080	100
1977	3	8,372	1,887	10,259	9,773	95
1978	1	560	101	661	661	100
Total	54	116,262	28,742	145,004	140,830	97

Sudan Agricultural Bank, New Halfa Branch 1980:11.

before sowing a particular crop and are collected at harvest time. The amount of each loan is relatively small and the numbers are large. Medium-term loans are issued for such projects as animal fattening, dairy, and poultry operations; fruit orchards; purchase of heavy agricultural equipment such as tractors and combine harvesters; and construction. To qualify for a loan for any of the first four projects, with the possible exception of poultry, an applicant has to show that he owns or has full control over a minimum of 5 feddan of freehold land; the loans thus are effectively limited to Nubians. The amount of each loan is much larger than the short-term ones and the number of borrowers much smaller.

For example, according to the Bank's 1980 annual report, only two loans were approved for animal-fattening purposes for the 1980/1981 season, for the amounts of £S3,210 and £S2,500. The same year, three loans were issued for dairy operations. One of the recipients was a Halfawi who had also received one of the two animal-fattening loans. The amounts of the three dairy loans were £S5,400, £S6,000 (for the man who also received £S3,210 for animal fattening), and £S7,800. Tables 3.8 and 3.9 show the amounts of loans issued to individuals, between 1968 and 1971 and in 1973, and between 1966 and 1972 and between 1974 and 1978, respectively, for the purchase of harvesters and of tractors and tractor attachments.

4

Shukriya Production Goals
and Labor Strategies

INTRODUCTION

Several cases are presented in the following two chapters to illustrate the differential impact of the New Halfa Agricultural Scheme on Halfawi and "Arab" tenants and to explore the relationships between production goals and labor strategies as well as access to the resources discussed previously. The cases represent categories of tenants differentiated ethnically, economically, sociopolitically, and by gender, education, and family. The term *tenant* is used loosely, since it also includes persons who hold tenancies and freehold lands but are not actively engaged in cultivation and those who are landless.

The cases involve "native administrator" tenants who use old political linkages to maintain and improve their socioeconomic and political position in the new environment; those who—although started on a rather small scale—were able to establish themselves as wealthy, successful tenants; others who—although not known as "successful tenants" to the Corporation—are acting very innovatively and making considerable profit; and also poor tenants, the majority of whom hold one tenancy and some of whom are landless, struggling to subsist.

None of the "successful tenants" achieved success by hard work only. The New Halfa Scheme, like the Gezira as described by Barnett (1977:59), has built upon and intensified the social differentiation that existed within settler societies before the inception of the Scheme and has widened the gap between the rich and the poor. The shift to a capitalist mode of production utilized these preexisting cleavages while vesting them with new significance.

If this depiction of the division of labor were complete—failed small tenant farmers joining the agricultural proletariat, small tenant farmers barely hanging on, and large farmers succeeding—we would be justified in issuing a negative evaluation of the Scheme: small islands of affluence within a sea of poverty. But, if we also examine the Scheme in terms of its contribution to the development of a larger region, the negative assessment becomes less firmly grounded. As Scudder has written:

> New Halfa was designed to include a major rural town and agro-industries with special emphasis on a sugar refinery and several cotton ginneries. Both industries have been established along with agro-industry associated with wheat milling, groundnut husking, and soap and oil making. This agro-industrial base, along with a wider range of business catering to the settler population . . . has generated a significant amount of non-farm employment, the magnitude of which has been seriously underestimated. . . . (1981:179)

The town of New Halfa is the largest nonfarm employer on the Scheme, and the government is the largest employer within the town, encompassing the New Halfa Agricultural Production Corporation, the Irrigation Department, local government councils, education services, health services, the courts, and the post office. Among these, the Corporation is the main employer, with a total roster of some 3,100, including technical agricultural staff, administrators, and workers; the other government services employ about 21,000 people (Agrar 1978, I, annex 8). The opportunity for off-farm employment is not restricted to the town of New Halfa and the various factories (see table 4.1). In every village, no matter how small, off-farm employment exists in shops, cooperatives, flour mills, schools, veterinary and health centers, and police. Khamsa Arab (Bireisi-j-Jadida), a Shukriya village on the western edge of the Scheme with over 3,000 inhabitants, offers an excellent example. The village supports fifteen shops, four butchers, a flour mill, a baker, three coffeehouses, a mosque, a clinic with village health workers, a coeducational elementary school up to sixth grade that employs six male teachers, a kindergarten with a female teacher, and a literacy school for adult women, also run by a female teacher. There are also several tailors who operate their sewing machines in front of shops, a shoe repairman, and several vendors who sell cigarettes, chewing gum, toothpaste, and tobacco. In addition to these, the village has some thirty *sabbabah*—men who

TABLE 4.1

Nonfarm Employment on the New Halfa Scheme

	Number of Employees May–June 1981[a] Permanent Employees	Seasonal Employees
Private Sector (excluding agro-industry):		
New Halfa Town	2,463	?
Sugar Factory Township	817	?
Rural Hinterland	1,014	?
Agro-industry:		
Cotton Ginneries	264	2,212 [7][b]
Sugar Factory	2,387	6,640 [4]
Soap and Oil Factory	134	50 [3]
Peanut Decorticators	—	416 [3]
Other	9	4
Government Departments:		
APC	2,817	5,731
Education	644	6
Irrigation	431	1,000
Health	945	—
Water & Electricity	355	—
Corp.		
Public Works	315	22
Post & Telephone	108	—
Veterinary	97	—
Forestry	92	626
Mechanical Transport	60	—
Other	121	5
Transportation:		
Taxis, Buses, Trucks	1,177	—
Cinemas:	18	20
Total	14,268	

[a]Not included are employees of the cooperatives (except for one cooperative cinema) and the Farmers' Union. Also omitted are the police force as well as the various illegal and legal businesses that have grown up in the refugee camps within the Scheme boundaries. Data were collected by Muhamed el-Hasan el-Tayeb.
[b]Figures within brackets show number of months employed.

engage in the buying and selling of animals—and about a half-dozen women who engage in petty trade from their own homes.

One of the shopkeepers, Babikir (pseudonyms are used in all case studies), from the Eishab lineage, was 25 years old in 1981 and had managed the shop for only a few months. Babikir had been a camel herder in Old Bireisi on the Butana, the natal village of most of the inhabitants of Khamsa Arab. He herded the family camels now left in the care of a younger brother. Babikir holds a tenancy, as do his brother and father. Now that he is on the Scheme, he will take care of all family tenancies in addition to keeping the shop. His parents spend the rainy season on the Butana and the rest of the year on the Scheme. Babikir sold four camels in ad-Damir, a market town to the north of the Butana, for £S1,200 to open his shop.

Except for grain, which he buys in Qadaref, Babikir usually buys all his goods in the town of New Halfa. Babikir does not intend to have his wife work the tenancies or herd on the Butana during the rainy season; they have a small boy. In January 1981, his shop held the following goods: twenty-six sacks of sorghum, which he had bought in Qadaref and was selling for £S17 a sack (since most people purchased the sorghum in small quantities, a sack often fetched a much higher price), tomato sauce, soap, salt, biscuits, cigarettes, candy, noodles, matches, henna, batteries, razor blades, cloth, rope, tea, dried hot peppers, dried tomatoes, aspirin, oil, flashlight bulbs, flour, dates, sugar, coffee, and spices.

The length of operation of the fifteen stores in the village is shown in table 4.2. Four of the shopkeepers—or their fathers or grandfathers—also owned shops on the Butana. All the village shopkeepers held tenancies and owned animals. Butchering, tailoring, vending, and female petty trading as well as the operation of a bakery, a flour mill, coffee shops, and health and education services are new occupations that did not exist on the Butana.

The agricultural Scheme, for all its shortcomings, has been responsible for an explosion in administrative, commercial, and agro-industrial employment, creating a growth point in a rural setting peripheral to the capital, Khartoum. While the data are not sufficient to draw firm conclusions, an overall evaluation of the New Halfa Scheme (and a number of others), in terms of its contribution to the income of large numbers of persons, may prove to be more attractive than one based narrowly on benefits to the tenants themselves.

Most tenants, whether rich or poor and irrespective of income or ethnicity, opt to combine, in their labor strategy, the exploitation of several economic activities, such as tenancy cultivation, animal husbandry, freehold land cultivation, rainfed cultivation of sorghum, sharecropping, wage labor, seasonal migration, teaching, and shopkeeping. However, the similarity ends here. Whereas affluent tenant farmers pursue this strategy to increase their holdings and

TABLE 4.2
Number of Stores and Length of Operation in an Arab Village

No. of Stores	Length of Operation
2	less than 1 year
3	1 year
2	2 years
2	3 years
1	4 years
1	5 years
0	6 years
2	7 years
2	8 years
Total 15	

optimize their economic opportunities, the majority of the tenants, who are poor, are forced to combine different labor strategies simply to reproduce the household. The 15-feddan tenancy, with its emphasis on cotton production to be sold to the monopsonist parastatal corporation, does not provide a sufficient return to the average tenant.

Indeed, since cotton is the least profitable component of the agricultural sequence (cotton, groundnuts, wheat), many tenants use the period when cotton is to be cultivated to concentrate on other activities. The cotton cultivation season coincides with the rainy season. For Arab tenants, this period involves running livestock on the Butana range and growing rainfed sorghum in the wadis, when these seasonal watercourses enjoy a short but intense watering. The consequent labor absenteeism (Sørbø 1977a, 1977b) on the Scheme reduces cotton yields and, therefore, the net income earned from the tenancy. Low yields and low returns lead to an adversary relationship between the Corporation and the tenant.

It is not the small size of the average tenancy per se that forces tenants into an unprofitable situation, in which the costs of inputs (seeds, fertilizers, insecticides, herbicides, mechanical traction, water, and sometimes wage labor) approximate or exceed returns from production, but rather the requirement that cotton be a component of every annual rotation. Arabs and Nubians agree that cotton is the least remunerative crop, grown only because the Corporation makes its cultivation a condition for remaining on the Scheme. No cotton whatsoever is produced on any of the freehold lands granted to Nubian farmers in compensation for lands lost at Wadi Halfa. Indeed, little in the way of groundnuts and even wheat, the preferred grain staple of Halfawis, is raised on these freehold lands, which are devoted instead to vegetables for household consumption and for markets in New Halfa, Qadaref, Port Sudan, and even as far as Khartoum. These fields are carefully protected, and there are few reports of animals damaging crops on freehold lands. Even on the tenancies, ruminant incursion is far more common on fields of cotton than on those of groundnuts or wheat, a point to be considered in some detail later.

The majority of the tenants cultivate one tenancy with household labor and supplement their incomes by other economic activities. Earnings from outside labor are used to bridge the shortfall between the costs of production and its returns. Because that bridge almost never is in surplus, these tenants have no capital available for investment in additional lands, equipment, or labor and are forced to remain in a basically subsistence posture year after year. Tenants who do have capital resources are in a position to accumulate holdings. Among the Halfawis, this accumulation includes highly remunerative freehold lands, where managerial decisions are entirely in the hands of the farmers themselves. Persons with capital resources are also able to offer hospitality to friends, neighbors, and, most importantly, Corporation and government officials, in return receiving valuable information and being favored in the allocation of scarce credit, fertilizers, improved seeds, and irrigation water.

Thirty-nine heads of household were interviewed in the Shukriya village of Sufiya-j-Jadida. The distribution of tenancies among them is indicated in table 4.3. Three of the eight household heads with no tenancies referred to themselves as farmers; two identified farming as their second occupation; two called themselves herders; and one, a woman, one of two female heads of households in the sample, called herself simply a housewife. The full occupational distribution of the thirty-nine respondents is shown in table 4.4.

Among the nineteen who identified themselves as farmers, seventeen, of whom two held two hawashat each, were tenancy holders. The farmer/animal owner held nine tenancies. Those who identified themselves as farmer/herder, farmer/merchant, wage laborer/farmer, health worker/farmer, housewife/farmer, and teacher, in addition to one of the government employee/farmers, held one tenancy each.

TABLE 4.3
Tenancy Distribution among 39 Households in Sufiya-j-Jadida

Number of Tenancies per Household Head	Number of Household Heads	Total Number of Tenancies
0	8	0
1	28	28
2	2	4
9	1	9
Total	39	41

TABLE 4.4
Occupational Distribution of 39 Households in Sufiya-j-Jadida

Farmer	19
Farmer/animal owner	1
Farmer/herder	6
Farmer/animal trader	1
Farmer/merchant	1
Herder	2
Gov. employee/farmer	2
School janitor/farmer	1
Wage laborer/farmer	1
Health worker/farmer	1
Housewife/farmer	1
Teacher	2
Housewife	1
Total	39

Those who identified themselves as herder, school janitor/farmer, housewife, and animal trader had no holdings.

When questioned whether they had any claims on rainfed lands on the Butana (table 4.5), seventeen of the thirty-nine responded no. Of the twenty-two remaining, fifteen had no personal claims but had some family claims. Only seven reported owning land on the Butana. The size of these lands ranged from 2 to 50 feddan (table 4.6). Animal distribution among the thirty-nine tenants is shown in table 4.7.

The data from Sufiya-j-Jadida indicate that the average villager holds one tenancy, has little land on the Butana, has a small number

TABLE 4.5
Off-Scheme Land Distribution among 39 Households

Tenants who own no land	17
Tenants with claims through family	15
Tenants with personal claims	7
Total	39

TABLE 4.6
Land Distribution among 7 Tenant Households

No. of Tenants	Feddan per Tenant	Total Feddan
1	2	2
2	5	10
1	10	10
1	25	25
1	30	30
1	50	50
7		127

TABLE 4.7
Animal Distribution among 39 Households

	No. of Tenants Holding Animals	Total	Number of Animals		No. of Tenants Holding Minimum No. of Animals
			Maximum per Tenant	Minimum per Tenant	
Camels	10	18	4	1	6
Cattle	32	166	25	1	2
Sheep	16	257	90	1	1
Goats	13	176	25	1	3
Donkeys	35	60	5	1	20
Fowl	21	97	16	2	5

of animals (which are kept on the Scheme all year round), and is largely dependent on farming as his or her major source of income. The average size of tenancy and off-Scheme land (in feddan) and animal ownership (head) among the thirty-nine tenants is shown in table 4.8. Disregarding the few tenants who own larger numbers of

TABLE 4.8
Average Tenancy, Off-Scheme Land, and Number of Animals
Owned among 39 Households

Tenancy	1.05 (tenancies)
Rainfed land	3.26 (feddan)
Camels	0.46
Cattle	4.26
Sheep	6.59
Goats	4.51
Donkeys	1.54
Fowl	2.49

Source: tables 4.3, 4.6, and 4.7.

tenancies, rainfed lands, and animals, average holdings are even smaller.

Most of the Arabs who assumed tenancies and moved to the Scheme to farm them were already poor on the Butana. Having neither large herds nor large amounts of rainfed land, it was easy for them to pack their few belongings and move with their animals to the Scheme. Returning to the Butana in favorable wet years for sorghum cultivation did not prove to be a problem. Of course, not all Scheme migrants belonged to this category. Some households with large numbers of animals split the herd, leaving most of it on the Butana, to give the Scheme a try. Many of these opted to return to the Butana after a year or two. Others from influential families moved to the Scheme for political reasons.

CASE STUDIES

Life on the Scheme

Ibrahim

Ibrahim, a Shukriya from the Sinnab lineage, was born in Reira on the Butana, around 1930. He had a relatively affluent childhood since his father had many animals. He was about 8 years old when his father sent him out with the herd—camels, cattle, sheep, and goats. A few months after he commenced herding, the Sinnab nazir of the Butana, whose headquarters were in Rufaᶜa, came to Reira on one of his periodic visits to the family. Upon returning, he took with

Cattle watering from an irrigation canal

Irrigation canal serving as a bathhouse

A Zibeidiya woman doing her laundry in canal water

Two Corporation agriculturalists mixing a herbicide with canal water

Irrigation canal as a fishing resource

A thirsty boy drinking canal water

A Halfawi boy working on his father's rented freehold field

Shukriya schoolchildren who have just finished picking cotton

Shukriya woman and her firewood

A Shukriya woman on her cotton hawasha (tenancy)

him three Sinnab boys, including Ibrahim, to attend school in Rufaᶜa.

Camels were then the only means of transportation. Ibrahim's father used to send camels from Reira to Rufaᶜa to bring the boys back during holidays. At a later date, Ibrahim's two younger brothers were taken to Qadaref, also for educational purposes. Later, the brothers joined Ibrahim in Rufaᶜa because the Qadaref school did not go beyond the elementary level.

Ibrahim was unable to sit for the final exam of his fourth intermediary year because his father had summoned him back to Reira to attend the funeral of his eldest brother. The nazir of Qadaref also attended and advised Ibrahim's father to send the boy to the agricultural school in Duweim in White Nile Province instead of sending him back to school in Rufaᶜa. Ibrahim's father agreed, and the nazir wrote the school board recommending Ibrahim strongly and explaining why he had been unable to take his exams.

Ibrahim began to attend the agricultural school in Duweim in the fall of 1946. He had only six months left before graduating as an agriculturalist when he was summoned home again to attend the funeral of his father's brother's son, who was an umda. After the funeral, the family decided that Ibrahim should assume the dead man's position. Since the *umoudiya* (the office of umda) was an elected office that required the formal approval of the candidate by a committee composed of the British District Office and local shaikhs, the district officer called a meeting in January 1949 to which fifteen local shaikhs were invited; Ibrahim was elected formally as umda within the Butana *khat* (an administrative unit within the Native Administration that included several umoudiya), of which his eldest brother was the head. That year also witnessed Ibrahim's first marriage, to his father's brother's daughter. In 1953, Ibrahim was appointed head of the court in the town of Subagh, a major Shukriya *damar* (hometown). He moved there along with his family and his youngest brother Hadi. Ibrahim started his term as judge by opening an elementary school for boys in the village; all Butana Sinnab boys immediately enrolled. An elementary school for girls followed in 1956.

Arabs first obtained tenancies in phase II of the Scheme, 1966/1967. Ibrahim and his brothers obtained tenancies but neither farmed themselves nor moved to the Scheme. They brought some of their people to the Scheme to attend to the land and compensated them in both cash and kind. Ibrahim remained in Subagh as the head of court and an umda. In 1968, he resigned both positions to run unopposed for the Butana chair in the Sudan National Assembly. He won the election and moved with his family to Khartoum for what was supposed to be a four-year term during which the permanent constitution of the Sudan was to be written. After only eleven months, the May 1969 revolution occurred. The Assembly was dissolved and the members sent home. This was a difficult time for traditional shaikhs since the new president of the republic also abrogated the Native Administration, thus depriving them formally of their privileges.

The members of the dissolved Native Administration did not remain out of favor for very long, however. Despite the newly created positions, the new government, and the rhetoric, the holders of key positions remained largely the same, especially in the first few years. This is attributed to several factors. First, literacy became a critical consideration in filling the new positions. Since the old native administrators were the only persons with any education, they emerged as the only eligible candidates. Second, although from the government's point of view the Native Administration was formally dissolved and the positions of shaikhs, umdas, shaikh khats, and nazirs were no longer valid, from the people's viewpoint the system remained intact, and the shaikhs, umdas, shaikh khats, and nazirs continued to be their legitimate representatives and only leaders. Because many of the new positions were elective, the traditional leaders had a clear edge over other candidates. Third, although the idea of a Native Administration was discrepant with the ideology of the new revolutionary government, the holders of such positions were the only people who had political or administrative experience or influence. As long as they were willing to change their rhetoric to suit the expectations of the new government, they were able to convey the government's socialist message to the people.

Ibrahim returned to the Butana, enrolled in the Sudan Socialist Union, and was made the party's representative on the Butana. He was also elected to the Kassala Provincial Council. During this period, he moved his family to a Shukriya village on the Scheme. He quickly found himself nominated and elected, for an initial term of three years, as representative of the Scheme's Sabaᶜat block in Kassala. Following the introduction of decentralization in the Sudan in 1981, Ibrahim was elected as a parliamentary representative within the Eastern Region. He was also an executive member of the New Halfa Farmers' Union, a member of the Saba°at Rural Council, and a member of the New Halfa Corporation Executive Board.

This sketchy outline illustrates the importance of political factors in the adaptation of an individual to a new situation. It is not surprising that a person like Ibrahim should pursue a political career — political ambition at the local, regional, and national levels has been a Sinnab way of life. Ibrahim's great grandfather, Ahmed Bey Abu Sin, was the first governor of Khartoum during the Turko-Egyptian period and remained in office for ten years (Holt 1976:9). Ibrahim's sociopolitical background played a key role in accomplishing his political goals. Note that most of what happened to him, especially in the beginning, was more a consequence of birth and circumstances than of a conscious strategy.

In 1966/1967 (phase I of Arab resettlement; phase II of the Scheme), although Ibrahim had acquired nine tenancies (two in his name and seven in the names of brothers, sons, and a nephew), he had no intention of personally settling on the land. The tenancies were cultivated by hired labor then as they are now. Ibrahim's political ambitions clearly lay elsewhere. The 1969 events changed the balance, and Ibrahim had little option but to return to the local arena and wait until things calmed down. The family moved to the Scheme in 1970 and 1971, and he was immediately elected and appointed to several key positions.

Tenancy possession among the Sinnab served two important functions. For poor Sinnab households, the Scheme presented an opportunity to improve their standard of living. Since basically every male Sinnab was eligible to receive a tenancy, no matter where he lived, his occupation, or his age, members of a household who did not wish to farm themselves could bestow the effective control over these lands to a poor brother who would settle on the Scheme and cultivate the different tenancies. A few politically ambitious and powerful Sinnab who acquired control over a great number of tenancies saw the Scheme as a suitable place for political operations after the 1969 coup and the abolishment of the Native Administration.

In two seasons, 1980/1981 and 1981/1982, Ibrahim continued to be successful and to develop his property on the Scheme. First, in 1980/1981, eight tenancies of 5 feddan each were grown in wheat. These were new lands that had just been opened and assigned for the season, through Ibrahim's intervention, to the village school. The school had been storm-damaged during the previous rainy season and the proceeds of the eight tenancies were to be used for its reconstruction. Ibrahim was put in charge of supervising cultivation and assuring that the money was spent properly. Among the nine tenancies under his direct control, four were cultivated in sorghum. The average production per tenancy was twenty-two sacks. All labor, from sowing to harvesting, was provided by hired hands.

Because of Ibrahim's connections with block inspectors, the whole harvest was transported on Corporation vehicles to a village store he owned, which also served as storage for the village's sugar quotas. Ibrahim had intended to grow wheat in five tenancies but later changed his mind—although the Corporation had supplied him with seeds and fertilizers—because the tenancies were infested with weeds. Since he relied totally on hired labor, production costs appeared too high. The Corporation then offered him two new tenancies to cultivate for the season. They were both in excellent condition: one produced thirty-two sacks of wheat and the other thirty-eight.

In the same season, he also had nine tenancies, of 5 feddan each, in cotton. Although some of them did not do well, on average the crop was successful. I was told by Shukriya one-tenancy holders that those who hold several tenancies have a great advantage over smaller holders in cotton production. The reason is not only that the latter have a larger area to cultivate. Several tenancies, although in a group effectively belonging to one man, are nevertheless registered under different names, to satisfy the "one man/one tenancy" principle. The accounts of the different tenancies are calculated and kept separately. Thus, a man who holds five tenancies in five different names can easily manipulate harvest distribution so that some tenancies produce the minimum while others produce more. Since the Corporation cannot charge the debts of one tenancy against another, debts continue to accumulate against some tenancies, while others keep on doing well and making profits. The tenant who is responsible for the "successful" tenancies acquires the reputation of being a successful farmer; this qualifies him to receive a share of limited inputs and loans since he is considered a better risk.

Second, in the 1981/1982 season, Ibrahim had ten tenancies of 15 feddan each: ten 5-feddan tenancies were grown in cotton, seven in sorghum, and two in wheat. During this season, the Corporation experimented with herbicides for the first time. Despite tenants' eagerness to try the new chemical because of widespread invasion of weeds, the Corporation was forced, due to limited supplies, to select only 200 feddan of cotton from each block. All ten of Ibrahim's cotton tenancies (50 feddan) were among those selected in his block. The same season, the Corporation tried to have "successful" tenants grow wheat for seed multiplication, with the Corporation providing all inputs, leaving tenants only the responsibility of watering the crop. At harvest time, after the costs of production were deducted, tenants were to receive three sacks of wheat per tenancy for their own use; the rest of the produce was bought by the Corporation at official government prices.

Ibrahim was able to use the advantages available to him after his initial political luck. He capitalized on kin to ensure effective production and also capitalized on his reputation, which was based on political and commercial success. Ibrahim is thus an example of the Shukriya tenant who combines accidents of birth and circumstances with shrewd business sense and political expertise to make life on the Scheme a successful venture for himself and his family.

Hamad

Hamad, an Eishab Shukriya, lives part of the year in an Arab village on the Scheme and the rest on the Butana. Hamad owns a Land Rover and a tractor. In 1981, he had owned the tractor for four years and the Land Rover for a few months. About 30 years old and recently married, Hamad has two small children. Before he became involved in the Scheme, he had been a herder, helping his father manage thirty camels. One year, he left his father on the Butana and moved to the Scheme with other relatives who wanted to try the new life. While many people decided to return to the Butana after a couple of years, Hamad, young, unattached, and ambitious, thought he might be able to make good profit if he remained on the Scheme and rented tenancies from people who lived elsewhere. Rent then was very modest: about £S5 annually for 15 feddan.

By 1981, Hamad had nine years of experience renting lands from absentee holders. He no longer rented whole 15-feddan tenancies, but rather units of 5 feddan for a single growing season, concentrating on specific crops in the rotation. For the 1981/1982 season, Hamad rented twenty-one plots slated to grow groundnuts and twelve plots in sorghum, paying £S35 and £S40, respectively, for each 5-feddan plot. Many of the groundnut lands were rented from Halfawis, while the sorghum tenancies were mostly from the area of his own village, rented from tenants who live in Qafala on the Atbara River, about thirty-five to forty-five kilometers away.

The year before, he had rented nine groundnut tenancies, all but one of which were destroyed by heavy rains. The surviving tenancy, located on higher, better-drained land, produced thirty sacks, which brought a total sale of £S600. In addition to land subtenanted on the Scheme, in 1981/1982 Hamad planted 1,000 feddan of rainfed sorghum on the Butana, claiming that both his father and grandfather had occasionally farmed them. Planting such a large area exposed him to a certain vulnerability, since these Butana lands, unregistered, could be seized by the state without compensation to current users. Yet he felt that even a single year's production on still-fertile land, given good rainfall, was worth the effort and, after a couple of seasons, fertility and productivity would decline to the point where further attempts at cultivation would not be sensible.

Hamad is a very clever trader. He does not rely solely on what he produces himself, but also buys from other farmers. In the 1980/1981 season, people assumed that groundnut prices would remain about the same as in the previous several seasons: £S3–4 per qantar. Being constantly on the move, which makes the receipt of information easier, Hamad realized early that the situation was going to be different that season. He very proudly related how he tempted farmers to sell him their produce at a deferred payment of £S5 per qantar and then resold the crop the same week for £S16.5 per qantar. On 600 sacks, he earned £S6,900 profit! Later, he bought 900 sacks of groundnuts at £S11, which he resold for £S20.25, a profit of £S8,325.

How did Hamad get into this privileged position, and why were so many others unaware of the true value of the crop? I spoke at length to Hamad and to some of the farmers who sold him the groundnuts. The attitude of the farmers toward Hamad's behavior was marvelously realistic and somewhat admiring. "Do not be deceived by his appearance," many said.

> Hamad is a wealthy man. His father owns camels, some of which Hamad was able to sell and buy a tractor. Hamad can go to New Halfa or elsewhere whenever he pleases. He knows people in the Corporation and in the groundnut market. Five pounds a sack is a lot of money when, as far as you know, the going price is between three and four. Of course, you become suspicious when someone like Hamad is willing to offer you five pounds per sack; you know he must be making a good

profit. He told us there were farmers in other villages who have promised him their crops. Information spreads around quickly here, but often one does not have the time to think a matter over, and five pounds per sack sounded very good.

I asked the farmers why they later agreed to sell him the remaining crop for £S11 per sack after knowing that the first batch was sold for £S16.50.

> There were problems at the groundnut market. We heard rumors that prices were falling. We knew of several farmers whose crop had been sitting in the market for days without being sold. We knew that Hamad would not pay us £S11 per sack if he thought the price would decrease, but Hamad has a Land Rover; he has money; he knows people; we do not have any of that. If we take our crop to the market ourselves, we would have to worry about transportation, first of all. Hamad can probably sell his crop directly to Khartoum merchants, without going through the market; it is illegal, but many farmers do that. We cannot do that; we do not know who the merchants are. Besides, we have heard they deal only in very large quantities. We would have to leave the crop in the groundnut market for only God knows how long.

Farmers who needed ready cash or did not want to risk the prices falling by waiting preferred to sell at £S11. The prices did fall at the end, from £S26 to about £S13—not as low as £S11, however.

In addition to renting lands, cultivating, and trading, Hamad has another activity that brings him substantial income: he rents his tractor to farmers, with himself as operator, for ploughing and sowing. Hamad had bought the tractor four years earlier by selling his share in his father's camel herd. In 1981, for ploughing a 5-feddan field, Hamad charged £S25, whether he was operating on the Butana or on the Scheme. Hamad said that he could plough and sow a 5-feddan field in less than one hour, if the soil was somewhat soft. Sowing with the *sallouka*, a traditional tool, is very time-consuming; thus, those who can afford it prefer to rent a tractor even though that means using a larger quantity of seeds. Some people rent tractors only for ploughing and do the sowing themselves. Depending on demand, Hamad can plough and sow about 55 feddan a day.

Hamad is another example of a successful tenant. His success did not derive from the possession of the same traditional resources and political influence as Ibrahim's, or from the ability to establish good connections with key Corporation people through hospitality or education. Yet neither is his success a result only of hard work and shrewdness. Hamad was in the privileged position of having enough animals to sell without endangering the household's subsistence and not having the responsibility of an immediate family (wife and children) to support, when he started.

Bayaki

Bayaki is a 38-year-old Shukriya woman from the Eishab lineage, the senior wife of a village elder in an Arab village on the Scheme. She refers to herself proudly as *Eishabiya hurra*, a free Eishabi woman. Bayaki came from a Butana village about fifty to sixty kilometers away from the new site on the Scheme. She likes living on the Scheme, saying, "It is much better here: plenty of money; nice cold water; nice clothes. Our village on the Butana does not have a *souq* [market]; it does not have anything."

Bayaki, like most other Eishabi women, is very hardworking. She awakens early, before sunrise, performs the early morning prayer, and recites the names of God. Afterward, she lights a fire using wood that was either collected the previous evening or bought (usually from older village women or children), milks the goats, and makes tea. After tea, Bayaki washes the dishes, sweeps the house inside and out, washes the faces of her younger children, and gives them warmed milk. The men drink sweet tea with milk and go out. Bayaki washes the dishes once more, and, if there is time, puts a few knots in a mat or a rug she is weaving.

Bayaki starts preparing breakfast around 7. Sorghum is always prepared the previous night. She rekindles the fire and prepares *lugma*, a porridge made with sorghum flour, milk, and clarified butter. The children, and at times the men, come home to eat breakfast. After breakfast, tea is once more brewed. If the men are around, she makes them coffee, a long process that involves roasting the coffee beans, grinding them along with the spices (cinnamon, ginger, cloves, and cardamom), brewing the coffee several times, and then pouring it into a small clay pot, known locally as a *jabana*. The coffee itself is known as jabana, after the pot in which it is served.

After breakfast, Bayaki goes into her own *quttiya* (hut), washes, and rubs her body with oils and perfume. If there is meat, she starts preparing a meal; if not, she repeats the morning porridge, now accompanied by *mullah*, a sauce usually made with onions and tomato paste. Bayaki never has an idle moment; even when she is visiting with her friends, her hands are usually busy spinning, weaving, or doing something.

Bayaki takes care of the animals from the time they return to the settlement in the late afternoon until they leave for the pasture the following morning under the care of one of her boys. Animals too small or too ill to pasture remain at home, where they are cared for and brought sorghum, hay, and water.

At home, animals stay in an enclosure or are tied to a metal fixture in front of the house. All animals are marked on their ears to identify the owner. Bayaki reports: "Animals need a lot of care: they need to be tied down; they need to be fed after they return from grazing to retain the nourishment they grazed during the day." A woman is responsible for the animals that belong to her husband and unmarried sons, as well as her own herd. In the evening, the animals are milked, usually by men. Then they are fed; lactating cows receive an extra portion of sorghum. Women warm the milk and feed the small children their supper. After that meal, they make *rowb*, a form of sour milk, for the following morning's breakfast. The leftover milk is saved in an animal skin or in a gourd to make clarified butter.

Bayaki sells surplus clarified butter when she can, although her husband does not totally approve, saying it is not appropriate for a village elder's wife to sell butter. Bayaki, with a big grin, says that men often say things they do not really mean, in order to save face. Bayaki makes straw floor and prayer mats from sorghum stalks and woolen rugs from camel hair, selling what she does not use herself. That income buys pots and pans, dishes, glasses, and sometimes cheap jewelry, perfume, or small animals.

Bayaki and her friends say that most men do not like to see their wives earning income over which the husbands have no control.

> Men always try to spoil things. If your husband sees that you have your own animals, he tries to take them away from you. He could not do that on the Butana because there was not much to spend the cash on. Now they want everything for themselves. If you work and give them all the money, then they are happy and do not complain. If you do not give them the money, then they start to complain and accuse you of spending too much time on your own economic activities, which interfere in the proper performance of your duties as wife and mother. Still, the Scheme is much better than the Butana; there are more opportunities here—a woman who knows how to braid hair finds women who would like their hair braided, and who are willing to pay for it; a

woman who can weave mats finds buyers. On the Butana there is no one to buy; they do not have any money so they want everything free.

Bayaki feels that women can make a lot of money on the Scheme only if men cooperate. Several Eishab women take the truck to New Halfa and buy utensils, perfumes, and other things to resell to village women. The most successful such woman in the village is one whose husband has been unusually supportive.

> When villagers started making her the target of their jokes, he defended her. Then they started making fun of him, saying he was dependent on his wife. Now they do not make fun of them anymore, since they [the couple] put their cash together and built a new quttiya. He could not have done that alone, since he is a poor man—he does not own a tenancy and has no animals. I could not do that because my husband would not allow it; I make things and sell them in the village and then buy things from the women who shop in New Halfa. My husband does not object too strongly because he knows he will never provide me with the kind of things that I am providing myself; especially with his demanding young wife. If you ask him, he will claim that he bought me all the things you see in my kitchen, but never believe him; most of the stuff that women own are things they have purchased themselves, with their own money. Life on the Butana was nice and simple but it is much easier here.

Not all relationships among Shukriya women are as starkly commoditized as these comments seem to imply. Particularly within the extended family, women do help each other in a variety of ways that are not directly compensated. But the desire and need for cash are progressively pervading many exchanges within villages on the Scheme, and women no less than men seek means to increase their income, even where those means seem to violate older notions of hospitality and community.

Salim Asad

Salim, a Shukriya from the Sinnab lineage, is of medium height, thin, handsome, and about 38 years old. Salim and his wife Sittana, his father's brother's daughter, have one unmarried son, a soldier stationed in Khartoum. With Salim and Sittana occasionally lives Ashsha, Sittana's sister's daughter, whose family lives in Reira, the Butana. Ashsha's father, a Sinnab shaikh, has four tenancies on the Scheme: one in his own name and three in the names of sons, the youngest of whom died several years earlier at the age of 18. The shaikh moved to the Scheme with some of his animals in 1972 and farmed for two years, after which he returned to Reira and left his tenancies in the care of Salim. The shaikh says he left the Scheme because his animals did not have the freedom to roam and were constantly harassed by the Corporation. He also did not find it practical to be separated from part of his herd most of the year. Although the animals were left under the supervision of family members and trusted shepherds, he felt his close proximity was essential to herd welfare.

Although Salim supervises the shaikh's tenancies, he neither labors on them nor receives any of the benefits. The shaikh relies totally on hired labor. Ashsha, his daughter, resides with Salim and Sittana only during short vacations; she boards at the girl's high school in New Halfa, where she is enrolled. She refers to Sittana as "mother" and to Salim as "father." This is in accordance with the Shukriya kin terminology equating parent's siblings with parents and their children with siblings. Occasionally, a Shukriya woman refers to her husband as her brother. Queried, she distinguishes between *akhouya wad^c ammi* (my brother, my father's brother's son [who might also be her husband]) and *akhouya shaqiqi* (my brother, the son of my father).

Salim has one tenancy. When tenancies were allocated, the Asad extended family from Reira and Rufa^c a on the Butana, and some of their former slaves, the Khadim family, were assigned an entire nimra of eighteen tenancies. Six of the tenancies went to Salim, his father, his father's brother, his father's brother's son, and two of the Khadim family. The Rufa^c a Asads received six, and the remaining six were distributed among the Reira Asads. The recipients of the last twelve tenancies never came to the Scheme and rely totally on hired labor.

In the early years, Salim divided his time between the Scheme and the Butana, moving to the Scheme for planting and harvesting. In 1970, the Butana was hit by a severe drought, rendering the pasture inadequate. Production on the Scheme, on the other hand, looked good, because the reservoir held sufficient water. Salim, his father, his father's brother, and his father's brother's son defensively moved with their animals to the Scheme, joining the two Khadim families that were already there. The following season, the others elected to move back to the Butana, but Salim and his wife opted to stay. "The tenancy was good at first," Salim says, "the land was giving and produced. There was plenty for both us and our animals to eat. Animals were not as persecuted then as they are now." But yields on the tenancies began slowly to diminish, due primarily to loss of soil fertility and to shortages of water.

What makes Salim stay on the Scheme when the rest of his family gave it up? When Salim first moved to the Scheme in 1970, he brought with him twelve head of cattle and forty sheep and goats. In 1981, after twelve years of hard work on the Scheme, he had only two cows and five goats left! Salim started selling off his animals gradually. I asked him and his wife why they did not quit after the first couple of years of having to sell animals. Sittana sighed, "toul al-amaal khalatna qaᶜdin" (high hopes made us stay). Every year, they hoped the next would be better and that they would be able to buy back some animals; every year, they lost more. "We invested money in building the quttiya [hut]; it is not like the *birish* [straw mat] tent that you can carry with you and go; we sat here to guard the house; every year, the loss was greater than the year before until we had very few animals left. We no longer have anything to go back to the Butana for." Salim and Sittana find themselves trapped. They no longer have the animals to support them on the Butana, and they no longer can afford living on the Scheme.

Salim is now cultivating only one of three crops in the rotation, sorghum, since cotton was not productive and, to his relief, the Corporation for several years recommended against its cultivation on his tenancy. Salim said that he grew tired of growing cotton and of owing the Corporation more and more money, year after year. At least, the way it stood, the debt would remain the same instead of increasing. Salim started growing sorghum in 1978/1979, when the Corporation, upon recommendations from the minister of agriculture, allowed its cultivation on the Scheme for that season. The following year, the government forbade sorghum; but many tenants, including Salim, grew it anyway and were lucky not to have the planted fields ploughed out by the Corporation.

In 1980/1981, sorghum was formally integrated in the Scheme rotation. Even sorghum production is not very good; in the Asad group of tenancies, for example, some tenancies produced twenty-three to twenty-five sacks, but the average production was eighteen, and some yielded only three to four sacks. Salim feels that it is nevertheless better to grow sorghum than cotton since at the end it all belongs to the cultivator.

Salim had not grown groundnuts for some time: the soil was no longer productive, labor demands were very high, the cost was high, and prices were very low until 1980/1981. Only his wife works with him since he cannot afford to hire labor, so Salim avoids labor-intensive activities. He wanted to grow groundnuts in the 1981/1982 season because of the previous season's very attractive prices, but he did not qualify for an agricultural loan.

Salim typifies those Arab tenants who, although not affluent, owned enough animals and had access to rainfed land on the Butana to support themselves and their families. The initial attractiveness of the Scheme, coupled with a bad year on the Butana, encouraged them to move. Having invested in building a permanent hut, they lost the freedom that pastoral life, with its easily erected and dismantled tents, had once afforded them, since they felt they should stay and, as Sittana put it, "guard the house." The longer they stayed on the Scheme and the more animals they lost, the more remote became the dream of returning to the Butana and resuming pastoral life.

ᶜAli

ᶜAli is a Shukriya from the Dreishab lineage. He has one 15-feddan tenancy, which is in his own name. ᶜAli, his wife, and their children, the eldest of whom is 15, moved to the Scheme in 1966. "The first three years were excellent," ᶜAli and his wife recalled. "All crops produced well. We used to make as much as £S100 a year from cotton alone, even when cotton sold at the price of £S9 per big qantar [315 *rotl* or pounds]. One man could produce 40 to 50 qantar."

The last time ᶜAli cultivated cotton was in the 1977/1978 season, when he harvested only 9 qantar. He says,

> Unless people have direct control over several tenancies, they no longer make money from cotton. Let us say a man has five tenancies. The Corporation advances him £S87.5 each [1980/1981], for a total amount of £S437.5. Instead of cultivating them all equally well, the tenant concentrates his efforts on only two, giving them more fertilizers, weedings, and regular watering. Now it is picking time. Let us say that he makes 8, 10, 15, 30, and 40 qantar, respectively, on the five tenancies. He can easily claim he made 3, 5, 8, 40, and 47 qantar, respectively. Since the tenancies are registered under different names, the first three will accumulate more debt; the last two will do very well. The tenant will make good money; the Corporation will think well of him, and he will be among the first to qualify for government assistance and loans.

ᶜAli did not appear to be either bitter or resentful as he was relating this.

In 1981, ᶜAli had been on the Scheme for fifteen years. Although his tenancy was no longer profitable as it once had been, he had no viable alternatives, since he never owned any animals apart from a few goats. In the early years, when the tenancy was productive, ᶜAli and his wife were able to buy a cow and a few sheep and goats, but these had long been slaughtered or sold to support the household.

In the fifteen years that ᶜAli had been on the Scheme, he grew cotton ten times. Thrice he ended the season in debt to the Corporation despite the fact that, in addition to the advances, he invested some of his own money and all his labor. By 1977/1978, his cumulative debt had reached £S134.

ᶜAli grew cotton again in 1980/1981, but as a partner on someone else's tenancy—someone who had migrated to the Rahad Scheme. He also planted sorghum in that tenancy, since he wanted to save his own field for wheat, in case the sorghum did not produce. The cotton tenancy produced about 15 qantar (anything below 20 is considered low). When he approached the block inspector to check the tenancy account to see if they had made any money, he discovered that it was £S323 in debt. ᶜAli claims that the year 1972/1973, when he made £S23, was the last time he received anything from cotton. In all the other years, the cumulative debt absorbed all earnings from cotton.

In the 1980/1981 season, ᶜAli grew three crops: sorghum and cotton on his partner's tenancies and wheat on his own. He provided all inputs and labor for sorghum and received three-quarters of the twenty sacks produced. In addition to sorghum being their staple grain, ᶜAli prefers it to other crops for various reasons. Although it requires both land preparation and weeding, it does not require fertilization like wheat and does not need as much water. The sorghum tenancy consumes about one-sixth of a sack of seeds, whereas wheat requires two and a half sacks. This inequality has to do with the difference in the sowing techniques of the two crops: wheat is sown by machine-casting; sorghum, on the other hand, is put in hand-dug holes, two or three seeds in each.

Sorghum is much more labor-intensive—most of the work is performed by the farm household itself, using simple tools. Sowing is done with the sallouka, a long wooden stick with a small piece of wood attached horizontally to the bottom; the farmer, holding the sallouka, steps on the bottom piece with one foot and turns around, making a small hole; he is usually followed by his wife or a small child who drops a few seeds in each hole and covers them with soil.

Weeding is done with the *malowd*, a hoe made of a wooden stick with a metal blade attached to it horizontally. Unlike wheat, sorghum needs to be weeded, in some years as often as four times. The tenancy is usually divided into eight basins. Some tenants do all the weeding themselves with household labor; some hire labor for the whole operation; others combine both. ʿAli spent £S10 to hire labor for two of the basins and weeded the rest himself. Since he is both labor- and capital-poor—and since his wife, during weeding time, was in bed for forty days following childbirth—the tenancy received only one weeding.

People who hire labor for the whole operation may pay as high as £S60–70 per tenancy. Some people employ the nafir (exchange work party) system, in which about ten tenants join together: they start in one tenancy the first day and keep on moving; on the eleventh day, they return to the first man's tenancy, continuing this way until the work is completed. When sorghum is ripe, it is harvested immediately—the ripe heads are cut with a sharp knife, by either men or women, and then gathered in one place where they are spread to dry for ten to fifteen days. During this period, the farmer has to camp out in the field to prevent losses due to theft, animal and bird incursion, or strong winds.

At harvest, a piece of ground where sorghum is spread to be husked is prepared. Husking is done by beating the grain with long narrow sticks. This stage is followed by the *mudhra*, where sorghum is thrown high in the air to separate it from chaff. It is then sacked and transported to the village for storage. ʿAli spent £S40 on his sorghum crop: £S10 for ploughing with a tractor; £S10 for weeding; £S18 for sowing, since he was too busy to do it himself; and £S2 for the purchase of seeds. Of the twenty sacks produced, he received sixteen, each valued at £S17.5, for a total value of £S280. Since he does not calculate the opportunity cost of his own labor, this amounts to £S240 net gain.

The wheat crop cost ʿAli £S10 for ploughing, £S10 for machine sowing, £S3 for building ridges, £S43 for four sacks of fertilizer, £S42.5 for seeds, £S5.5 for cleaning the canals on and along the tenancy, £S10 for spraying with insecticide, and £S30 for harvesting. Since the harvest yielded eleven sacks, ʿAli also had to buy burlap containers, which cost him £S8.25. The cost of production was £S162.25, again not counting the value of his own, his wife's, and his children's labor. ᶜAli sold the wheat immediately at £S176, for a net gain of only £S13.75.

ᶜAli supplements his agricultural income by serving as the village imam, teaching in the village literacy school, and occasionally serving as a guard in the block's agricultural headquarters. He and his family represent the many Shukriya tenant households who were not well-off before the Scheme and are not well-off after it. With only one marginally profitable tenancy and very few other resources to draw from, ᶜAli and others like him are trapped. Although their condition is perhaps somewhat better after the Scheme than before in an absolute sense (because of greater economic and sociocultural opportunities—e.g., better education and health), they sometimes perceive it as having deteriorated, since the Scheme succeeded in raising expectations that for many Arab tenants were never even minimally fulfilled.

Life Off-Scheme: Ahmed, Awad el-Karim, and Hasan

Three Sinnabs—two brothers, Ahmed and Awad el-Karim, and Hasan, the latter's son—reside on the Butana throughout the year. They spend the dry season in their damar of Reira, where they have permanent wells. The only "strangers" there are some dependent households that have been with the Sinnab for generations. The settlements are scattered, with nearer kin in greater proximity to each other than to less closely related households. Each settlement consists of several tents, depending on the number of married women who live there.

Ahmed holds three tenancies on the Scheme: one in his own name and two in the names of his sons, Mahmoud, who lives in Khartoum, and Hamid, who lives in Subagh. Another of Ahmed's brothers, who lives in an Arab village on the Scheme and holds two tenancies of his own, is in charge of all the tenancies; the income goes mostly to pay for hired labor. What little is left goes to the on-Scheme brother himself, since he does not have many animals. Ahmed says:

> I am a man of animals. I went to the Scheme because my sons pressured me, told me that I was getting old and that it would be better for me to settle. They also thought my boys would be able to live at home and attend school at the same time. That is why I went. Both myself

and my brother Awad el-Karim decided to give it a try. It does not work. The Scheme is all right if you have only a few animals like my brother, but with large herds, it is not good. I know all about animals; I understand them and they understand me. I do not understand irrigated agriculture and I cannot start to learn in my old age.

Ahmed owns a large herd — four camels, thirty head of cattle, over three hundred sheep, thirty goats, and ten donkeys. In addition to being a better way of life, pastoralism, he feels, is much more profitable than agriculture if one has a minimum number of animals. "I can work on a tenancy for three or four months, day and night, and not make £S100. Here on the Butana, I can sell one cow for £S100 to £S150, a sheep for £S40 to £S50. Of course, tenancy cultivation can be very productive if one has control over a large number of tenancies, but how many people are so lucky! I can count them on one hand." I asked him why he does not abandon his tenancies altogether.

> There is no way we will give up our tenancies. You never know when conditions might change, and what you own is gone. A disease might strike your animals and carry them all off, or maybe a drought. If that ever happens, at least there will be the tenancy to turn to. You send your daughter and sons to cultivate, turn away your hired labor so that the money that goes to pay for them can be saved, and then purchase some more animals with your profits. Thus, someday you might be able to go back to the Butana. There is nothing but herding for people of my generation.

Ahmed herds his animals with the help of two sons and two hired shepherds. The whole herd remains in Reira in the dry season. At the end of the season, when water is scarce in Reira, only his goats are watered there. The cattle and sheep are walked to Sufiya every other day for watering. Ahmed's elder son does most of the watering with the help of a hired hand; when the rains begin, this son goes to the wadis to sow sorghum and later returns for the harvest. The younger son herds. Ahmed pays one shepherd £S30 a month in addition to food and clothing. He hires the second hand only during the dry season to help with watering and pays him £S20 a month.

Ahmed has several pieces of land on the Butana — in Um Hashima, al-Khasa, al-Bahowqi, and al-Rawyan. Before tractors were introduced, he relied totally on the sallouka, but now he uses tractors whenever he has cash to rent them. With the help of a tractor, he often sows

40 to 50 feddan a year. It costs him £S20 to plough each 5 feddan. Ahmed rents some of his lands to others to cultivate. The rent depends on the condition of the land. In 1981, a good piece of land without too many weeds fetched £S20 to £S30 per 5 feddan. If the land has many weeds, it is rented for £S10–15. If the land is infested with weeds, Ahmed rents it out in exchange for two days of labor—one day of sowing and one of weeding.

I questioned Ahmed about livestock marketing.

We sell mostly sheep, since they bring the most money. Last year, I sold four or five cattle but between sixty and seventy sheep. Goats we do not sell too often since the prices they fetch are low. We keep them for milk, mostly for the children, and for meat. Animal traders [sabbabah] come to us here. We separate market animals from the rest of the herd. You see, sheep give birth every *khareef* [rainy season]. Today's market animals are all the males that were born last autumn, in addition to any females that have not given birth after a year. They are referred to as *mi*ᶜ*addi*, meaning a year has passed without their becoming pregnant. They are as good as males. We agree with the *sabbabi* [singular of sabbabah] about the prices. If we know and trust him, we do not require him to pay the full amount at purchase time. He is only required to post a deposit, and later on, after he sells the animals, he pays the balance. We might also walk the animals to the different markets in Tamboul, New Halfa, or Qadaref ourselves; however, experience has taught us to wait here for the sabbabah to come; it is less risky. If we are here and we do not like the offered price, we do not have to sell. The sabbabah, on the other hand, do not like to go back empty-handed, having made the trip. Some people make more money by taking their animals to the market. In ordinary situations, an animal that brings £S225-230 on the Butana might bring £S250 or more in the market; it is riskier though.

Ahmed continues:

Experienced herders sell their animals in the *darat* [beginning of the rainy season], when the animals have put some weight on. A herder should estimate how much money he requires for the whole year. If he spent £S2,000 last year, he should estimate this year's expenditure at £S3,000, to allow for the increase in the cost of living. He should sell £S3,000 worth of animals, in order to have enough money to last all year long. A fatter animal earns about an additional £S50 in a cow and £S10 in a sheep. When I have money, I go and buy animals to fatten them for profit. The sheep that I buy for £S30 in the dry season, I can easily sell for £S50 in the darat; a calf that cost me £S100 can be resold for £S150-170. Owners sell their animals in the dry season only when they are forced to: either because they desperately need the cash or because they no longer can feed and water the animals.

Ahmed sells animals in other times than the darat only when he needs large sums of money or if the money is required for reasons other than food purchases. He buys most of his food from a certain shopkeeper in Sufiya (known on the Butana as Sufiyat ad-Dreishab or the Sufiya of the Dreishab lineage), whom he pays annually. Sorghum often forms a most essential part of the purchased goods. It is required not only for human consumption but also for animals. Sorghum is used as a supplementary diet for livestock, especially lactating cows throughout the year, and as a major feed in the last part of the dry season, when the grass is gone.

Awad el-Karim and his married son Hasan live in the same camp as Ahmed. His married daughter Nafisa and her husband and his unmarried son Sayyid also live with him. Awad el-Karim was born in Reira and is about 65 years old. All his children were also born in Reira. He moved to the Scheme, but after two years returned to the Butana, leaving his four tenancies (in the names of himself, his sons Hasan and Qasim, and a son who drowned in the Khashm el-Girba reservoir in 1968) under the supervision of a relative.

Like his brother Ahmed, Awad el-Karim and his family spend the dry season in Reira. The animals are watered in Reira or in Sufiyat ad-Dreishab, about twenty to thirty kilometers away.

Animals like to stay in *batn el-wadi* [the bottom of a wadi] in the dry season because of the shade provided by trees. When the rains come, they move up to higher grounds to avoid flies and floods. In the beginning of the rainy season, the animals move within the Butana; this is referred to as the *nushouq*. They start moving to Hafir al-Bahowqi [reservoir] after the rains stop and water in shallow reservoirs starts to dry up. When the water in the hafir starts to dry up, the animals are moved back to Reira till the following rainy season. This schedule is more or less followed unless there is a drought, when we have to move the animals wherever grass is. We do not like moving the animals to the Scheme if we can help it, to avoid arguments with the officials and the police, but we do go there when we have to—at the risk of having to pay fines if our animals are caught on anyone's field.

Awad el-Karim has lands in Um Hashima. If it does not rain there, or if the rains are insufficient, he rents from others whose lands have been favored with rain, always for cash, he says. If his own lands receive sufficient rain, he usually rents some out.

Awad el-Karim has 4 riding camels, all his own; 25 cattle, 20 of which are his own and 5 the family's; 150 sheep; 30 goats, of which 5 are Hasan's; and 2 donkeys. The camels stay around the camp all year long, moving only short distances. If he had a large herd of camels, he would hire a shepherd for long-distance herding. The cattle and goats stay close to the camp when the household is in Reira. The sheep stay away with a hired shepherd and come back only for watering. The cattle and the goats stay in Reira from October to May. From October to about January or February, they water from rainwaters in the *jalouth* (a rock depression where rainwater collects) in an area called Qalʿa. After January or February, they are watered from the wells. The cattle usually herd without supervision when they are in Reira, coming back to the camp each evening. The goats herd with Hasan. The sheep, tended by a hired shepherd, graze in al-Bahowqi and water in Reira. They have to be watered every third day.

Awad el-Karim sold five cattle—two old cows and three male calves—and fifty sheep in 1980/1981. The cows were sold for about £S200–250 each, and the calves for £S150–170. As with Ahmed, goats are rarely sold, since they represent meat for the family and year-round milk for the children; moreover, goats do not bring much money.

Hasan had five years of schooling, but he was not doing well so his father withdrew him to attend the animals. Hasan does not like living on the Butana under the present circumstances since he does not have many animals of his own. Although he owns a tenancy, he does not think he would be able to support himself, his wife, and his children from that alone if he decided to move to the Scheme. On the Butana, although he is not an independent herder, he and his family will not go hungry while his father is alive and has animals. He would really like to go to Saudi Arabia and work for a few years, after which he could come back to the Butana and purchase enough animals to become independent.

In the beginning of the rainy season, Hasan and his father leave the animals under the care of Sayyid and go to Um Hashima to sow sorghum. They leave again at harvest time. Hasan's position vis-à-vis the land is similar to that with animals: although he has some claims, the land belongs to his father.

Summary

Let us look at these cases within a framework of what J. I. Prattis refers to as situational logic:

> Situational logic refers to the actor's position within any given power or wealth structure in terms of his access to and control over resources. This involves a consideration of the actor's social location, his motivations, and prior experience, and the available means by which defined ends could be attained; and stipulated that the framework for choice, and therefore action, occurred within these parameters. (1982:213)

The first case is a man born in a politically prominent family with considerable power and resources. His position within the local administration and the fact that members of his immediate family were able to acquire tenancies for which they had no personal need led to his control of nine tenancies, only two of which were actually in his own name. In the beginning, the tenancies were merely a source of investment in addition to his Butana activities, requiring neither residence on the Scheme nor actually being involved in cultivation. His ambitions lay in another arena, the central political one to which he was elected after going through a series of local political positions.

The situation changed following the May 1969 revolution, when the local shaikhs found themselves deprived of power, at least temporarily. The Scheme then appeared a lot more promising as a point from which the center might again be penetrated. This does not mean that the old roles had been totally terminated. Ibrahim continuously drew on them to advance his political gains, but he did so selectively, overstating or understating them depending on his perception of the situation. The understatement of the old role is seen clearly in events that took place in 1973, when a group of educated young Halfawi and Arab men combined to remove the traditional leadership from executive positions in the Farmers' Union. Ibrahim, who joined the group, was criticized during that time by members of his own family, who accused him of forgetting them and siding with the others. They told him "inta ma bageit minnana; ma bageit Sinnabi; inta nasseit-al-beit wa mashi ma\u02bfal-wileidat" (You are no longer one of us; no longer a Sinnabi; you forgot the *beit* [house, tent, people of the house, kin group], and sided with the young).

For Ibrahim, the tenancies served to further his political ambitions by enabling him to entertain, offer hospitality, and spend money campaigning, but his political position had enhanced his ability to acquire several tenancies in the first place and to obtain control over other tenancies in time. He was the first to hear about and qualify for the new opportunities in herbicides, selected seed multiplication, fertilizers, and so forth. His position in the Farmers' Union and on the Corporation Board gave him a great advantage over other tenants. An agricultural inspector, for example, would never dare ask a man in his position to leave his office or accuse him of stupidity or incompetence, as is often done with other tenants.

Ibrahim's family is in a position to offer him cash gifts in addition to loans when he is in need. His brothers, two of whom are university professors and one who was a regional minister, feel they partly owe their present positions to him; it was he who supported their education in preference to his own. Besides, having two brothers in the national capital and one in the regional capital means that he has a place to stay when he is in either place to petition a case, ask a favor, or pay a social visit to a government official. His family's political position opens all doors. The fact that he represents the Farmers' Union, and to a certain extent the Corporation, enables him to use these roles when he is arguing his personal interests.

The remaining cases indicate important differences, both from the first case and from each other. Hamad gives the superficial impression of being entrepreneurial. Having had animals to sell and at that time being without wife or children to support, Hamad was able to rent several tenancies and profit considerably. He sold animals to buy a tractor, whose rental generated a good return. Mobility and capital gave him better access to the market and the Corporation. He was in a privileged position to learn the prices of different crops before the information became public. Hamad was not taking any risks when he offered £S5 a sack for groundnuts when the tenants, based on previous years' prices, thought the going price was between £S3 and £S4. The farmers who sold him groundnuts on a deferred payment basis knew better than to believe that Hamad would offer them more than the market price, but, not realizing that the discrepancy between the two seasons' prices would be so high and not having the transportation to check the market for themselves, they felt Hamad had made them a very good offer. Actually, what Hamad did was not unknown to the Shukriya, who have had the sheil system for generations.

Bayaki is the only woman in these case studies; like most Shukriya women on the Scheme, her presence there is a consequence of her husband's decision to move rather than her own economic strategy. Although she enjoys living on the Scheme, she could not have refused to join her husband had she felt otherwise. Her husband can force her back to the nomadic life any time that he feels the Scheme no longer fits his needs. Although divorce is not uncommon among the Shukriya, I know of no cases caused by a wife's refusal to move with her husband. From a life on the Butana, which consisted of constant movement, putting up and pulling down tents, collecting firewood, and caring for the animals, Bayaki was brought to a settlement life.

Although she did not participate in the decision, she is pleased with the outcome. Her husband never had many animals on the Butana, and being on the Scheme offers her different economic opportunities, a possibility of visiting the town occasionally when accompanied by her husband or her eldest son, and easy access to canal water. She also likes having a school for her children to attend. As the wife of a village elder, Bayaki has to work under more constraints than some other women. Within those restrictions, she feels she is doing the best she can. She sells mats and rugs, purchases utensils, buys small animals for resale when she needs the cash, and so on. Since she is rarely allowed to go to New Halfa other than for medical reasons and unless accompanied by her husband or her son (both of whom refuse to take her to the market), she relies on other village women for the purchase of her goods, knowing that the price she pays is higher than her own costs would be in town.

Salim and ʿAli, respectively a Sinnabi and a Dreishabi, are both poor, with only one tenancy each and very few animals. As a Sinnabi, Salim has relatives who are in a position to help him in case of dire necessity. Both Salim and ʿAli are very hardworking. Unlike Ibrahim, who does not labor in the fields himself, they are almost totally self-reliant. They plough, sow, weed, and harvest. ʿAli also acts as the village imam, for which he receives a small payment from the government, and occasionally as a guard at the block headquarters. Both Salim and ʿAli are aware that if they had more tenancies and closer linkages to the block and to the Corporation main office, their economic situation would be much better. After witnessing the high 1980/1981 prices for groundnuts, they expected that those high levels would be maintained the following season. Yet neither of them grew groundnuts because neither could afford the up-front cost at the beginning of the season, and neither qualified for an agricultural loan.

If the situation on the Scheme becomes much worse, Salim feels he can always return to the Butana and its pastoral life. There are enough Sinnabis there with large herds who might give or lend him a few animals to start a herd and would not let him starve. ʿAli does not have supportive agnates and feels going back to the Butana is out of the question. If conditions worsen on the Scheme, he will have to become a wage laborer. ʿAli hopes that his eldest son, who was 15 in 1981, will finish high school, get a job as a village teacher, and help support his parents in their old age.

Ahmed, Awad el-Karim, and Hasan are examples of Shukriya absentee tenants. The reasons for their absenteeism are different, however. Ahmed and Awad el-Karim each tried the Scheme for two years, after which they decided they were better off on the Butana since the Scheme cannot accommodate their herds, at least not as easily. To them, the Scheme tenancies represented a novel source of investment that they were willing to try. They never considered it an alternative source of income. They abandoned the Scheme as soon as they decided that it did not serve the best interests of their ani-mals—their first priority. The tenancies are left under the supervi-sion of relatives and worked by wage laborers; the small profits that might accrue after deducting expenses are left for poor on-Scheme relatives. They are nevertheless unwilling to abandon the tenancies altogether: they are regarded as an alternative to total destruction if a disaster strikes and wipes out the herd.

Hasan's position is somewhat different. Although one of the tenancies under his father's control is in his name, his claim to it is vague—the tenancies distributed to him and his two brothers were entirely for the benefit of their father. Hasan has since married and has children; being the head of a household, he can settle on the Scheme and cultivate his tenancy if he wishes. If he leaves his father on good terms, he can probably take charge of the other three tenancies. His father is reluctant to have him leave, however, since he needs him for the animals. Besides, Hasan has never lived on the Scheme, has no knowledge of irrigated agriculture, and worries about not being able to make it there, even with four tenancies, since he would probably have to rely on expensive wage labor for cultivation. He sees that little if anything will be left beyond the costs of production. Hasan also knows that his brother Sayyid does not have to give away his own tenancy to Hasan if he does not want to. Sayyid has an equal right to his father's and deceased brother's tenancies.

To a certain extent, Hasan's position is similar to that of Salim and ᶜAli. They all have the feeling of being trapped, Salim and ᶜAli on the Scheme and Hasan on the Butana. Hasan's position vis-à-vis his father and the herd is not unique. Most present herd owners, including Awad el-Karim, Hasan's father, have gone through this stage in their early manhood. Hasan's situation differs from theirs in the type of opportunities, real or imaginary, that exist today but that did not in the past. During his father's youth, it was common for young men with wives and children to be in this dependent state, without sufficient animals of their own to establish independent households. Today enough young men are able to leave the Butana and get relatively well-paying jobs in Saudi Arabia, Kuwait, and the Arab Emirates. They come back after several years and buy larger herds or build modern houses in towns. This makes it extremely difficult for the peers they left behind to accept contentedly what they consider an unsatisfactory situation.

5

Halfawi Production Goals and Labor Strategies

INTRODUCTION

The preceding chapter illustrated alternative labor strategies utilized by Shukriya tenants on the New Halfa Scheme. This chapter presents six examples of Halfawi adaptations. Three of these, Majid, Malik, and Nabil, represent highly successful tenants who own large parcels of land, tractors, and animals and have good connections within and outside the Scheme. A glance at their earlier lives reveals why they were able to make such a success on the Scheme when so many others have failed. Sammy represents another group of Halfawi tenants, those who own one tenancy each and who have a few animals and some freehold lands. Their holdings enable them to live a life considerably more comfortable than many one-tenancy or landless farmers. The final two are landless farmers who moved to the Scheme with the rest of the settlers from Wadi Halfa but did not qualify for a house, freehold lands, or a tenancy, because they owned neither home nor land in Nubia. They live on the Scheme by laboring for wages, sharecropping, and renting; they depend on the availability of land, owners' preferences, and their own ability to provide inputs and labor if they opt to rent rather than to work for wages or share-crop.

CASE STUDIES

Majid

Majid was born in Wadi Halfa about 1932. His father sent him to Umdurman at the age of 10 to attend the American Missionary School. His admission was made possible by the intervention of his father's sister's son, who was then a judge in Khartoum. The judge had enrolled a sister's son in the school and was very impressed by it; on one of his visits to Wadi Halfa, he was able to persuade Majid's father to send the obviously bright boy away to school.

Majid recollected his early days at the boarding school:

> My father was a very religious man and extremely strict. We fought constantly. I knew that the school was my only chance to get away. Although at home I had the reputation of being very mischievous and always got in trouble, at school I became an example of the good and obedient student because I quickly learned it was the only way to guarantee my stay there. I even attended the Christian church to please my teachers. The principal's wife, who was childless, took a liking to me. I started having most of my meals at their house. I was eating very well when the rest of the students were fed rubbish. Another student, also from Wadi Halfa, became very jealous. He sent my father a letter telling him that I had converted to Christianity, citing my regular church attendance as evidence. The judge had been transferred to al-Obeid by then. My father came to Umdurman and took me back to Wadi Halfa after I had been at school for less than two years. This was in 1944. I was about 12 years old.

To keep him at home, Majid's father opened a store for him in 1945. The boy was not old enough to carry such responsibility, however. He would leave the store unattended to hike five kilometers home, where his mother would have lunch waiting. The father was heartbroken and did not know what to do with his son. A father's brother's son, who owned a garage at the time, suggested training Majid in his garage as a mechanic; both the father and the boy welcomed the idea. Another of Majid's father's brother's sons had been in Egypt for some time, working for a pasha. Hearing of the boy's recent training in automobile mechanics, he sent Majid's father a message in 1949 asking him to have the boy sent to Egypt, where he could get Majid a job in one of the pasha's workshops. Majid spent about a year in Egypt as an apprentice mechanic. He had just bought a small used car with his savings when the news of his father's death reached him; he returned to Wadi Halfa in his car to attend the funeral.

Majid rented his car to the Wadi Halfa customs office for a while and later sold it for a large profit. With the money he started a business, buying good used cars that belonged to Egyptian pashas and other rich families, performing all needed repairs, and selling them in the Sudan for at least twice the purchase price. This venture came to an end in 1955, when Nasser's ascendance to power made such types of trade very difficult to carry out. Majid recollected, "At the time I had just purchased two cars. I cleaned, scrubbed, and fixed them really well. They looked very attractive. I started renting my cars to hotels and tour groups. The government, which did not have any decent vehicles in Wadi Halfa, started renting my cars when any government officials or delegations visited. They would take the cars and put a little flag on the front to make them look official."

Gradually, Wadi Halfa became an attractive tourist area, and three or four tour companies opened offices there. They brought tourists by boat from Egypt to visit the archaeological sites. Because of his experience and assertiveness, Majid quickly emerged as the agent for these companies: he brought them cars, met them at the airport, and took them to their hotels. He recalled:

> I knew that the *khawajat* [singular *khawaja*; a term used in the Sudan to refer to foreigners, especially Europeans and Americans] were obsessed with punctuality, so I made sure never to be even a minute late for an appointment. Very quickly, I acquired the reputation of being reliable and had a virtual monopoly over car rental in the area. They knew that if they wanted me at a certain place at five in the afternoon, I would be there at five and not four hours later. I met many tour groups and their guides and became very friendly with them.
>
> After a few years, those who were once mere guides became the managers of their own home offices. Whom do you think they remembered in Wadi Halfa for being hardworking and reliable? Me, of course! They took away representation rights from all the other offices in town and gave them all to me. I closed out five offices that way. There were at least twenty companies abroad who dealt exclusively with me. I met many professors of archaeology, and they all mentioned me in their reports. I became the king of Halfa, but the Aswan Dam came and destroyed everything I built over the years. My work had to do with the ruins: no ruins, no work. All my work went under the water. For twenty years, I had dealt mainly with Europeans and Americans; all of a sudden I had to deal with uneducated, uninformed people after having dealt with civilized people all my life.

Majid came to the Scheme in 1964; after a few months, he went back to Wadi Halfa and remained there for several months. A group of tourists was arriving for a last visit to the ruins, so he decided to go and meet them. However, just before they arrived, a presidential decree was issued to close the Halfa Town airport.

> I came back to the Scheme. I was heartbroken, but I decided I could not afford to dwell on my own misery. I became friendly with the

afandiya [white-collar workers] — the judge, the police chief, doctors, and people from the Corporation. I used to get together with them and sit around and drink beer; I drank in those days. Little by little, we became good friends. One evening I would go to their homes, and the following evening they would come to mine.

In the beginning, Majid had only one tenancy, which he had assigned to the village agricultural cooperative for cultivation. He would listen to the Corporation staff talking about agriculture — when to plant cotton, wheat, and groundnuts, when to water and fertilize, and how often to weed; he memorized every word they said. In 1965, he was asked to become the New Halfa agent for a bus company that operated between Khartoum and New Halfa. Shortly thereafter, he also opened a transport office of his own. Majid described his duties in his role as transport lord:

> For example, if a Khartoum merchant wants to buy 5,000 tons of cottonseeds from the Corporation, he comes to me to arrange for their transport. I receive a commission, which ranges between 5 and 10 percent of the value of the crop, from both the buyer and the truck owner. The bus company I am managing was originally owned by an Italian firm. They made me their agent because I was recommended to them by an Italian archaeologist who had worked in Wadi Halfa.

In 1967, Majid became the resident representative in New Halfa for a large tractor firm. He sold their tractors to agricultural cooperatives and to individuals. He reported, "I was very keen; I knew how to sell tractors. If a person came to me with 40 percent intention to buy a tractor, I would make him 110 percent sure by the time he left my office an hour later." How had he managed to do that? He explained:

> A tractors cost only £S1,580 at the time. These low prices continued till about 1969. The ridging attachment cost £S320, the sowing disc about £S900, and the *namousa* [the attachment used for opening on-farm canals] £S130 — £S2,930 altogether. When a person came to me, I would say to him, "How much money do you have?" He might have said, "Well, I have some." I would say, "Well, how much? Is it £S300? £S400?" He would say, "It is about that much." I would say, "What if I show you a way to buy a tractor now and to pay me and the bank back within three months?" This always got them very excited. I made buyers mortgage their homes and borrow money from the bank; or I would mortgage the houses for them myself. I knew that by renting the tractor out a man could easily pay me and the bank back, so there was no danger that they might lose their homes; my customers also knew that.

If someone had only £S300 and no home to mortgage, I would still let him have a tractor but kept it in my name until he finished paying for it. No one ever failed to pay the money back. Most paid everything back within three months, as I had predicted.

Majid's predictions were based on the calculation that a tractor was capable of preparing twenty 5-feddan tenancies a day for £S1.5 each. This meant £S30 per day. At the time, a drum (45 British gallons) of diesel fuel cost £S4.05 and lasted for several days. A man was in a position to make £S900 in one month or £S2,700 in three, not counting fuel cost and value of labor. Majid recollected, "Once the company's Middle East branch manager, who was stationed in Beirut, visited the Sudan. He came to New Halfa and was very impressed with the number of tractors I had sold. In his report he wrote that I was the company's most active agent in the whole country. This lasted for three years, until 1970, when the government nationalized everything. That was when I started cultivating on a large scale."

Majid learned a great deal about Scheme agricultural operations through his dealership and his association with Corporation officials. He started cultivating his own tenancy while he had the dealership; after 1970, he began farming on a very large scale. He owned five tractors and was able to plough his own tenancies as well as those of others. Majid said that he had ploughed most of the area that extended between his village (approximately five kilometers from New Halfa) and the Saba'at section in the northern parts of the Scheme. He did this until 1974, when the Corporation bought about fifty tractors and issued a regulation restricting the open use of commercial tractors on the Scheme. Majid then sold his tractors, keeping only one for his own use. He cultivated wheat, cotton, and groundnuts in addition to fruits and vegetables.

In 1978, Majid became the agent for a very large oil-pressing factory in Khartoum, in charge of purchasing cottonseeds and groundnuts. At that time, the groundnuts were transported to Khartoum unshelled. In 1979, the company purchased four groundnut strippers with a capacity to produce 15,000 tons of shelled groundnuts annually and put Majid in charge.

Majid started a fruit orchard in 1971, for which he purchased 10 feddan of freehold land. In his orchard he had about six hundred fruit trees, including two varieties each of oranges, lemons, grapefruit, and guavas, in addition to mangoes and dates. In 1974/1975, he started a livestock breeding and fattening farm adjacent to the orchard. Cattle and sheep were kept separately. The farm also had a fodder storage place, which in October 1981 contained hundreds of sacks of groundnut shells in addition to some barley. Majid acquired the shells at no cost from the four groundnut strippers he controlled. In September 1981, his farm had thirty-six head of cattle; his holdings often went as high as ninety head, consisting mainly of calves, about fifty of which he sold each year.

In addition to those he bred, Majid bought calves from Arab pastoralists, desperate at the end of the dry season when prices were at their lowest. All the purchased animals were inoculated before being brought onto the farm. Majid always kept purchased animals separate from his regular herd to lessen the chances of contagion. The animals were fattened for about three months and then resold as soon as an attractive price became available. From each calf he earned £S40–50 over the purchase price. He bought from forty to sixty calves each year and bred about twenty. With his own animals, Majid followed a different strategy. The male calves were kept until they were between one and a half and two years old. Females were always kept for breeding unless they proved barren or became too old or sick.

Majid also kept sheep. The flock was divided between those bred on the farm and those purchased young for fattening and reselling. He sold about seventy sheep a year, trying to get rid of them before the beginning of the rainy season to avoid a hoof disease caused by muddy grounds. The animals that were bred on the farm were not allowed to graze during the rains; feed was brought to them in their enclosures.

Animal waste was used as fertilizer for fruit trees, while commercial urea was used for other crops. Majid usually composted collected animal manure and fallen tree leaves in a hole dug five meters deep. When full, the hole was filled with water, sealed with mud, and allowed to ferment for a full year.

Different combinations of feed were used: remains from groundnut tenancies and strippers, molasses bought from the sugar factory, and cottonseed residues. Majid mixed the groundnut and cottonseed residues (*umbaz*), molasses, and a small amount of salt, for fodder. He never marketed milk produced by the animals. He took some home for his two households (he had two wives), but the rest was left for the calves. He believed that it was more profitable to feed the milk to calves than to sell it—since milk was relatively inexpensive while meat was very costly—and that calves were much healthier when allowed to suck their mother's milk.

In December 1981, Majid was in the process of establishing a chicken farm. He had constructed eight compartments with a capacity to hold 6,000 chickens. He had also constructed a pigeon loft large enough to hold 5,000 pairs. Under the loft, areas for fodder storage were to be constructed.

Majid was in control of five 15-feddan tenancies, one in his own name and the rest in the names of other family members. In the 1980/1981 season, he cultivated cotton, groundnuts, and wheat. All five cotton tenancies were attacked by animals. He complained to his block inspector, but nothing was done about it. His five groundnut tenancies did extremely well, with average production of 140 sacks each, a total of 700 sacks. He sold the crop for £S13.3 per sack, making £S9,310. I told him that I found it very surprising for a man with his linkages to wait too long and to have to sell his crop at the lower prices, when he could have obtained over £S20 a sack, had he sold it earlier. He responded:

> Look, when I took my groundnuts to the market, the crop was very clean. People who rushed their crop to the market before proper cleaning probably lost a great deal. Merchants deduct a certain percentage for dirt. A man who took 70 sacks to the market was paid for about 50, after deductions. I have my name and reputation to protect. When I take 700 sacks to the market, it is 700 sacks. Groundnuts are sold by weight and not by the sack. A sack should contain one qantar [100 rotl]. Actually, my sacks had more than one qantar each. In effect, I had more than 700 sacks.

Besides being a producer and seller of groundnuts, Majid also acted as a large-scale buyer in his role as an agent representing Muslim, an influential Khartoum man who, in addition to being a very successful trader, owned several oil and soap factories in various parts of the Sudan. Majid purchased groundnuts for Muslim, had them shelled in the four strippers owned by Muslim's family, and transported the shelled groundnuts to Khartoum and Port Sudan for processing and export. Majid related:

> In 1980/1981, agents of certain Khartoum merchants, upon instruction from their bosses, also factory owners, raised the price of groundnuts artificially to £S22 per qantar, to drive me and my boss out of the market. They knew that Muslim would not pay such high prices for the

crop. When the prices rose so high, I declared publicly that I was boycotting the market, took off to Fau [the Rahad Scheme], purchased, on behalf of Muslim, 63,000 qantar of groundnuts, and brought them back to New Halfa for shelling. I also spread the rumor that what was purchased was actually much more than the quantity brought back to New Halfa and that Muslim's company had already satisfied its needs for the season. When the other buyers got wind of this information, they were sure that I was no longer interested in reentering the market. They had a conference among themselves in which they agreed to bring the price down from £S22 to £S13. They announced their decision to the Farmers' Union that supervises groundnut marketing and attempts to get the best deal possible for the tenants and threatened to boycott the market if the Union insisted on a higher price.

The Farmers' Union and the assistant commissioner's office were concerned. They demanded a higher price without specifying how much that price should be. The merchants went on strike and stopped purchasing altogether. Meanwhile, the groundnuts, including my own, were sitting in the Crop Market. The farmers were very upset. The crop sat in the market for forty-six days. The merchants insisted that £S13 per qantar was their highest bid. If the Farmers' Union and the tenants did not like the price offered, they should look for better prices elsewhere. It was not going to come from them.

A meeting was called by the assistant commissioner and the Farmers' Union to which all merchants, including myself, were invited. The Union's president opened the meeting by thanking me and Muslim's company for our honesty and mentioned how, when we promised to buy the whole groundnut crop the previous year, we carried out our promise and purchased the whole offered crop. The president continued to speak about how the merchants artificially raised the price to drive me and Muslim out of the market, an action that forced me to turn to the Rahad Scheme to purchase my needed groundnuts and that the merchants brought the price down to £S13 as soon as they learned I was no longer buying. I spoke and put the full blame on the Farmers' Union itself—"You forgot your traditional customers when the price was more attractive and you forced them to turn to other markets," I said. "You forced me to buy my groundnuts from the Rahad Scheme. You forced me to benefit other schemes and other farmers while ours were still sitting here. It was with a broken heart that I brought back the groundnuts I purchased from Rahad, knowing that I was benefiting another council, when the New Halfa Council, our own council, badly needed that money."

Majid told me that he had a well-thought-out plan in his head when he made that speech. He wanted to get the assistant commissioner, who was already very angry at the merchants because the Council had lost a great deal of money due to the halt in sales, even angrier. Throughout the meeting, Majid acted as if he had no interest at all in the crop, having already satisfied his needs. He also had a valuable piece of information that Muslim had discovered: the New Halfa local merchants were under instructions from the real buyers that under no circumstances should they raise the price above £S13 a qantar without consulting them. Majid checked to make sure that the minutes of the meeting were being recorded. He looked at each merchant individually and asked, "Do you undertake on yourself, and in front of everybody, to purchase the whole crop if it is offered at £S13 a qantar?" The unanimous answer was an absolute no. No one wanted to take sole responsibility for purchasing the whole crop. Majid suggested that all merchants should sign the minutes as further evidence of their intentions. They all did.

Later the same day, Majid went to the Farmers' Union and met with the president and some of the executive committee members. He offered them £S13.2 per qantar. In his mind, he told me, he was prepared to offer another 10 piasters per qantar. The Farmers' Union discussed the offer briefly and then asked Majid to raise the price to £S13.3 per qantar to "at least cover the cost of burlap sacks, which you will be getting back anyway since they will contain the crop." Majid agreed and signed a contract with them to buy the whole crop for £S13.3 per qantar. The other agents came back several days later offering £S16 per qantar, but it was too late; Majid had the contract. As he put it: "misikta-s-souq wishtareitu, qashartu, w-saffartu" (I got hold of the market, bought it up, shelled [the groundnuts], and transported it).

This incident reveals the mechanics of groundnut marketing in New Halfa. Although the crop is supposedly the tenants' property, in fact that applies only before harvest. After harvest, the tenant has little control over what happens. The forces that manipulate the market are beyond his control, if not his understanding. The minimum price is dictated by the government for tenant protection, but that price is sometimes so much below the current market prices that assuring it is in effect meaningless. During the 1980/1981 season, for example, when the official minimum price was £S5.3, the market price fluctuated between £S13 and £S22. These fluctuations were due to atypical circumstances that do not occur every year, however.

The Sudanese government introduced the Crop Market to provide some protection for tenant farmers who previously sold groundnuts to merchants at very low farm-gate prices. But it also reduced peasant control over the marketing process by making the Crop Market the only legitimate arena for these transactions, and peasants now bear the costs of crop transport from farm to market. While peasants are not required to accept market prices, if they do not they are saddled with the further costs of transporting unsold produce back to the farm.

All tenants belong to the Farmers' Union, which acts as marketing representative for its members. Once the Union accepted Majid's offer, individual tenants did not have the right to agree to alternative higher prices offered by other merchants. Many of the poorer peasants carp about their Union or rather about its officers, claiming that they identify more with the Corporation than with the rank-and-file membership. It is clearly the case that these officers, although elected by the tenants, tend to come from more affluent strata and have more in common with Corporation and government officials and with private sector elites than with their own members. The officers often have large holdings and are favored by the Corporation and the Agricultural Bank in the provision of agricultural inputs, irrigation water, and financial credit.

Majid himself had insufficient water on his wheat tenancies during the 1980/1981 season. He attributed this to a conspiracy against him by a "leftist" block inspector.

> I am a good and clever farmer. I even received, a few years ago, the Corporation's best farmer prize. My tenancies are always cited as examples of good farming. When guests visit the Scheme — ministers, bank managers, expatriates — they are always brought to see my fields. Last year, the Corporation did me harm. It was all the fault of the first inspector of our block; I am sure you have heard of him. He was finally arrested in May. He was against me from the beginning. He did not like me because I was a successful farmer. It is a plot; they want to overhaul the system. They achieve that by bankrupting agricultural schemes and industries, so that the prices will keep on rising up to the point that the people could no longer stand it and revolt. I heard this from the inspector himself. "It is not you that I am against," he said, "it is the system." I sent a letter to the agricultural manager of the Scheme, with a copy to the police, in which I complained about cutting off the water to my tenancies, and pointed out the reasons. Afterward, I went to see the manager and told him to take back his tenancies if that was the way I was going to be treated. "It is not your tenancies that we will take away," he said; "it is him that we will get rid of; you just wait." I waited. He was arrested in May.

I asked Majid exactly what the inspector did.

He used to withhold water from the crop on purpose. This did not apply only to my tenancies. He did it to others as well. He particularly disliked successful farmers. He wanted to crush our self-esteem so that we would no longer care about work. He also had the authority over harvesters. He would harvest the tenancies of people around me and leave mine till the end. This is forbidden, since animals start entering the Scheme right after harvest. It is impossible to keep them off your land when all the tenancies around you have already been harvested. Thus, the animals ate most of my wheat before harvesters arrived. I used to produce more wheat on my tenancies than anybody else. In 1979/1980, I made between forty and forty-five sacks from each tenancy. Last year, I made only sixty-one from all five; an average of twelve sacks per tenancy. I told the manager, "You can go back to earlier accounts and see for yourself the kind of farmer I am. Things were going extremely well until you brought in this man."

Majid and his family owned 85 feddan of freehold land, plus a 10-feddan orchard. Each year, he left about one-third of the area fallow, a conservation luxury not available to many smallholders, who need to keep all their lands in continuous production. In the 1980/1981 season, about 32 feddan were used to grow melons and watermelons. After deducting expenses, the profit came to £S7,200. Melons had brought in a total receipt of about £S2,000 per 5 feddan the year before. He also had squash, *muloukhiya* (a leafy vegetable that looks like spinach), okra, eggplants, and tomatoes. He said, "I always look around to see what the others are sowing or planning to sow, and I sow something else." His profit from the squash and muloukhiya crops was about £S1,500; from each 5 feddan of tomatoes he made about £S3,000.

Majid employed four farm laborers for £S25 per month each. They lived in huts on the farm, took care of the animals, watered and harvested the fruit trees, and guarded the farm and the adjacent orchard. In addition to their salaries, they received an incentive of £S0.5 for each sack of fruit they collected. "That way they treat my trees as if they are theirs. Collecting fruit is not merely a question of picking them off a tree and throwing them in sacks. Fruit picking is an art in itself. If you are not careful, you may damage a tree; you may break off a branch or something. I take all of this into consideration when I pay them the incentive." Fruit is picked during a six-month period, on an average of twenty days per month. Majid grosses about £S6,000 yearly from the fruit. Prices tend to rise in the month of Ramadan, and there are other fluctuations during the year.

For example, a sack of lemons might sell for as high as £S20 or as low as £S8.

Majid owns three vehicles: a Land Rover, a small Toyota pickup, and a large truck with its own driver, used for transporting crops within and outside the Scheme. In addition to operating his tenancies, freehold lands, farm, fruit orchard, and several franchises, Majid opened a small spare-parts shop in the industrial area of New Halfa in 1981. "I bought lots of old parts and hired laborers to clean them with kerosene and to polish them. When my laborers were done, the parts looked almost brand new. Instead of throwing them into one big pile as you usually see in this type of store, I had some nice shelves constructed, arranged the parts neatly, and hired *afandiya* [white-collar workers] to run the shop."

Three days before Ramadan in 1981, an auction was held at the Corporation. Majid attended, intending to pick up a crane and a generator. Instead, he bought 179 tractors.

When I arrived, bids for the tractors had reached £S300–600, and a few were already sold. The Corporation people looked hot, tired, and bored. I was immediately inspired. I took one of the officials aside and said to him, "Look, Ramadan is only two or three days away. You have been here all morning and have sold only a few tractors. The way you are going, you will be here for weeks. You do not really want to stand here under the hot sun and do this during Ramadan! Why don't you sell me the whole lot for £S240 each? As you see, some of these tractors are worthless and would not fetch £S100." The official said he wanted to discuss my offer with his colleagues. It did not take these men long to arrive at a decision. I found myself the owner of 179 tractors. The people were very angry. They called me an *intihazi* [exploiter]. I said to them, "Don't stand there and call me names; if you are real men, outbid me; offer the Corporation more." Of course, I knew when I said those words that nobody could. Naturally, I did not have to pay on the spot. One of the reasons that many people were so upset was because they wanted to buy only one tractor, and they regarded it as unfair to sell them wholesale. I turned around immediately and told the people, "You were angry with me because you wanted to buy single tractors, so I will give you the opportunity to do just that. Start with your bids." I sold several right away for a minimum of £S500 each. From the 179 tractors I have about 30 left, which I will dismantle and sell as spare parts.

Majid's 1981/1982 ambition was to build in New Halfa what he called "a small, first-class hotel, with about 20 to 25 rooms, in addition to some shops with apartments above." He felt that, with the number of foreigners who frequent the Scheme, it would be a great success.

> I bought a very nice piece of land to build the hotel on, right in front of the gas station. There was a government land auction. Since I have a city map, I know the location of every single piece of land. The auction took place in front of the Wataniya Cinema. People were bidding and buying; they paid between £S2,250 and £S3,325 per piece.
>
> When the auctioneer announced the sale of a certain piece of land, I stood up since it was the one I had had my eyes on for some time. Although no one there recognized the value of the land and some did not even know the precise location, they became interested when they realized I wanted it. People tend to think that I always know what I am doing. They started bidding against me. I was furious and let them know it. I told them I had been sitting for hours, watching them bid on land and buy; did I start bidding against any of them? No. In fact, I congratulated them. Now that it was I who wanted a piece, everybody is dying to get the same piece. "Good then," I said, "bid against me. I will outbid any of you. Let the government become rich on the backs of the Nubians, if that is what you wish." I started walking back and forth without even looking up and started bidding against myself, "1,000, 2,000, 3,000, 3,500, 4,000. Come on; let me hear one of you outbid me; 4,100, 4,200, 4,300." They gave up, saying that I was crazy; that no one could stand up against me. I got the land for £S4,300.
>
> After that, I bought five other pieces, real nice pieces. Since no one wanted to bid against me after the earlier scene, I got each of them for £S2,800, thus bringing the average price down to £S3,050. After that, a group of bidders disagreed among themselves and started raising the bids to £S5,000–6,000. Some put the blame on me saying that Majid *talla⁽ha lissamal-ahma* [raised the bids to the red sky].

Majid prides himself on having been clever all his life:

> Even as a child, no one could get ahead of me in cleverness. You know the Corporation agricultural manager. His father was one of the teachers at the missionary school I attended; now he is the principal. The son was my classmate. I had to drop out of school while he graduated and attended college. I said to him the other day, "Don't you remember when we were in the same class, how I always outsmarted all of you? Now many of my old classmates are college graduates, and look at

me, a plain farmer." The manager said to me, "Don't go too far; you were ahead of everyone there, and you are ahead of us all here as well."

Majid lives in the most up-to-date house in the village. It has a colorfully painted gate, is nicely furnished, and contains fans and air conditioners, a color television, and a new videotape machine. As I was sitting in his living room one day, sipping iced lemonade and chatting with him and his wife, he very proudly recited all the improvements that he had put into the house and asked me if it made me feel homesick. "My whole house is screened off very tightly. There are no mosquitoes here. Others complain about mosquitoes in their houses, but not me. People try to copy what I do but it never comes out as well as mine. They lack my expertise; they have not been around."

Malik

Short and stocky, 47-year-old Malik continuously joked about his waistline, telling me that he was at least seven months pregnant. He is a Nubian village tenant farmer and the principal of one of the boys' schools in New Halfa. His wife Muna, also short, ample, very good-natured, and hospitable, and his nine children—seven girls and two boys—were our constant companions and loving and caring friends while my daughter Tamara and I were in the field.

Malik and his family moved to the Scheme in 1964. In Wadi Halfa, they lived in Digheim. He explained:

> Wadi Halfa was organized differently. We did not have a city of Halfa as we do here. It was just a market and was referred to as such. Some people lived in villages that were close to the market, and others lived far away. Wadi Halfa consisted of umoudiyas [the sites of umdas], and Digheim was an umoudiya that included several villages. Most of the villages were along the banks of the Nile. The Aswan Dam flood was not the first that we suffered from. I remember the 1957 flood, when villages had to be moved away from the Nile. The first villages to move to the New Halfa Scheme were the ones closest to the Egyptian border. It took several months to move everybody. Villagers who lived close to the market in Wadi Halfa were resettled in villages that are close to the town of New Halfa on the Scheme.

Malik had been married for two years when migration to the Scheme started. He left on 5 July 1964, leaving behind his wife, who had her second baby that very day. People chose their new villages while they were still in Wadi Halfa. Those in the Digheim umoudiya were resettled in Villages Eighteen, Twenty-one, Twenty-two, Twenty-three, and some in Village Nineteen. Many of the inhabitants of Digheim refused to move and are still in Wadi Halfa. Malik recalled:

> In Wadi Halfa, villages were much closer to each other. We used to be able to walk to many of the villages, especially the ones in the same umoudiya; that was because they were not separated from each other by agricultural fields. In Wadi Halfa, Angash, for example, was only about two kilometers from Digheim. The present inhabitants of Village Sixteen lived in an area known as *ardh al-hajar*, the land of rocks, a very difficult area to cultivate and far away from the market. They were considered very fortunate since they were resettled in a village very close to New Halfa.

The inhabitants were shown maps of Scheme villages, and people were asked to select their houses accordingly. Relatives were given houses in the same village or town block. Everyone who had a house in Wadi Halfa received a house and a tenancy on the Scheme. Those who did not have houses were given nothing on the Scheme. Those who had several houses or a very big house in Wadi Halfa were given one house and cash compensation, or in some instances two houses. Malik's brother, who lived in Khartoum, received two houses and one tenancy, while his father received a house and a tenancy.

Malik was a schoolteacher in Wadi Halfa in 1958 and 1959. At the end of 1959, the government sent him to Khartoum for two years to attend a teachers' college. After graduating, he was transferred to the town of Atbara. His stay in Atbara was brief; he managed to be transferred back to Wadi Halfa through the aid of a Nubian friend at the Ministry of Education. He married Muna in 1962 and taught in the town of New Halfa from 1964 to 1970, when he was promoted to principal.

Malik has full control of fifteen tenancies. Of these, only one is in his own name. The rest belong to his dead father, his brother, and other relatives. Malik started cultivating on a large scale about four years after settling on the Scheme. Since all village tenancies were under the management of the village agricultural cooperative, he started by cultivating in other areas. One year he farmed in the Saba‘at section, about one hour's drive from his village. During the cultivation season, Malik made daily trips to Saba‘at, including the month of Ramadan; usually he traveled after getting out of school in the early afternoon, remaining on the farm until after dark.

Why would he leave his family tenancies with the village cooperative and cultivate in such faraway places?

> When we first moved to the Scheme, we, the villagers, had a meeting. We decided to establish an agricultural cooperative. Almost all Halfawi villagers had permanent jobs elsewhere, and we needed a way to take care of our lands so that we would not risk losing them through repossession. In addition to losing the land, repossession would have meant the possibility of bringing strangers into our midst. I was made president of the cooperative. We agreed that each family would receive two sacks of wheat a year. The rest of the produce would be sold and profits used to buy shares in the flour mill. To this date, profits are reinvested to buy more shares. We also bought tractors. Now the flour mill is expanding. They want to start a textile factory. The cooperative did not want to bother with the groundnut tenancies because most Halfawis, at that time, did not know how to grow groundnuts and because it was too labor-intensive. After a few years, when the cooperative became successful and better-established, I decided to pull out my tenancies and those of my family and to cultivate them myself. Many villagers did the same thing.

Malik cultivated in Saba⁢at in 1967/1968, prior to the completion of all Scheme phases in 1969/1970. Land was free for the asking. He cultivated about sixty-eight tenancies (340 feddan) that season and was the only person in the village to do so, renting a tractor when needed. It cost him about £S2 to plough a 5-feddan tenancy. All the tenancies were cultivated in wheat, producing from thirty to fifty sacks each. Some yielded as many as sixty sacks.

The almost daily commute to Saba⁢at proved to be too difficult. Malik searched for and found tenancies closer to his village. He cultivated those rented fields with a partner on a sharecropping basis, wherein Malik supplied, in addition to the land, all inputs and received four-fifths of the produce. He also rented freehold lands—he personally owned only 6 feddan.

In 1980/1981 and 1981/1982, Malik rented thirty-one, 5-feddan freehold fields, totaling 155 feddan. He had rented twenty-five of these fields for several years, paying an annual rental of £S40 per field when the going rate was £S50. How had he managed to do that?

> I rent them every year but never exhaust the soil. Although I never cultivate all of them in any one year, I nevertheless pay the rent to assure their continued availability. I never cultivate the same piece of land more than twice a year; normally only once. People in the village

know that they are better off with me than with a stranger who would intensively cultivate the land for the whole year and leave it utterly exhausted, so that no one would want to rent it the following year.

In the 1980/1981 season, Malik had two fields (10 feddan) in tomatoes, one (5 feddan) in sweet potatoes, and thirteen (65 feddan) in melons. He also planted eggplants, okra, and onions, purchasing £S270 worth of seeds and sowing them to start the seedlings, but nothing grew. He tried again and ended with a few weak seedlings that produced low-quality onions. He explained, "Agriculture is a very risky business. If a loss like that is going to break your neck, you should not get involved, since you cannot afford it. You have to have enough money so that a big loss does not mean starving." On the freehold lands Malik followed various strategies. He farmed some of the vegetables without assistance, others with the help of wage labor, while still others were cultivated on a sharecropping basis. For example, of the 10 feddan in tomatoes, 5 he farmed by himself and 5 in partnership with a sharecropper, on a fifty-fifty basis, each providing half of the inputs—Malik the land, and the partner the labor. The same arrangement was carried out for 45 feddan of melons. Normally, Malik does not sharecrop more than two tenancies with the same person, especially in arrangements where the partner receives up to 50 percent of the produce; Malik does not think the partner would devote the attention to larger pieces of land that he pays to smaller ones.

Tomatoes are ready to market in three months. Sowing starts either in the rainy season or in the cold season, and seeds that are sown in the beginning of December can be marketed in March. A field of 5 feddan is divided into twelve terraces. Each day, the mature crop of one or two terraces from each field is picked, producing between twenty and thirty boxes. Malik usually sells his crop wholesale. In 1981/1982, prices averaged £S8–9 per box, with a range from £S6 to £S10. Marketing continues for about one and a half months. Tomato seeds are sown again with the rains in May. In May 1981, Malik bought five boxes of seeds for £S150.

It is very risky, but if one is successful, one can make a bundle from agriculture. The seeds that I had sown in December produced an excellent crop, although many people had advised me to avoid tomatoes. When you are a farmer, you have to be willing to lose as well as gain. Otherwise you will always be afraid of trying anything because you are unwilling to lose £S70. If you can afford to lose that much money, you might gain thousands if the crop is successful.

Dealers came and bought sweet potatoes from the farm. Malik hired fifteen to twenty laborers for three to four days, to dig the potatoes out. A field averaged between 180 and 200 sacks, sometimes producing as much as 300 sacks. Malik spoke disdainfully of farmers who considered 100 sacks per field a good return. When he marketed his crop, a sack of potatoes sold for £S10–12. Later, the price rose to £S16–17. After deducting expenses and his partner's share, his net income amounted to £S2,000.

Melons are always auctioned in the vegetable market. Malik takes them there early in the morning. In those periods, he usually wakes up at 4:30. By 6:30, he has already transported three to four carloads, the first of which was loaded the previous evening. In 1981/1982, he sold about 250 loads at an average price of £S60 (ranging from £S40 to £S130). He grossed some £S15,000 from melons alone, before expenses (table 5.1). The out-of-pocket expenses were not usually this high, because Malik carried out his own land preparation; but since he had a sharecropper, expenses were calculated as if all labor was hired at current market prices.

Malik employed a full-time tractor driver whom he paid £S50 per month in addition to an incentive: any day the driver ploughed more than five tenancies (either Malik's own or those of others who rent the tractor), he received £S0.25 for each additional field; ploughing eight to ten tenancies in one day is not uncommon. For other agricultural operations, Malik hired help on a permanent, seasonal, monthly, or daily basis, depending on each crop's requirements. Malik avoided sharecropping on his own wheat fields since the crop did not require constant surveillance. When help was required, it was hired on a piecework basis.

For cultivating most of his freehold lands, Malik often hired sharecroppers. In April 1981, he had several freehold fields under cultivation. There were six fields (30 feddan) northeast of the village, three of them sharecropped with a village farmer. Two full-time Eritrean laborers were temporarily hired to work the six fields. They were paid £S30 a month in addition to food. Malik paid for one of the laborers, who was in charge of his three fields; the other, who was in charge of the sharecropped fields, was paid by his partner. Malik did not have to participate in supporting the second man

TABLE 5.1
5-Feddan Field Expenses for Melons in £S

Heavy disc ploughing	30
Light disc ploughing	15
Ridging	15
Terracing	30
4 cans of seeds @ £S15	60
3 guards/2 months @ £S30/month/each	180
Expenses per field	330
Total expenses for 13 fields	4,290

because the partner was supposed to provide all labor, Malik having provided the land. In addition, a full-time worker was hired to guard the crop. Malik had four fields (20 feddan) in another area, two farmed independently and two with a sharecropper. In addition to providing labor on 10 feddan, the sharecropper also guarded all four fields. One of two fields grown in tomatoes was sharecropped with a Fur farmer, and the other was worked with hired labor.

Malik said that he ploughed the land very carefully and allowed it to rest and air out. In 1981/1982, he cultivated all his wheat-growing government tenancies. He would have liked to rent additional ones for cultivation, but nothing that he considered suitable was available.

In 1981/1982, Malik also cultivated fifteen groundnut tenancies, nine in partnership with Husam, a man whose brother was a senior-level Corporation official. The other six he farmed on his own. For the first nine tenancies, Malik provided only ploughing; Husam was responsible for everything else, including the provision of labor. Malik had grown no groundnuts in the 1980/1981 season.

> In 1979/1980, I grew groundnuts in fifteen tenancies. They were doing beautifully. At harvest, I could not find any laborers to harvest the crop. I had to water the tenancies three times to make the pulling easier. This caused the roots to weaken so that when the plants were pulled out, most of the groundnuts remained underground. I lost a lot that way. Because of this, combined with the very low prices that were available at the time, I swore never to grow groundnuts again. The following season, prices rose higher than ever before. So this year I am cultivating fifteen tenancies, nine of them with Husam to relieve me from having to provide labor for them.

I discussed the sharecropping arrangement with Husam. Although he lived in Khartoum, the previous year's high prices of groundnuts tempted him to come to New Halfa to try growing them. His brother introduced him to Malik, who agreed to sharecrop nine tenancies with him. Malik would get one-fourth of the produce from the nine tenancies before any deductions were made. Malik prepared the land, but Husam paid for everything else, including seeds and labor. Husam did not plan to spend the whole season in New Halfa, since he was cultivating other farms in the Khartoum area. He had hired a full-time attendant and was going to hire labor. He commented: "Groundnuts require a lot of work. They need constant weeding; otherwise the crop could be totally destroyed. Weeding is very labor-intensive and very costly if performed by hired labor; but if the land is worked properly and water is not a problem, a tenancy will produce between 120 and 150 sacks." Husam hoped that the price of groundnuts would continue to rise. He believed that it would not be too closely tied to international market prices since large portions of the groundnuts in the Sudan are consumed locally in the form of cooking oil.

The same season, Malik cultivated thirty-six wheat tenancies, fifteen of his own and twenty-one of the Corporation's. Eight tenancies were sown with the variety jiza 157, ten with a Mexican variety, and the rest with jiza 155. The twenty-one tenancies granted to him by the Corporation had been left uncultivated by the villagers because they felt that the land was not well suited for watering since the location was too high; considering water shortages, they were afraid the crop would die of thirst. Malik went to the Corporation, where he had many friends who visited him several nights a week; he provided food and drinks and asked to be allowed to cultivate these fields, saying that he was willing to take the risk.

The output from the thirty-six tenancies was variable, depending on the variety grown. Jiza 157 was a disappointment, producing only 7 to 9 sacks per tenancy. The Mexican and jiza 155 varieties did better; average production for all thirty-six tenancies was 20 sacks, a total of 720 sacks. Malik did not sell any of the wheat to the Corporation to reimburse cultivation advances.

In theory, tenants are not allowed to store wheat. Except for what is needed for family consumption, they have to sell everything to the flour mill at official government prices, which are usually much lower than market prices. In 1981/1982, the government bought

wheat at £S14 a sack; a few months later, the market price rose to
£S23–24. The government also tries to stop tenants from transporting wheat outside the area. Considering the close kinship ties that
exist in the Sudan, tenants resent having to obtain permits to send a
couple of sacks of wheat to their families in Wadi Halfa. I was told
that regulations tended to be much stricter in the past, with threats
of household searches for hidden wheat. In fact, however, affluent
tenants usually store their entire crop and start selling gradually, as
prices improve. Sales are most vigorous in October and November,
when prices are highest.

In addition to his government tenancies and freehold lands, Malik
raises livestock. Muna, his wife, says that they started raising animals
on the Scheme when they lived in another Halfawi village, where
Malik was a schoolteacher. He started by buying one cow for family
use, since, with several children, they had to buy about 10 pounds
(weight) of milk per day. The cow calved. He bought another cow
and then a third. The cows produced more milk than required by
the family, so they started selling the surplus on a very small scale.

By 1981/1982, Malik had twenty-eight head of cattle, including
thirteen calves, of which five were male. They were all marketed at
about two years of age since, after that, they became too expensive to
feed. At the time, a two-year-old calf fetched about £S170. A good
milk cow brought £S450. Malik had eleven milk cows, each yielding
about 20 pounds of milk a day, during its five-to-six-month lacta-
tion. Eleven cows thus produced approximately 220 pounds of milk
a day. About 20 pounds were consumed by the family and distributed to relatives and neighbors. The rest was marketed at about 10
piasters per pound of milk, for a total of £S20 a day. I asked Malik,
who hired his own shepherd, why he did not get involved in livestock raising on a large scale like Nabil, a well-known Nubian livestock owner from another Scheme village (see discussion below). He
replied:

Nabil has been a merchant from the beginning; besides, he does not
cultivate as extensively as I do. Keeping a large number of animals
requires a great deal of labor. I teach every day, six days a week, except
for holidays, from seven in the morning until two in the afternoon. I
do not have that kind of time. This year, I am planning to retire from
teaching. That will give me the chance to concentrate on farming.
Then I will start buying young calves, fatten them for a couple of years,
and resell them for at least double the original price. Now I care for

animals along with cultivation. Nabil concentrates mainly on animals. He has many tenancies and freehold lands, but most of the area is grown in fodder.

Malik did retire from teaching in late 1981.

For the third consecutive season, in 1981/1982, the Corporation decided not to require cotton in the rotation in Malik's village, where the soil is poorly suited to it. Malik was delighted, for despite his general success in farming it had been years since his cotton account had shown a positive balance. "As a matter of fact, I think the tenancies are in debt, but I do not know for how much, and I do not care to find out." He was optimistic about the Corporation's intention to eliminate the joint-account system for cotton tenancies, but he remained critical of its overall operation. "What I am angry about is their decision to charge a water fee that includes an overhead charge. I heard from one of the officials that it might be £S200 a year for each hawasha. Not many people make that kind of money from their tenancy, especially not from cotton, and with those fees no one will bother to farm." What did he think of the continuously reduced capacity of the reservoir to store water? He blames Arab tenants for shortages of water.

> The Scheme was designed for us, and the reservoir's capacity was calculated on that basis. Then they brought the Arabs in. They did not consider the water issue. Those Arabs do nothing to benefit the government, which provides them with seed, fertilizer, and cash advances to grow cotton. Before the harvest, they bring their animals onto the fields and the crop is eaten. The government spends more and more every year, and the Arabs feed it to their animals.

Malik did not acknowledge that many Nubians seem to follow the same strategy of allowing their livestock to graze unharvested cotton.

Malik's salary as a school principal was about £S170 per month, a very modest fraction of his overall income. That salary could not cover even a week's hospitality for the friends who gathered at his home every evening for food, drink, and conversation. Yet despite seriously considering early retirement from teaching to devote himself to the agricultural ventures that generated most of his income, he always referred to agriculture as his hobby. Malik did not want either of his two sons to be farmers.

Malik claims that he never leaves too much money sitting in the bank. Each year, he expands and intensifies his agricultural activities. "When you are generous to the land, the land is generous to you. I do not conserve on fertilizers, seeds, insecticides, weeding, or anything else the land might need. I plough the land several times if needed, air the soil, and allow it to rest. I never abuse the land because if I do, it will take its revenge. Whatever I make goes back to the land. I increase the amount of land I cultivate year after year."

Malik explained what he viewed as major Scheme problems:

1. The fertilizers are very expensive. Poor farmers cannot afford them. The government should subsidize them and sell them cheaply.
2. The Scheme is infested with weeds. The present tractors cannot remove them, since heavier equipment is required. They have been telling us for years that the new tractors are coming, that the World Bank is bringing them, but we have not seen a thing yet.
3. Crop diseases are widespread.
4. Water shortages are a major problem. The Corporation cuts off the water according to a fixed schedule, without regard to crop needs. They cut off the water for the wheat crop in March without any consideration for the farmer who planted late. No one starts sowing late if he can help it, but sometimes farmers are forced to because of unavailability of tractors, seeds, and water. Farmers are supposed to finish sowing by the first of October but that almost never happens.

Malik tried to assure that his crops received enough water by appealing directly to the chief water engineer. He applied the same principle, involving friends at the top if necessary, when he needed fertilizer. Malik preferred to buy his fertilizer from the Agricultural Bank rather than from the Corporation because it was less expensive. In 1981/1982, the Bank sold sacks of fertilizer at £S8 apiece, while the Corporation's were sold for £S11.8. The difference in price is considerable. Each wheat tenancy requires eight sacks, and Malik farmed thirty-six tenancies. Buying from the Bank he spent £S2,304, a savings of £S1,094.4 from what the Corporation would have charged.

At least two of Malik's relatives whose tenancies were under his control were not pleased with the arrangement. They were an older woman and her daughter, both widowed, living next to each other. The daughter's husband had worked and lived in Port Sudan with his family and therefore had been unable to take care of his tenancy. The mother was too old to assume direct control. Both tenancies had been assigned to the village agricultural cooperative, and each family received two sacks of wheat a year. When Malik recovered his tenancies from the cooperative, he asked these families to assign their lands to him, saying that he would give them whatever they had received from the cooperative and perhaps more.

After Malik took over, the families received no money from cotton or groundnuts, and only three sacks of wheat yearly. Both women felt they should be receiving more. Neither, however, wished to have a confrontation with Malik. Since the daughter's sons were too young to work the land and she herself had too many other responsibilities to assume direct control—and her mother was too old—they were resigned to the situation. They genuinely liked Malik: he was nice, patient, and dependable when needed. The daughter knew that Malik benefited greatly from the tenancies under his control, but she also realized that she could not make them as productive as he did since she did not have the necessary resources. If they took the tenancies away from him, it would not be appropriate for them to seek his help, especially financially, if things did not work out.

Both women also owned freehold lands that were under Malik's control. The daughter said:

> He has all the family tenancies and freehold lands—his dead parents', his sisters', brother's, cousins'. Most of these people cannot work the land. His brother is a successful merchant in Khartoum and will not live here for anything. Both his sisters are high school teachers, and their husbands have excellent jobs. He is very energetic and hardworking, and he knows many important people. A tenancy requires much money before it begins to produce—ploughing, seeds, fertilizers, weeding, and water. Watering could be a severe problem. Your whole crop could burn before your own eyes, and you could not do a thing about it. You have seen how hard he worked the last few days when the wheat crop required its last watering. He was out every night until the early morning hours, chasing water guards, going to the water engineer. People do things for Malik because he puts them under his obligation. I can never do that. I have no transport, no money, and no connections.

Majid and Malik exemplify Halfawi tenants who, through various resources and labor strategies, have managed to make the Scheme very successful for themselves. It would be unfair to deny that personal qualities, such as shrewdness, intelligence, and entrepreneurship, are relevant in obtaining their goals. They invest a great deal of effort in learning about agriculture. Yet these qualities were likely to have been underexploited or directed toward more modest goals had it not been for their access to external resources, including experiences learned and connections made in Wadi Halfa for Majid, and education that gave him an edge over many other tenants for Malik.

Both also have financial resources to mitigate the uncertainties of innovation.

Majid's entrepreneurial qualities surfaced in childhood, but it was due to his father's financial and human resources that he was able to attend a missionary school, be trained as a mechanic, and get a job as a mechanic in Egypt. His experiences in Wadi Halfa equipped him with visibility and a reputation for shrewdness and capability that paved the way to Scheme success. Easy access to family tenancy and freehold lands facilitated his ability to draw on the relations established with Corporation staff in the early years of the Scheme. His initial resource inventory allowed for an investment cycle and progressively increased accumulation, enabling him gradually to become one of the most successful Scheme tenants.

Malik is a hard worker, but his success could never have been achieved by work alone. In addition to his education, which contributed to his Scheme success, Malik came with other connections, evidenced by his ability to attend a teachers' training college in Khartoum and his being transferred back to Wadi Halfa by involving a Nubian friend. As a schoolteacher in New Halfa, Malik was not only a neighbor to many Scheme residents; they were also his students, or fathers, brothers, uncles, and other relatives of students. The Arabic proverb says, "man ᶜalamani harfan surtu lahou ᶜabdan" (He who taught me one letter, I will be his slave). Coupled with material resources and willingness to work hard and to experiment, his position as schoolteacher and principal was advantageous on the Scheme. He immediately established good relationships with Scheme administration and had access to large parcels of land—greatly facilitated by the fact that, because it was still the first stage in Scheme resettlement, vast areas of cultivable land had not yet been allocated. Hospitality played a major role in reinforcing Malik's ties with Scheme officials and other people of influence, and he received guests every evening.

Nabil

Although animal rearing is associated with Arabs and other pastoral-nomadic groups in the area, the Halfawi population is becoming more and more interested in livestock. Like most Arab tenant households on the Scheme, most Halfawi households own only a few animals to supplement their agricultural and other incomes. A few affluent Halfawis have made livestock rearing a major labor strategy, however, and have profited greatly. Nabil, a Nubian Halfawi whose village lies within eight kilometers of the town of New Halfa, is an excellent example of Halfawi involvement in animal rearing, as are nearly all of the other members of the village. Among the 238 village households, most own a tenancy and a few animals, although some own larger numbers of animals and control numerous tenancies. Nabil is one of the biggest livestock owners in the village.

Nabil has control over seven government tenancies, one of them in his own name and six in the names of family members. In addition, he has control over 60 feddan of freehold land that is largely cultivated in sorghum used mainly for animal fodder. While animal husbandry was the dominant form of production and subsistence on the Butana prior to the Scheme, fodder production is an innovation that reflects the increasing commoditization of ruminant livestock. Nabil tries to keep half of the area fallow each year for higher production.

In addition to the land, Nabil owns at least eighty head of cattle that are corralled at night in the village, leaving with their herder for open-range grazing at seven in the morning and returning to the enclosure at four in the afternoon. Upon their return, they are fed sorghum to supplement the day's grazing. Two full-time herders are employed to care for the animals and to do the milking. Nabil's 1981 cattle herd contained ten lactating cows. He started the year with thirteen male calves; by August, twelve had been sold. Usually, Nabil waits till the calves are three years of age before they are marketed, but that year a shortage of graze led him to sell them at a younger age. He tries not to sell females unless they are incurably sick, old, or barren. Nabil said that he owned sixty fertile cows, but he never allowed them all to get pregnant at the same time. That would make feeding difficult, especially in rain-deficit years. Also, by controlled breeding, he assured the availability of milk for domestic use and sale throughout the year. Nabil said that he had different kinds of cows: one kind gave milk until it delivered; others for just a few months; others for up to six months. He preferred the red Butana cattle because they were good-natured and good milkers.

The milk output of the herd ranged from 10 to 20 rotl (1 rotl = 12 fl. oz., 0.35 liter) per cow, per day, a total of 100 to 150 rotl of milk. It was transported to New Halfa daily in one of his two vehicles, where between 80 and 100 rotl were sold to the agricultural school and the rest to a dairy shop in the town. Although the going price per rotl of milk was 10 piasters, Nabil got 15 because of its high butterfat content and because the supply was dependable.

Nabil had been raising cattle for over twelve years. Some of his better milking cows were purchased at about £S400 per head. He said that he would never sell a milking cow at any price, although he might consider lending one to a very dear friend who was trying to start a herd; however, he said, even this was unlikely. In addition to the cattle, he owned over 250 sheep that grazed on the Butana with a Shukriya herder. They usually spent the dry season in Wad Naᶜouma near Qafala and the rainy season on the Butana. The sheep were raised strictly for meat. Between 25 and 35 male sheep were marketed yearly, while the females were retained for breeding. He felt that raising sheep had both advantages and disadvantages: the advantage was that they grew and reproduced quickly; the disadvantage was that sheep were more prone to diseases and infant death than cattle. In normal years, he lost between 10 and 15 sheep, mostly newborns.

Although Nabil had owned a few cattle, sheep, and goats in Wadi Halfa, most of them did not make it to the Scheme; those that did became sick and were quickly slaughtered, died, or were stolen. Five years after settling, he started with one cow, purchased from his sister's husband for £S20. He would have invested in cattle earlier, but his father would not allow it, considering it unbecoming for a Nubian to herd. After his father's death, he bought a few cows from an acquaintance on the Butana, caring for them himself, taking them out at the end of the day and bringing them feed. After experiencing herding with five cows, he decided it was profitable, increased the size of his herd, and hired a full-time herder. Nabil said that he employed the herder for two reasons: he was really a merchant with a construction materials shop, so he could not effectively take good care of both; besides, as a Nubian, taking out a few cows and walking with them as they grazed at the end of the day was one thing, but devoting himself totally to the herd was entirely discrepant from Nubian values.[1]

Once he decided that animal husbandry was a sound investment, Nabil began buying cows regularly, sometimes one every month, sometimes more, paying for them with profits from his shop, until

---

[1] Michael Horowitz (1972) makes the same argument concerning Manga farmers' reluctance to become herders despite the assumed wealth of the latter, since the pastoral life-style is so contrary to their own. See also F. Barth (1967) on Darfur.

he had a herd of some thirty cows. Luck was with him, and most of the newborns were female. Within ten years, he had built up the basic breeding herd to over eighty cows. Rather than feeding them entirely on the open range, he converted his freehold lands from wheat to sorghum (a crop that at the time was not permitted on the tenancies), exclusively for fodder. The sorghum variety grown is called *abu sab‘een* in New Halfa (literally, the father of seventy), referring to the seventy-day period from sowing to maturation. The seeds are very small and the stalks as sweet as sugarcane, so sweet that Nabil's own children—as well as livestock—had to be kept out of the fields. The fields were worked with rented tractors and hired labor, and still he found the process profitable. Each year, four or five sacks of sorghum were stored to provide seed for the following planting season.

Nabil said that he learned herding from the Arabs. "Cattle are very good, but most Halfawis do not like looking after animals. They prefer farming since they like to be comfortable. Animals and comfort do not match." Nabil referred to himself as a merchant/farmer/herder. He started his construction business in 1969. "When we first moved to the Scheme, I noticed that people were always building something or another, but there was not even one shop in the town that sold construction materials. I investigated the issue fully and decided, in partnership with my brother, to start such a shop. It was the first of its kind in the area. My son joined us a few years later."

Nabil said that initially Halfawis were very surprised by his interest in animals.

"You have money," they would say to me, "why would you want to run after animals?" I was the first man in my village to start cattle herding on a large scale. Others started five to seven years after me. Before, people had at most a cow or two. People were also afraid; they were afraid of theft. The Arabs knew the area well, and we did not. They were armed and thought that killing a man was not much more serious than slaughtering a chicken. I used to advise people to invest their money in animal raising, but they would not listen to me. I am sure many thought that I was losing my mind. Their attitudes changed when they realized how successful I had become. I would tell them that I made £S400 per month from milk alone, and they would go out of their minds; some were very jealous. They learned from me.

Milk sales averaged about £S300 a month, but much of that money was spent for cattle feed, and the cost has increased markedly in recent years. "In addition to graze, lactating cows must be fed, mainly on sorghum and umbaz, the residue of cottonseeds after the oil has been pressed. Years ago a sack of umbaz cost only £S5.5; now it costs £S44. I also need about ten sacks of bran each month. In the past, the flour mill sold bran at only £S1 per sack; now it costs £S3.7." With two full-time herders at £S35 per month each, and the cost of supplemental feed, the milk herd required monthly expenditures of £S120-130, in addition to the sorghum grown on Nabil's freehold lands. Toward the end of the dry season, when graze was exhausted, all the milk earnings were spent on purchased feed. "This does not worry me, however. I gladly spend the whole income on my animals when they need it because it pays in the long run. Lactating and pregnant cows that are properly fed give more and better-quality milk, with high fat content, and healthier calves. People gladly pay 15 piasters per rotl for my milk when it can be bought for only 10 piasters elsewhere; even 20 piasters when milk is scarce. They know I am not stingy with my cows."

Nabil's milk cows are divided into two groups, the larger group milked in the early morning for immediate transport to market, and the smaller herd milked in the evenings for household consumption. Since he had to drive one of his vehicles—he owns a Toyota and a Land Rover—daily from home to his shop in New Halfa, transporting milk to the urban market entailed no additional costs.

Planting of the sorghum fodder crop on Nabil's freehold lands was timed for harvest in April, the height of the dry season, when open-range graze was scarcest and purchased feed most costly. Sorghum stores well, and any feed not consumed at that time was stored on the farm. He has also integrated his other crops with livestock rearing. "I never miss a year of groundnuts, even when prices are not attractive, since I feed the remains to the animals."

During the 1981/1982 season, Nabil grew groundnuts, cotton, and wheat on his government tenancies. The previous season, he had wheat and groundnuts only. He said he sold £S3,000 worth of wheat, all jiza 157.

In our village, people are mainly dependent on agriculture, especially wheat and groundnuts. Both men and women participate in cultivation and work the tenancies. Cotton problems are all caused by the government. If a farmer finds a good piece of land he will cultivate it; for seventeen years, the land has not been properly ploughed; they are not using heavy enough tools for deep ploughing. Farmers are afraid to throw their money into cotton and risk losing everything. In 1969/1970,

I myself made £S1,000 from cotton after the government deducted its share. If the soil was good and we did not have a joint account, a farmer could easily make 50 qantar per tenancy. All problems are caused by the authorities themselves, not the farmers. Now the farmer is putting all his effort into wheat production. He will plough the tenancy four times if necessary. The government will not plough the cotton fields four times, only once. If you decide it needs more ploughing, you have to pay the full cost yourself. Why should I? You think the government is poorer than me, so I have to pay all expenses and then share profits with them? They are very stupid. Groundnuts are as important as wheat. With these two crops, because we do not have partners, we do not care if we spend £S300 on one tenancy; the whole profit will be ours, unlike cotton. Why should the farmer spend money for the benefit of the government?

In 1979/1980, Nabil had cotton in seven tenancies that produced 104 qantar, an average of 15 each. He claims that he spent £S400-500 of his own money. "The government advanced me £S10 for the first weeding when it cost me £S30-35. That is ridiculous. I have not received any money for that season yet." In 1980/1981, he did not grow cotton. He grew wheat in seven tenancies and groundnuts in only three. "That was because the rains were a bit heavy, so I could not prepare the land in advance. Besides, the price of groundnuts in the previous year was not very high. Because of my animals, I grow groundnuts every year to use the remains as fodder. Luckily, last year the early price was high, and I received £S20 per qantar, moving fast in case the price dropped."

In the seven wheat tenancies, he made over 200 sacks, an average of 30 per field. Although he knew the price would rise if he waited, he sold 120 sacks right away at £S25 each. Why did he not wait? "Because I am a merchant. It is more beneficial for me to sell early and have access to the cash, which I can invest in trade, rather than wait for several months for a few extra pounds per sack." The 80 sacks he kept were for his extended family and for seeds. Nabil never bought seeds from the government unless there was a new variety he wanted to try, and he never experimented on more than one or two tenancies at a time.

Despite the high groundnut prices of 1980/1981, Nabil cultivated only four tenancies in 1981/1982 because of labor scarcity. "In the past, labor was available and cheap. The land was in a much better condition, without too many weeds. Now labor is scarce and expensive; the land requires more work. Experienced groundnut laborers today are reluctant to work for wages in preference to sharecropping. I do not want sharecroppers in my fields. I do not want to cultivate seven tenancies to discover at the end that I cannot recruit enough labor to work them."

Sammy

Sammy was 54, rather short, with thinning, carefully combed hair, and a thin mustache. His wife Foziyya died in 1979. Sammy's father's mother, who was also Malik's mother's mother, and Foziyya's father's mother were sisters. Sammy had seven years of education and worked in New Halfa for the health office in charge of the malaria section. His monthly salary was £S90.

Sammy and Foziyya had eight children, four girls and four boys. Two of the girls, ages 27 and 22, were married; the elder lived in a Scheme village and the younger in Khartoum. The elder daughter's husband worked at the Corporation as a cashier. Sammy's third daughter became engaged to a Nubian village man who worked in the Arabian Gulf. The eldest son, a 21-year-old graduate of a two-year Egyptian college, worked in Khartoum for his sister's husband, who had an office supplies store. The second son, 17, was in high school and hoped to attend the University of Khartoum.

Sammy and his family came to the Scheme in 1965. He had a government tenancy and inherited freehold land from his father, as did his brother Samir, who lived next door, his sister Insaf, who had lived on the other side of him and had recently died, and his other two sisters, Ikhlas and Hamida, who were married and lived in another village. The family was given three houses when it came to the Scheme, one for Sammy, one for his brother Samir, and one for their father.

The family's freehold land was in two villages, 20 feddan in the father's name in the village where most of the family lived and 19 feddan in the mother's name in the village of the two married sisters. When the family moved from Wadi Halfa, the father divided the land that way so his married daughters in the other village would have property of their own. Before he died, the father was in charge of the three government tenancies, his own and those of his two sons, in addition to the freehold land in the main village. He usually provided inputs, his sons provided some of the labor, and the produce was divided equally among the three.

After his father's death, Sammy took the three government tenancies, and Samir the freehold land in the main village. The land in

the other village remained for the daughters. Sammy explained that
he and his brother divided their holdings in that manner because
freehold land calls for expensive inputs, especially when one does
not have the time to do the work oneself, and Samir's economic status was better than his own. Samir was an accountant at the tele-
phone company, making £S180 a month. After their father's death,
Sammy and Samir initially helped their sisters cultivate the lands in
their village and divided the produce in three parts, for Sammy,
Samir, and the two sisters. Recognizing that it was taking too much
travel time, since neither Sammy nor his brother owned a vehicle,
they decided to leave the land totally in the care of their sisters. The
two women started cultivating the land themselves with the assistance of hired labor. They grew wheat and vegetables and usually
sent two or three sacks of wheat a year for their two brothers.

Comparing his situation with that of an affluent farmer like Malik,
Sammy said:

Malik has fifteen government tenancies under his direct control. In
1980/1981, he had thirty-six tenancies under wheat, about seven of
which did not do too well, yielding only 7 to 8 sacks each, but the rest
produced between 27 and 35 sacks each, some as high as 40. He had
over 1,000 sacks, of which about 100 went for *zakat* [Islamic charity].
In addition, Malik usually distributes wheat to poor relatives and villagers so that God may increase his fortune. Last year, he gave away
between 80 and 90 sacks to people like Ibtisam, a widow whose tenancy is under his control, and Hamid. He sold 300 sacks right away at
£S20 each for a total of £S6,000 to pay back his debts to the Corporation and the Sudan Agricultural Bank. Malik pays the Corporation by
check, so he does not have to have the cash ready in his hands at harvest time. Since it takes about two weeks for a check to clear, he has
time to sell wheat on the open market and to deposit the money in his
bank account, instead of selling them [the Corporation] the wheat at
official government prices, as many farmers are forced to do. He does
the same with the Agricultural Bank—he buys his fertilizers from them
instead of from the Corporation. It is cheaper there: £S8 as opposed to
£S11.8 per sack. Not everybody can do that since the Bank has requirements that not everyone can meet. One has to have something to put
down as collateral or someone willing to serve as guarantor. Besides,
Malik knows all these people. He does them favors all the time. They
always come to his house, eat his food, and drink his water.

Malik saves the rest of his wheat to sell right before sowing. People
want good seeds for sowing. In July, a sack of wheat sold for £S27.5. By
the time people start preparing for sowing in October, it can go as high
as £S30. Of course, one can never be sure. Sometimes seeds arrive on

time, although that rarely happens. If enough seeds arrive on time, the price of wheat will drop sharply. Another man in Malik's position would be a millionaire by now. Malik does not know how to save money. His hand and his house are always open. People come and borrow money from him and do not pay him back for months; sometimes years. A couple of years ago, he took a trip to Europe.

In the 1980/1981 season, Sammy grew wheat on all three tenancies. He rented two of the groundnut tenancies to a Fur sharecropper on a fifty-fifty basis—all expenses and all profits were divided equally: Sammy provided the land and the Fur provided the labor. Cotton tenancies were left uncultivated. The two groundnut tenancies produced 120 and 130 sacks, respectively. After washing and cleaning, about 112 sacks remained, since the reduction in volume was substantial; 12 sacks were put aside as seeds for the following season. From the remaining 100 sacks, all production expenses—ploughing, seeding, sowing, weeding, harvesting—in the amount of £S280 were calculated. The 100 sacks of groundnuts fetched only £S11.5 each— they were sold right after harvest, before the price went up, for a total of £S1,150. After deducting expenses, £S870 was divided evenly between Sammy and his sharecropper.

During the preceding eight or nine years, Sammy had grown groundnuts by himself, with occasional hired labor. He was forced to seek a sharecropper in 1980 because of his wife's illness and eventual death. In the same season, he farmed five wheat tenancies, two of which were rented from other holders at a fee of 20 percent of the harvest. One of his own tenancies was attacked by a herd of cattle four days before the harvester was scheduled to harvest the whole nimra of thirty-six tenancies. Sammy explained:

> It must have been a herd of over 300 head. They attacked the whole nimra of tenancies, and eight, among them one of mine, were totally destroyed. All this happened in one evening. The owners were never identified. When a large herd attacks a tenancy, what does not get eaten is stamped over, making it impossible for the harvesters to do their job, since they can deal only with standing crop. The tenancy would have produced between 30 and 35 sacks. My neighbor had his harvested despite the attack, and his tenancy yielded one and a half sacks! I did not want them to harvest mine, as it would have been a total loss financially. The few sacks it might have produced would have been less than the harvester's rental fee, £S30.

The tenancy was already in debt because the Corporation had provided all inputs and prepared the land; payment, in cash, was due upon harvest. Since the three tenancies are under different names, the two productive ones were not charged for the other's debt.

On his remaining tenancies, Sammy made 30 sacks from one and 35 from the other. The two that he rented yielded 20 and 25, with one-fifth, or 9 sacks of wheat, given to the owners. This left him with a total 101 sacks of wheat: 10 percent was immediately donated as zakat to the village poor. He gave 5 sacks to his brother Samir and 10 to relatives and needy villagers; 15 sacks were sold at £S20 each for a total of £S300, from which he paid £S120 owed to the Corporation for harvesting, to the City Council for back taxes, and to Malik for money borrowed to buy seeds and fertilizers. He stored 9 sacks as seed stock for the following season, and the remainder were sold off gradually as needed. While his wife lived, Sammy said, they consumed about 13 sacks of wheat a year because she baked the bread herself and they entertained more. Since her death, and with the unmarried girls at school, Sammy has bought bread from the market, requiring only about 3 sacks a year for household consumption.

Although he could have borrowed money from the Agricultural Bank to finance his groundnut crop, Sammy preferred not to. He found the process to be too complicated, requiring too much paper work.

> I manage. I keep my own seeds. Malik ploughs for me and I pay him back when I can. He always charges me a little less than the going rate since we are cousins. Sowing costs me £S15–20 a tenancy, which I again usually borrow from Malik. With hired labor, one watering costs £S1.5 per tenancy. If I do not have the money or if I find that I have the time, I water the tenancies myself. Weeding is about £S20 for each tenancy. I take the money out of my salary, or I borrow from Malik or from Salah, a village shop owner from whom I borrow between £S100 and £S130 a year. I pay him back when I sell my crop. He does not charge me any interest since I also buy most of my foodstuff from him at about £S80 a month.

In the agricultural year 1981/1982, Sammy wanted to grow wheat on his own three tenancies and on as many tenancies as he could rent on a one-fifth basis. By December 1981, he had managed to rent five. He was planning to grow groundnuts in only one tenancy since, because of labor shortages, he was afraid the cost of each weeding would go up to £S50–60 per tenancy. Malik was to plough the fields with the ridging attachment, charging £S12 per tenancy.

Sammy owned four cows. They were not producing milk—they were all pregnant and due to deliver in a month or two. He also had two calves. Sammy usually kept heifer calves and sold the males after three to four years. In 1981, he had been keeping cattle for about five years, during which time three were lost: two drowned in one of the canals on the Scheme, and one was bitten by a snake and died. Cattle drown, according to Sammy, because of a disease known locally as *al-heish*. The animal's body gets so hot that it dives into water to cool off and drowns when the water is too deep, as in canals. He had begun animal husbandry with two cows.

> Raising cattle can be very profitable, but it is difficult for the Halfawis. The most important thing is to find yourself an honest herder. That is very hard. With animals, you either have to take care of them yourself as the Arabs do, or find some one trustworthy to do it for you. For us Halfawis, it is very difficult to do the former. We have to live in houses, to drink clean water, and to eat clean food. The Arabs do not care. An Arab can live on milk alone for months at a time. We cannot do that. Besides, people will make fun of you if you do that. They say, "He is becoming an Arab." It is shameful for us. Now the only people around to work as shepherds are the Hadandawa and the Mallo [a term used to refer to some of the people of West African origin], but you cannot trust either group. Then there are the Beni Amir. Some of them are trustworthy, but they are mainly cowards. They are afraid of the Hadandawa and the Mallo. When you have a herd, you have to be willing to fight for it; Beni Amir cannot fight. If it were not for that problem, cattle raising would be very profitable. If you have enough cows to give you five or six calves a year, you can sell them for between £S100 and £S900 each, depending on the time of sale and the size, sex, health, and age of the animal. This is not counting the milk. If you have five or six milking cows, you can sell about £S3–4 worth of milk a day.

Sammy said that a few years earlier he had entrusted six family sheep to a Mallo shepherd. Sammy, his brother, his married sisters, and his daughters were planning to slaughter the animals during the feast of sacrifice, ʿId el-Kabir, which celebrates the end of the pilgrimage to Mecca. Five days before the day of feast, the shepherd came to him, claiming that the animals were stolen. "We all went out and looked all over the place for them, but there was not even a trace. I was furious and very embarrassed, but what could I do? I could not kill the man for six sheep. I could not prove they were not stolen. I am sure this was a deal between the shepherd and his brother; the brother must have come after dark and collected the animals to sell elsewhere and the two must have divided the profits; but there was no way I could prove it."

Sammy is an example of the many Nubian tenants who, in addition to their tenancies and possibly freehold lands, have steady jobs that constitute their main earnings. Cultivation and sometimes animal husbandry are important additional sources of income. They do not have the resources and perhaps the personal qualities of Malik and Majid that would enable them to compete with the affluent tenants, but neither are they totally at the mercy of nature, the Corporation, the outside world, or the Agricultural Bank.

Hilmi

Hilmi, 49, his wife Wasfa, 40, and their seven children are a Halfawi tenant family living in a Nubian village. In addition to their seven unmarried children, Hilmi and Wasfa have a married daughter, Siham, 25, who has four children, including a newborn baby. Siham's husband had been in Saudi Arabia for about six months, but she and the children still lived in New Halfa. She came to visit her family several times a week, and her new baby was born at their house. Hilmi and Wasfa's second eldest daughter was Hind, 21, a rather good-looking, tall, slim girl. Hind was illiterate; since she did not have a birth certificate, and her father was never interested enough in the girl's education to get a doctor's certificate estimating her age, she had never been able to attend school. Hind did most of the housework: cleaning, cooking, taking care of the children, and doing the laundry. She also helped on the farm. She was very excited whenever I went to their house or accompanied them to the field, urging me to look at this or that or to take a picture of her working in the field.

The other daughters—Nada, 18, Salma, 16, Huda, 14, and Samira, 8—attended school, the first two in New Halfa since they were beyond the elementary school stage, and the others in the village. The three older girls helped with housework and, after school, worked with their father in the field. The older boy, Muhamed, 12, was in the fifth grade. Although he sometimes helped his father, especially during school vacation, he was usually urged to stay home and study. His father felt that his eldest boy should at least finish high school and perhaps become a schoolteacher. The younger boy, Mustafa, was only 6 and was not to start school for another year.

Since Hilmi had been without property in Wadi Halfa, he was entitled to neither a tenancy nor a house on the Scheme and had to rent land and a house in the village. In 1980/1981, he was able to rent several parcels of freehold land: 1. two and one-half fields of 5 feddan each from the village school principal; 2. one field from a retired government employee in the village; 3. two fields from a tenant who resided in Wadi Halfa; 4. one field from a villager who was employed by the New Halfa Town Council. For each of the six and a half fields, Hilmi paid £S50 per year to the landowners at the beginning of the season.

Hilmi cultivated the rented land during most of the year. From March to July, he grew melons and watermelons and some okra and eggplants. In the 1981/1982 season, he had three and a half fields in melons, half a field in okra, half a field in tomatoes, one in sweet potatoes, and a feddan in eggplants.

Hilmi bought seeds for the okra, eggplants, tomatoes, and pumpkins from the New Halfa market. A container of seeds cost about £S8–10, depending on the species, and a 5-feddan field required three to four containers. Watermelon and melon seeds were usually imported; farmers sent to Khartoum for them. In 1981/1982, a container of melon seeds cost £S10–11. A field required from six to eight sacks of urea fertilizer at £S11.8 a sack. Hilmi bought his fertilizer from the Corporation and applied it himself—hiring labor to apply fertilizer usually cost £S5-6 per field. Using a small hand pump, Hilmi sprayed each field with insecticide an average of three times. Each spraying required one gallon of insecticide per field, costing about £S6. Hilmi paid £S25 to have each field disc-ploughed and £S10 for ridging. He said he never hired labor for weeding since he himself, his wife, and the girls were able to do all the work themselves. Taxes were paid on marketed vegetables in the amount of 10 piasters per box of tomatoes, or per sack of eggplants or other vegetables, and £S2 per carload of melons and watermelons.

Okra was a very important crop to Hilmi and his family since it matures fast and does not require much care. The family started eating okra one month after sowing and started marketing it about two weeks later. Four to five sacks were collected twice weekly by Wasfa and the girls. A sack brought anywhere from £S3–4 when the market was flooded to £S10 when okra was scarce. Money received from okra sales paid for the family's daily requirements of sugar, tea, coffee, spices, and sorghum.

During the cultivation season, Hilmi was always in the field. His wife or one of the children brought him both breakfast and lunch every day except for Friday, when he came home around noon, attended the village mosque for prayer, ate lunch, and went back to the field. Hilmi prayed in the mosque every morning, then came home for his sweet tea with milk before leaving for the field or the market around 6 A.M. At the end of 1981, Hilmi hired a laborer who had just arrived from Upper Egypt. In addition to providing his food, he paid him £S15 a month.

In 1981/1982, Hilmi was able to keep four of the fields that he rented the year before and to rent three new ones. One was prepared for tomatoes, and two were in sweet potatoes, which were planted in May. They stayed in the ground for about six months before being harvested. A field of sweet potatoes could easily produce 100 sacks in one season, said Hilmi's family enthusiastically. Since they were not very popular on the Scheme, Hilmi usually transported them to Port Sudan for marketing. This required preparation—obtaining a permit to carry the produce outside the area and renting a truck, which cost £S50-70. A truck could carry from 60 to 70 sacks that usually sold for £S3-4 each, although occasionally they fetched more. A truckload could bring him £S500–600 when prices were good.

Hilmi preferred renting land to sharecropping. The last two seasons were the first in which he was able to rent. Before that, he had sharecropped on a fifty-fifty basis, where the owner provided all inputs—including land preparation costs—which were to be deducted from the harvest, and Hilmi provided the labor—his own and his family's. Having been able to put some money aside in 1979/1980, he decided to take the risk and try farming on his own the following season. Hilmi said that what he made each year was usually enough to take care of the family members because their requirements were modest. Sometimes, however, they were forced to borrow money because of a bad harvest. In those years, he borrowed from his fellow farmers, whom he tried to pay back the following season. He was never charged interest since they were all in the same position: if he needed them this season, they might need him the following. Hilmi and Wasfa estimated their household's monthly expenditure at £S40. They preferred to pay cash for all their purchases; but, as their income was seasonal, they were invariably forced to seek credit from a village shopkeeper.

The New Halfa Agricultural Scheme exemplifies a situation where different production strategies based on available resources coexist: where, although everybody lives in the shadow of the capitalist world system, some are more darkly shaded than others; and where, although the majority of tenants eke out a living and subsistence activities function to support the metropolis's needs for cheap raw materials, some tenants make profits that are reinvested internally toward localized expansion. Instances of local accumulation and reinvestment are crystal clear with Malik, Majid, and Nabil. Looking at their earlier life histories and their later development helps us understand why they, but not Hilmi, were able to prosper despite the general economic and environmental deterioration of the Scheme, annually expanding their agricultural and livestock holdings. If Scheme conditions continue to deteriorate, the value of tenancies and even freehold lands will continue to decline, and these affluent farmers will be able to accumulate more holdings at an even lower price.

Hamid

Hamid was a 45-year-old non-Halfawi farmer living in a rented house in a Nubian village, with neither government tenancy nor freehold land. Thirty years earlier, he had migrated from Upper Egypt. "In the past, Egypt and the Sudan were like one country," he said. "I was brought to the Sudan by a laborer to dig canals, and I never went back." In the Sudan, he did agricultural work in Kosti, Duweim, Khartoum, and later on the New Halfa Scheme. In Khartoum, he was able to rent land along the Nile for vegetables. These rich alluvial soils were divided into narrow stretches of about 600 square meters, renting for £S10 each. Hamid rented twenty sections and made a reasonable living. When the value of riverine land skyrocketed with the explosive growth of the capital city, the fields were reclaimed by their owners. Hamid and many other tenant farmers were left landless. Seeking agricultural employment, he moved to the Scheme in 1969, leaving his wife and children in Khartoum. Hamid never liked being so far away from his family, and after a year he returned to the capital. But in 1974 he once again moved to New Halfa, where he has been ever since. His wife and children despaired of life in the Sudan and returned to their home in Egypt. Hamid immediately remarried a 26-year-old Halfawi woman, Farida.

Farida had been married twice before, the first time when she was only 13. Her father chose the groom, whom she first saw on the wedding night. She could not accept being a wife and was divorced within a year. When she was 15 she married her father's brother's son, Ahmed, with whom she had a daughter. This marriage also ended in divorce, when Farida and her baby girl, Maryam, returned to Farida's father's home. Ahmed moved to Khartoum, where he remarried. When Farida and Hamid were married a few years later, Ahmed tried to reclaim his daughter. But Ahmed's own mother sided with Farida in refusing to allow Maryam to live with Ahmed's new wife. Ahmed was adamant that Maryam not live with Hamid. The dispute was resolved when Farida's mother, who lived in the same village as her daughter and Hamid, took the girl. A few years later, Maryam moved in with Farida, where she has lived ever since.

Farida and Hamid have three children of their own, two of whom attend the village kindergarten; the youngest, a girl, was 6 months old when I left the field. Maryam attends elementary school in the village. In the morning, when the children leave for school and Hamid for the farm, Farida devotes herself to the baby, bathing and feeding her, then fixes breakfast for her husband and children, who return at mid-morning to eat. After Farida cleans the house, does the laundry, and prepares the afternoon meal, she awaits Maryam's return from school and then joins her husband in the field, leaving the baby in Maryam's care.

Malik both hires Hamid as an agricultural wage laborer and provides him with 10 feddan of freehold land planted in melons and watermelons to farm on shares. Melons are planted in March, at the height of the dry season, and harvested in June and July, during the rains. Watering is critical. It is required every four or five days during the dry season; the plants are extremely sensitive both to drought and to overwatering. During the harvest, Farida and Maryam join Hamid in the field. The fruit is picked every other day and immediately transported to market in New Halfa. Malik takes the produce there himself in his Land Rover, carrying some fifteen carloads during the season. Prices have varied according to the quantity of melons in the market, from a low of £S20 per carload to a high of £S100. Malik and Hamid hoped to gross from £S800 to £S1,000 by the end of the season, with expenses of about £S280 for seeds, fertilizer, and land and canal preparation deducted from the gross, leaving a net of about £S260–360 each for the owner and the tenant.

While some people attempted to grow okra, eggplants, and squash on freehold lands following the melon harvest, Hamid preferred to let the field go fallow. The heavy rains that often fall in July and August turn the fields into thick mud, and cultivation during those months is exceptionally difficult. Rather than work the land at that time of the year, Hamid customarily traveled to Khartoum and sought employment as a porter. Earnings were not good, but he spent little on food and nothing on lodging, sleeping with the other porters in the market or in half-finished buildings, and was able to return to the Scheme with between £S50 and £S100 for his labors. At this time, Malik sowed his tenancies in wheat, and Hamid worked for him as a wage laborer. In 1980/1981, he earned £S340 laboring on Malik's twenty-one wheat tenancies.

Hamid had found employment with Malik every year since his return to New Halfa in 1974. "Malik is a good man," he said.

> He also has money, so he can pay for everything: ploughing, seeds, fertilizer, which he deducts at harvest time; what remains is divided in half. I could never sharecrop with someone who expects me to put up half of the cost at the beginning. I can go to Malik for money when I need it, and repay him several months later. I would be better off renting land than sharecropping, if only I could afford it, as Malik himself does. But you have to lay down the cash in the beginning, and if the crop does not succeed, you have to bear the full cost. The only things I own are my hands.

Were it not for Malik, Hamid says, he might not have survived in the village. Malik helped him rent a house from an absentee owner and advanced the monthly £S5 rental, reimbursing himself from the melon harvest proceeds. He even spoke on Hamid's behalf when he wanted to marry Farida. Malik's intercession was sufficient to overcome the Halfawis' reluctance for a local woman to marry a "stranger," an Egyptian. Hamid's rented house consisted of just the four original rooms built by the Corporation. Unlike many Scheme residents who invested in expanding and improving their homes, Hamid had added nothing but a simple kitchen, constructed from metal sheets. The furnishings were also meager: a few knotted rope beds known as *ʿangarib*, common throughout the northern Sudan, some kitchen utensils, and a couple of chairs.

Hilmi and Hamid settled on the Scheme with none of the benefits that were accorded to persons who had to give up homes and lands in Wadi Halfa: they received no house, tenancy, or freehold lands. Wage laborers and occasional sharecroppers, their only resources are their physical strength and that of their wives and children. Hence their fortunes largely reflect the household development cycle, lowest when children are too young to assist in the fields and when wives are pregnant or devoted to the care of infant children and rising somewhat when household labor is more available for farming. Both men are hardworking and skillful farmers, but it is unlikely that either will ever have the capital to obtain land in his own name.

Hilmi's immediate prospects were brighter than Hamid's because his wife Wasfa, without infant children that required her close attention, was prepared to join him in the fields. Hilmi could then assume the greater risks, and potentially greater rewards, of sharecropping and put wage laboring aside for a while. Hamid was dependent entirely on his own labor, which he marketed on the Scheme during most of the year and in Khartoum during the slack summer season. He could not even temporarily obtain lands on either a rental or a share basis and anticipated never graduating from wage labor. On the contrary, a physically incapacitating accident or illness would render him and his family totally destitute. The same is true of Hilmi, who also would be reduced to continuing poverty by a bad agricultural season or poor market prices for the crops, since he has no resource cushion to weather adversity.

6

Political and Ethnic Conflicts

INTRODUCTION

In 1964, the New Halfa Agricultural Scheme began the resettlement of Halfawis forcibly relocated from their homes and farms when Lake Nasser, the reservoir for the Aswan High Dam, flooded the region of Wadi Halfa. In subsequent years, local pastoral populations—Shukriya, other Arabic-speaking groups, and Hadandawa—some of whose grazing lands were lost to the Scheme, were also permitted to obtain Scheme tenancies.

The approach to settling the latter groups was dramatically different from that taken with the former. In addition to their new tenancies, most Halfawis were provided with well-made houses in planned villages equipped with domestic potable water and sometimes electricity, grade schools, and clinics. Many of the villages are in close proximity to the town of New Halfa, which is accessible by road. As noted earlier, former landowners among the Halfawis were also granted freehold fields on the Scheme, twice the size of the farms abandoned in Wadi Halfa. These freehold lands are exempted from all the cultivating constraints imposed by the Corporation on the tenancies—individual farmers may plant whatever crops or maintain as many animals as they wish—and the freehold lands may be rented for cash or a share of the harvest or even sold outright. In contrast, settled herders received tenancies only and, in some cases, materials with which to build homes. Their villages are more remote from the administrative and commercial center of New Halfa, and access to them is often difficult in the rainy season.

Settlers from pastoral groups greatly resent the advantages accorded to Halfawis. Resentment is especially strong among the Shukriya, who regard themselves as the traditional masters of the Butana, forced to give up to the Scheme prime grazing land along the Atbara River and to suffer the added indignity of being denied Halfawi residential and farming privileges.

The relocated Halfawis also have grievances, which are intensified by a tremendous sense of loss, especially among the older generation, and nostalgia for Wadi Halfa. To them, the local herders are unsophisticated and uncivilized, basically primitives despite Halfawi efforts to educate and modernize them. Where the Arabs and Hadandawa fault the government for settling strangers on their traditional lands and granting them special privileges, Halfawis argue that the government should never have permitted Arabs on the Scheme at all. They particularly resent allowing Arabs grazing rights on the Scheme between April and July, noting that, although this is the dead season on the tenancies, it is the period of intense vegetable cultivation on freehold lands, which are particularly vulnerable to animal incursions.

Yet Halfawis themselves are increasingly taking to raising livestock. Since they are unwilling to assume a pastoral way of life with its reduced material consumptive profile, these Halfawi herd owners consign their animals to the care of pastoralists during at least that portion of the year when cattle, sheep, and goats must be kept off the Scheme. Thus, there is a relationship of hostility and dependency, evidenced in Halfawi accusations that pastoralists abuse their trust, being at best casual in their concern for the consigned animals and at worst selling or slaughtering them and then claiming that they were stolen. This problem was more severe during the early years of the settlement, when Halfawis had little experience in animal husbandry.

As one settler explained: "You see, they used to come and steal our animals. Since we did not know the area very well, it was very difficult to search for and recover lost animals. We have learned a great many lessons here. Now Arabs know better than to steal a Halfawi cow. They know that we will follow them as far as it takes to recover it. Arabs now believe that all Halfawis are armed, and we are happy with our new image." Arabs and Hadandawa continue to be accused of intentionally bringing their herds to graze Halfawi fields before the harvest, while Halfawis insist that they themselves have a better sense of responsibility toward their neighbors.

Despite having been relocated by official government action, Halfawis feel the insecurity of being foreigners in their new homes.

> Things were better in Wadi Halfa where we were at home and there were few outsiders. A stranger coming to town was immediately identified. He could not do anything bad, since he could be spotted at once. That is because our ties are like those of a strong family. Any Nubian will watch over and assist any other Nubian. Arabs do not care about family ties. A 7-year-old boy is given a sword and sent to herd thirty camels on his own. He brings his animals to your land. You ask him to take his animals out, but he tells you they are hungry and need to eat. You protest that the crop is yours so he challenges you to remove him by force. If you kill him, the government puts you in prison. If he kills you, you are lost. These Arabs are really bad, even the Shukriya.

Butana Arabs expressed surprise and confusion over Nubian reluctance even to carry, let alone to use, weapons, an attitude balanced by the Nubians' contempt and fear of what is considered the pastoralists' adoration for their swords. "Halfawi influence on us is bad," said one Shukriya.

> People are not as attached to their weapons as they once were. Before these strangers came from Halfa, it was out of the question for a man to leave his home without a sword, even if it was only for a short walk to his brother's tent. Only a man afraid to fight would present himself without a weapon. That is because it is unthinkable for an Arab to attack an unarmed person. The Halfawis do not carry swords; they are afraid of them. To us Arabs, dignity, pride, and honor are very important, and we defend them with our swords. We Arabs do not anger easily, but once aroused we resolve problems with our swords.
>
> Halfawis really confused us at first. They would get agitated and angry very easily, hurling insults at us. We interpreted this as a challenge to fight, and drew our weapons, expecting the other to do the same. But the unarmed Halfawi would then withdraw, saying "I was only joking; I take back whatever I said," and run away! Arabs found this behavior unmanly; it was so foreign. Arabs *never* take back their words, whatever the risk might be; it is simply unheard of. It is shameful to be so afraid of death, shameful to cling so to life.

To Halfawis, as one resettled Nubian explained, shame attaches to the very act of appearing in public with a weapon. "You cannot do that among Nubians. Even carrying a heavy stick is shameful, for any villager might ridicule you, saying, 'So, why are you carrying such a heavy stick? Whom are you planning to fight?' "

Nubians recognize if not appreciate Arab resentment toward them. When I discussed this with several Halfawi men, they made the following points: "Let's face it, we try to be civil to each other in public but inside they dislike us and we dislike them. Arabs are very selfish, claiming this was their land before we came. That is a lie. Nobody lived here. We came and developed the area, and now everybody wants to move in. That is not what the government promised us; they told us we would live by ourselves." But surely, I queried them, there were people in the area before the Scheme was established. "Well," they reluctantly agreed, "maybe some Shukriya were here, passing through with their herds. But what about the others, those who came from Rufaʿa, Qadaref, Kassala, and the Red Sea area, who now have tenancies on the Scheme? New Halfa was supposed to be for Nubian resettlement; now most of the tenancies are owned by the others, and they dominate the Farmers' Union. They always vote against us, and they often get their way because they are more numerous."

The following cases indicate some of the kinds of conflicts that occur between Arabs and Halfawis and among other ethnic groups. Despite the animosities, alliances occasionally form that cut across ethnicity, as interest groups emerge in opposition to ethnic claims. The final case illustrates such an alliance between old enemies against their own peoples.

HILLAT ALI KARRAR

The neighborhood (*hillat*) of Ali Karrar is a section of the town of New Halfa settled by Arabs, mainly from the Shukriya, who came as squatters in 1964 to provide milk and dairy products to an urban hospital. Each year, the area expanded, as more and more formerly pastoral households moved in, constituting an encysted population surrounded by Halfawis. Halfawi claims that these settled herders engaged in practices that were unsanitary and dangerous—using the irrigation canal as a latrine—were supported by the departments of Health and Irrigation. The Irrigation Department wanted the settlers to move at least a kilometer distant from the canal, but they refused.

The Shukriya settlers have countered attempts to have them evicted by trying, since 1966, to obtain legal titles to the neighborhood. They argue, with the support of other Arabs, that New Halfa was built not as a Halfawi but as a *Sudanese* town, and they therefore have as much right to reside in it as anyone else. They grant Halfawis exclusive residential access to their Scheme villages, but not to this commercial and administrative center. In 1967, the Town Council denied a petition to grant the Arabs titles to 50 house plots of 400 square meters each. A similar petition emerging from continued illegal Arab settlement in Hillat Ali Karrar, for twice the number of house plots, was denied several years later. Finally, in 1980, the Town Council did allow Arab settlement in New Halfa, but only in another part of the town, granting 105 house plots near the landing strip where Corporation planes used for aerial spraying of agricultural chemicals were based. The agreement provided that no Halfawis or other non-Arab Sudanese would be permitted to settle among them.

This was not a satisfactory solution for the Shukriya, who then tried a different approach. For many years, the national government in Khartoum had been under pressure to bring administrative functions closer to the people. The huge size of the Sudan, the largest country in Africa, and its rudimentary and poorly maintained internal transportation network, with every significant official decision being made in the capital, meant that government efficiency was modest at best. A program of decentralization was initiated in 1981 with regional ministries corresponding to the national ministries in Khartoum. The Eastern Region's capital was in Kassala, and a Sinnabi was appointed to a ministerial post. The Shukriya ceased to direct their petitioning to the unsympathetic New Halfa Town Council and sent a delegation directly to Kassala to obtain the minister's support for their permanent residence in Hillat Ali Karrar. The minister appeared responsive; but when word got back to New Halfa, Halfawis formed a delegation of their own and, bypassing the minister, went directly to the governor, pleading their case that the Arabs should not be allowed legal settlement in Ali Karrar or, at a minimum, should not be allowed to settle both there and near the airfield.

The governor and the minister realized the potential explosiveness of the situation. Since any resolution was bound to offend one of the groups, administrative wisdom persuaded the authorities to "defer" a decision until some later, unspecified date. By the end of 1981, no official decision had been made.[1]

MAJLIS RIFI HALFA

During the summer of 1981, a group of Arab villages on the Scheme that were members of a local council dominated by Halfawis sought to be reassigned to an all-Arab grouping. Prior to the decentralization and the establishment of a new regional government in eastern Sudan, Kassala Province was composed of districts, of which New Halfa (sometimes called the Middle District) was one. New Halfa District had been divided into five councils or *majlis*: al-Madina (the town of New Halfa), Rifi Halfa (literally rural Halfa, the planned Halfawi villages on the Scheme), Khashm el-Girba, As-Saba^cat, and al-Masna^c (the settlement area of the Scheme's sugar factory). Rifi Halfa included not only the twenty-five planned Halfawi villages, but also sixteen Arab villages, of which half were in the western border region of the Scheme and half along the Atbara River.

When decentralization created the Eastern Region by joining Red Sea Province and Kassala Province, people expected a general administrative reorganization, in which subregional boundaries might be redrawn. Taking advantage of what they hoped would be a friendly response in the regional capital, where two of the newly appointed ministers, a Sinnabi Shukriya and a Hadandawa, came from pastoral communities, some of the Arabs sought separation of their villages from Rifi Halfa majlis and incorporation within the all-Arab majlis of As-Saba^cat. They suggested that the simplest solution that would best respond to the needs of the settlers was to divide the Middle District into two units: one for the *iskan* (planned Halfawi villages) and the town of New Halfa and one for the Arabs.

The situation was discussed by men at the Farmers' Union, an organization that is supposed to represent all tenants, regardless of ethnic identity. Initiating the discussion with traditional pleasant-

---

[1] During a brief field mission in the northern Sudan in 1987, I met several former residents of New Halfa, including two physicians from the hospital near Hillat Ali Karrar. They all remembered the incident clearly, but none knew how it was resolved. The short time I had in Sudan and the difficulties in obtaining fuel did not permit me to return to the area myself. In a May 1988 meeting with Ibrahim Ma^couda of the Farmers' Union, he confirmed that the Ali Karrar case was still on hold.

ries, a Halfawi notable, with good humor, asked the Arabs present, "So, why do you want to leave us? You do not like us anymore? We are not good enough for you?" A Shukriya farmer diplomatically suggested that in fact the idea of a separation was not theirs, but rather came from the regional government. "But you don't have to agree with the government, do you?" responded the Halfawi.

Then one of the Shukriya said he would illustrate their point of view with a little story. "Arabs slaughter animals quite often," he said.

> Animals are slaughtered to entertain guests and to offer hospitality. Unlike some people we know, it is not an Arab custom to allow a guest to depart without offering him a meal. We slaughter at weddings, funerals, births, and circumcisions. Any occasion, for an Arab, merits the offering of an animal. Now each animal has two parts. The liver and the kidneys are most desirable, delicacies, and usually these are reserved for honored guests. Liver and kidney are so good that we don't even bother to cook them, preferring to eat them raw. The remainder of the beast is also good to eat, but is not special. Now, there was once a butcher. Every time he slaughtered an animal, he reserved the liver and the kidneys for himself and shared only the other parts with family and neighbors (and even of these parts he kept the largest part again for himself). He did this for many years. His neighbors hoped that some day he would end this shameful practice, but year after year the butcher consumed all the liver and all the kidneys. Such shameful behavior finally proved too much for the people, and they killed the butcher. This has been our story with you Halfawis. For years, we watched as you butchered animals and kept the choice parts for yourself. Finally, it became time for us to be our own butchers and eat some liver and kidneys too.

A Halfawi replied, insisting that only a minority of Arabs, those with political ambitions of their own, sought administrative autonomy. In fact, just the opposite is the case. The Halfawis would love to see the Arabs on their own, but most of the Arabs are unwilling to leave.

> They are eager to remain with us, but we no longer want them. You see, Arabs expect us to stand still and wait for them to catch up with us. Why should we? They are asking for elementary schools in their villages while we need more high schools. They want running water; we want more electrification. Arabs think it is not fair for us to have high schools when they don't even have elementary schools. But why is that our problem? And then, many of the Arabs, especially the old ruling families, like the Abu Sin, want to remain with the Halfawis. The sep-

aratists are those newly educated Arabs, like the president of the Farmers'
Union, who want to take the leadership away from the old families. It
definitely does not do *us* any good to have the Arabs remain in our
administration.

In a May 1988 meeting with Mr. Ibrahim Ma'ouda, the president of the Farmers' Union, I learned that the Arab villages were
eventually successful in their attempt to separate from the Halfawis
and found their own village council. This council, know as *majlis
qura nahr atbara* (the council of the villages of the Atbara River), is
composed of 135 villages both within and outside the Scheme, in
addition to the town of Khashm el-Girba and the sugar estate.

Instances of Arabs opposing Halfawis, as well as competition and
conflicts among Halfawis residents in Scheme villages and those in
the town of New Halfa, were manifested during the April 1980
regional elections. One Halfawi man said:

We people from the planned villages do not like the people of the
madina, most of whom are not true Halfawis but Egyptians. They are
sons of merchants who lived in Wadi Halfa before we were forced to
move, but their origins were elsewhere. Two men, one from Village
Twenty-three and one from Village Two, competed to be elected assistant commissioner for the Middle District. We residents of the Scheme
favored the man from Village Twenty-three because he was educated
and would be good for us. Unfortunately, he was also supported by city
merchants and people involved in the local government whom we wanted
to see removed. We asked our preferred candidate to disavow their support, but he refused. Do you know what we did? We organized a serious campaign against him and in favor of his rival, whom we really did
not like as much. Tempers began to flare, and the authorities brought
in additional police from Khartoum to forestall any unrest. Our candidate won.

Now there will be new elections [in October 1981]. The Halfawi
villages are seeking a formal separation from the Arabs prior to the
election. Some Arabs went to Khartoum to block our action, for they
want to remain with us. But we don't want them, and for good reasons.

You see, during the April 1980 elections there was a third candidate, an Arab. When the votes were totaled, the man from Village
Twenty-three received 12,000 votes, the man from Village Two, whom
we supported, received 12,500, and the Arab received 7,000. Now there
aren't 7,000 Arabs in the area who could have voted for him, and he
surely received no votes from any resident of the twenty-five Halfawi
villages on the Scheme. Many of his votes must have been cast by residents of the town who, even though they come from Wadi Halfa as we
do, are not real Halfawis. They have no real reason to prefer a Nubian

over an Arab, and in some future election they might give all their votes to an Arab candidate. That way the Arabs might win against the Halfawis in an open election. Those shrewd Arabs who went to Khartoum to block our attempts at separation understood that, and that's why they want to remain within our political jurisdiction.

LOCALIZED ETHNIC CONFLICTS

Instances of conflict that expose tensions both between and within ethnic groups are found in the records of the Farmers' Union. Some of these have wide-reaching implications, as in the cases outlined above. Others are more modest, involving just a few households, camps, or villages and focusing on livestock incursions on tenancies and freehold lands, animal theft, and the purported immorality of strangers. Three of the recorded cases took place in 1973, in the first decade following the initial settlement of the Scheme.

In July of that year, residents of the Arab village of Wad Nabar on the Atbara River complained to the administrative officer of the New Halfa Town Council about a camp of Arabic-speaking Zaghawa who had migrated from Chad. The villagers protested the increasing number of Zaghawa, implying that they were responsible for the theft of village livestock. A week previous to the complaint, several animals that had been missing were discovered in the Zaghawa camp, already butchered. While the Wad Nabar residents were able to collect payment from the strangers, they feared that in the future they would be unable to resolve problems so readily and sought official intervention to prevent any recurrence.

Nubians also complained about the Zaghawa. A letter from the residents of Village Twenty, addressed to the Farmers' Union in May 1973, noted with displeasure a Zaghawa camp of eighty huts "an arm's throw from our homes. They make wine [that corrupts our farmers] to the detriment of their health, morals, and finances. Our complaints to the authorities fall on deaf ears. . . . [Although they are nomads, they give every sign of remaining on the Scheme] for we see them buying tenancies from Arabs whose fields are adjacent to our own. This is a danger that must be stopped."

A third complaint, also about Zaghawa wines threatening community morality and also dated May 1973, was submitted to the New Halfa authorities by residents of Subagh-aj-Jadida, an Arab village in the north of the Scheme. The petitioners reiterated their demand that the Zaghawa camp be relocated.

INTRAETHNIC CONFLICTS

Ethnic units are not internally homogeneous—competition for resources may flare up among persons generally defined as belonging to the same group, although from different lineages and subtribes. In 1975, two Shukriya subtribes, the Bawadira and the Miheidat, fought over water rights, a fight that led to years of hatred and violence before peace could be restored. This fight began in April 1975, when a Miheidat man tried to water his animals from a Bawadira well over the objection of a Bawadiri who was present. The lone Bawadiri was attacked by a group of Miheidat men and killed. Nine Miheidat were implicated in the murder and imprisoned. A month later, another Bawadiri was killed by a Miheidat; the murderer was caught and sentenced to twelve years in prison. A few days after the killing, Bawadiris in vengeance killed four Miheidat and wounded five others, for which acts two Bawadiris were arrested and given life sentences. The Miheidat responded to this last act of violence with the killing of two Bawadiris, for which six men were arrested.

As these acts of vengeance and countervengeance, which had continued for about five years, threatened to continue indefinitely, a committee of reconciliation was formed. Composed of elders from various groups of Shukriya, including representatives of the warring subtribes and a number of Sinnabi notables, the committee held a hearing at the Farmers' Union in January 1980, where a face-saving resolution to the conflict was adopted. The authorities agreed to an immediate halt to the arrests, prisoners from both sides were freed, and blood money of £S1,000 was paid by both tribes for each of the murdered victims' families. To avoid future conflicts, the authorities defined new mutually acceptable boundaries for grazing lands and water, which were formalized by order of the governor of Kassala the following June.

In the case cited above, homicide, although extremely important, was not the only cause of the extensive proliferation of the problem. Although the conflict arose over water use, the moment the first man was killed it was transformed into an issue of tribal honor. The loss of honor could be restored only after killing a member of the opposing group. The problem quickly escalated, with more and more killings. Had the first killing taken place between Arabs and Halfawis, or among Halfawis, it would probably not have resulted in so many additional killings, but would have been left to the police and the courts to decide.

As a matter of fact, such an incident did occur in May 1975, when a Halfawi policeman shot and killed a Shukriya herder. The case was presented to the court right after the murder took place, and several hearings were held to discuss it. After long and heated discussions, a reconciliation between the two families was reached, with the killer's family agreeing to pay £S775 to the victim's family. In the Bawadira and Miheidat situation, however, neither party was in a position to relegate the affair to either the court or the police without the risk of losing honor, since that would have been an open acknowledgment that the other group was more powerful. The police were directly involved in this case only in the imprisonment of the murderers. Resolving the problem through the involvement of tribal elders and abiding by their recommendations, however, was not a loss but a gain of honor, since reconciliation was reached out of respect, not fear.

THE FARMERS' UNION ELECTION OF 1973

At the inception of the Scheme in 1964, a Union of Halfawi Villages, composed of two representatives from each of the twenty-five new settlements, was formed to assist the relocators in adjusting to their new environment. The Union also pressured the government and agricultural authorities for the benefit of Halfawis, to eliminate the costs of irrigation water for the wheat crop, for example, and to limit the number of hawashat allocated to non-Halfawis in proximity to their own tenancies. As more and more non-Halfawis were granted lands on the Scheme, members of the Union of Halfawi Villages decided that it would be to their advantage to have a single voice speaking to the administration on behalf of all tenants rather than being segmented by ethnic affiliation. A joint committee of Halfawis and Arabs drew up the new charter, and the Farmers' Union came into being in 1966.

For the first seven years, the president of the Farmers' Union was a very traditional older Nubian man from Village Three, with persons from the traditional Arab and Halfawi elites filling other Union offices. Despite frequent differences among them, on one point the Arab and Halfawi elites were in complete agreement: the leadership should remain with them, and they should resist attempts by younger, better-educated persons to challenge their dominance.

Dissatisfaction with gerontocratic rule among the Shukriya predated the establishment of the Scheme. A Butana Students' Association was formed during the 1950s; Ibrahim Ma'ouda, a member of the Diweyhiyeen religious elite, which was closely allied to the Shukriya aristocracy, was elected president. Students from the Umdurman Islamic University, from which Ma'ouda graduated, from the University of Khartoum, and from foreign universities joined the Association. Although most of the members were themselves from elite families, they joined together to challenge the power of the local shaikhs and of the Native Administration. Experience gained in the Association became relevant on the Scheme—many of its members were granted tenancies or belonged to families with tenancies. The Butana Students' Association, although initially an Arab group, became the point around which politically ambitious younger Nubians rallied, challenging the traditional leadership.

Thus, as the conservative older Nubians found common cause with conservative older Shukriya in the Farmers' Union to promote their aims to the administration, so more progressive younger Arabs and Nubians joined forces in opposition to their elders. Members of the older generation were totally outraged by this challenge from their own children. A younger Sinnabi man told how he was reproached by elders from his own family, who declared: "Inta ma bageit minnana, ma bageit sinnabi, inta naseital-beit we maashi ma'al-wileidat" (You are no longer one of us; you are no longer a Sinnabi; you forgot the beit and side with the young). The elders and their traditionalist supporters were not about to retire in this confrontation with their educated children and fought to keep them out of power.

A Nubian man, who was supporting the Arab opposition in a forthcoming election, recalled with wry amusement the occasion when the president of the Farmers' Union, then a Nubian and his elder kinsman, summoned the younger man to meet him the following morning in a coffee shop, ostensibly to discuss family matters. The younger man arrived on time, but the president did not come. When the older man finally arrived, several hours late, he at first feigned not having remembered the appointment. But when the younger man reminded him of the previous day's conversation, the old man turned suddenly and in front of all the other customers in the cafe said, "I want your support in the election."

Telling the story some years later, the younger man said that he had had no choice but to discontinue working for the opposition. He could not publicly repudiate his elder, a former umda. He admitted to a reluctant admiration of the strategy the old man had employed to obtain his loyalty: arranging a meeting in public, making him wait, and so piquing the curiosity of the others who would witness the command and the reply. The president not only insisted that he should support him in the election, but that he should use his influence with other young Nubians to remain loyal. This the young man said he could not do. While he would personally support the old man, he was in no position to instruct others how to vote. The old man interpreted this as an act of defiance and slapped his younger relative — already in his early forties — across his face in public, as a father would discipline an impolite child.

Traditional Arab leaders also tried to restrain their younger kinsmen from supporting the challenge to established authority. An Arab man, who had identified himself with the challengers, said that on election day, as he was entering the Farmers' Union building, he noticed a group of Shukriya elders sitting in the shade across the street. One of them summoned him, addressing him insultingly as *walad* (boy)! The younger man disregarded the offensive tone of the summons and respectfully asked the old man if there was something he might do for him. Ignoring the young man's polite question, the elder asked instead, "Addouk shinou deil alli sanidhin" (What have they given you and done for you, those you are standing behind?), implying that the young man had been bought by the opposition. "Yiddouni shinou" (What could they give me?), he replied. "ʿAmalouk ra'is" (Have they made you president?), the old man responded sarcastically, pointing out that the young man was betraying his family and his heritage and not even getting the top prize.

Despite their best efforts, the elders were defeated in the election by the educated young challengers, and these young men assumed control of the Farmers' Union. The traditionalists protested, claiming the elections were unconstitutional and demanding new ones. When the authorities denied their demand, the elders refused to turn over the Union's records, account books, and even its official vehicle. Finally, the deputy minister of social affairs in Khartoum sided with the victorious challengers; the recalcitrant elders were threatened with court action if they continued to refuse to recognize the election results.

CONCLUSION

Except where tenant settlers as a whole combine in opposition to the New Halfa Agricultural Production Corporation management, the conflicts and competitions engaged in by Scheme residents as *groups* illustrate the incompleteness of the transition to a fully capitalist mode of production. These conflicts emphasize cleavages along precapitalist lines: between lineages and subtribes of Arabs, between herders and farmers, between Arabs and Nubians, and between younger and older generations. It would be a mistake, however, to see these conflicts merely as continuities with pre-Scheme days. Although they align people on the basis of descent, ethnicity, and age, the disputes involve both traditional elements—such as animal incursions on cultivated fields and competing claims over water rights— and modern elements—such as control of the Farmers' Union. As the articulation of local and world economies becomes more complete, I anticipate a more clearly class alignment to emerge in the competition for resources, involving, for example, landless agricultural workers in opposition to tenants and freeholders, and small-scale landholders in opposition to those with large holdings. New Halfa Scheme settlers are well aware of their location in a class hierarchy, but have not moved from that awareness to actual organization. I suspect that such organization is imminent, although its emergence will not immediately or perhaps ever totally replace ethnicity, tribe, descent, and age as bases for asserting common interests.

7

Conclusions: Considerations for Policy

What are the lessons to be learned for development in the Third World from this examination of the transformation of rural Sudanese economies under the influence of large-scale, capital-intensive irrigated agriculture? And what is its relevance for social science theory?

Let me very briefly approach the latter question first. While the data from New Halfa do not unambiguously challenge major theoretical perspectives, they underscore the inadequacy of dependency models in accounting for the variety of adaptations that are found under situations of peripheral capitalism. Dependency models (see, for example, Bernstein and Campbell 1985) effectively define the political economic position of the Sudan as it relates to northern industrial market states and to the world capitalist economy. They lead us to anticipate the subordinated status of small-scale tenant producers on the New Halfa Agricultural Scheme.

They do not, however, prepare us for the tremendous range of socioeconomic differentiation that has occurred during the past twenty years, in which ethnic, gender, demographic, educational, and other factors generate different opportunity situations for Scheme residents. Despite the general subordination of the Sudanese peasantry, the peasants differ in their ability to control the productive factors of land, labor, and capital. Dependency models prepare us to expect internal homogeneity. The discovery of considerable internal differentiation calls for other explanatory approaches; here I have drawn eclectically on decisional, transactive, and situational analyses in the attempt to bridge the macro political economy and the micro differentiation of resident households.

It is curious that the expectation of internal homogeneity in Third World communities under development is found both among critics of development who embrace dependency models and among establishment planners in host governments and international development financing organizations, who, ostensibly, are more likely to identify with competing modernization theories. The accumulation of tenancies in the hands of an elite minority of Scheme farmers was certainly not anticipated in the design of New Halfa, which assumed that the "one household, one tenancy" principle that was supposed to guide the original distribution of lands would endure indefinitely. Had the planners appreciated settlers' differential access to strategic resources, they might better have predicted their subsequent stratification.

The naïve assumption of homogeneity is dysfunctional with respect to effective economic growth because it ignores the equity basis of sustainable development:

> ... it is becoming increasingly clear that the "engine" that initially moves development forward in agrarian nations is the rising disposable income of hundreds of thousands, indeed millions of small-scale *rural* household production units. Not only does most agricultural production come from such households . . . , but their increasing consumption of local and nationally produced goods and services as they move beyond subsistence can be expected to generate significant amounts of enterprise development and farm and nonfarm employment. (Scudder 1988:18)

It is most unusual for a large-scale agricultural development Scheme in Africa to be cost effective when assessed totally in its own terms. These Schemes rarely meet either production objectives or anticipated financial rates of return. I suggest that the recurrently poor evaluations these schemes receive is at least partly due to the absence of interventions that enhance economic returns for the majority of settler households. Even if there has been a general improvement in the economic well-being of many — perhaps most — tenant households on these irrigated Schemes, when compared with their pre-Scheme conditions of life, this improvement is much less than it might have been had there been adequate planning for tenants with little access to labor and capital.

As I have shown, the costs and the need for timely availability of critical production inputs — water, fertilizer, credit, machinery, labor, and information — favor the affluent and discriminate against poorer farmers. One lesson for development, therefore, is that an anticipation of socioeconomic differentiation can assure more equitable access, with the result that a larger number of tenant households would both improve their own economic standing and demand the kinds of goods and services that multiply benefits and spread them both within and beyond the scheme.

The second lesson for development to be learned from this study is that tenant farmers on large-scale agricultural schemes should be encouraged to invest not only their labor but also their knowledge and initiative to assure optimum economic performance. For the first fifteen years or so of operation of the New Halfa Scheme, peasants were required to grow what they felt were nonremunerative crops, especially cotton, and were forbidden to grow sorghum and raise livestock on the tenancies. Farmers who nonetheless engaged in these prohibited activities might have their animals seized or their grain fields plowed under and, in some cases, were actually evicted from their holdings.[1] Yet, had Scheme management allowed each household to make its own production decisions, there would have been far better adaptation to the declining availability of irrigation water caused by the rapid siltation of the Khashm el-Girba reservoir.

It seems clear, too, that farmers, especially Arabs, would have invested more of their labor and capital on their tenancies had they been permitted to grow sorghum and fodder crops. Agricultural development schemes often make false distinctions between subsistence and cash crops, failing to understand that, for farmers, domestic marketing of food crops is often financially more rewarding than selling export crops to monopsonistic purchasing corporations (Little and Horowitz 1987). A producer of cotton on the New Halfa Scheme has no control over the disposition or price of the crop. A producer

---

[1] In 1981/1982, when Corporation administrators were already preparing to accept sorghum because of its more frugal requirements, 265 tenancies were actually repossessed because their holders planted the crop in a rotation other than that specified by management. All but nine of the lands repossessed were farmed by Arabs, who prefer sorghum to wheat for domestic consumption. In previous years, there were also such repossessions (1977/1978: 77 tenancies, of which only 2 were held by Halfawis; 1978/1979: 10 tenancies, all Arab; 1979/1980: 52 tenancies, of which only 3 were held by Halfawis; 1980/1981: 40 tenancies, all Arab), but normally the fields were simply assigned to another member of the same household or family. In 1981/1982, a decision was made to the effect that neither the evicted farmers nor their kin could recover the tenancy (personal communication with NHAPC general manager).

of grain operates in a much freer market—much of the crop circulates among neighboring households and grain can be stored on the farm and consumed by the producing household itself.

Nonetheless, there were multiple effects, and the Scheme did contribute to economic development through a diversification of the sources of income and the generation of off-farm employment. In fact, when assessed in a *regional* context, a negative evaluation of the New Halfa Scheme is less firmly grounded. The modern town of New Halfa, though excluded from the World Bank's evaluation of the Scheme, owes its very existence to large-scale irrigated agriculture. Muhamed el-Hasan el-Tayeb's survey of nonfarm employment in that town estimated the presence of "1,408 businesses, including 500 tailors, 335 retailers, 91 cart owners, 60 wholesalers, 40 restaurant/coffeeshop owners" (cited in Scudder 1981:100). In addition, there are government officials, Corporation employees, hospital personnel, police, market inspectors, and the like. Even el-Tayeb's figures are probably underestimations. While he records 26 specialized vegetable sellers for the New Halfa market, I counted at least 80 in a single morning. The town of New Halfa has grown from the simple administrative center envisaged in Scheme planning documents to a large and vibrant secondary city (Rondinelli 1983), providing both public and private sector economic opportunities for thousands of families and supporting thousands more.

My study did not allow for a calibration of the economic impacts of nonfarm employment and business, but they are clearly substantial. They provide a range of investment opportunities that were totally unanticipated in the creation of the Scheme and ignored in its evaluations. That lack of knowledge necessarily leads to a truncated understanding of what is actually going on.

The crisis of African production is genuine, and I do not mean by this study to denigrate the contribution, however partial, that large-scale irrigated agriculture can make to its resolution. There is no doubt that the potential to increase production in low-rainfall areas through control of water is very great (Moris 1987; Moris, Thom, et al. 1987). The recurrent problem has been that the costs of this production, especially the infrastructural costs of dams, canals, and perimeters, have been greater than the returns. Construction of perimeters in Africa is today estimated to cost between $20,000 and $30,000 a hectare. Governments and managers of irrigated schemes have attempted to recover part of these costs by requiring production of high-value export crops and by holding returns to producers at little more than the costs of physical maintenance. This strategy may work in the short run, but production and income decline over time, and the unanticipated or underbudgeted costs of rehabilitation escalate, tempting management to become even more appropriative of the surplus value of peasant labor. Over time, what is bad for labor also proves unsatisfactory for the Scheme itself.

The data from New Halfa support, if they do not confirm, an alternative approach: the Scheme should encourage each production unit to make those decisions that seem most appropriate to its own opportunity situation. This means that the peasants should participate much more actively in management, should be allowed to decide for themselves how best to allocate labor and capital, and should themselves decide what to produce and how and when to market it. The role of management should be to facilitate household production agendas, not to determine them.

The rehabilitation plan for New Halfa does correspond more closely to production agendas as expressed by the majority of Scheme households, because it permits raising livestock and grain for domestic consumption and local sale. The intention of the rehabilitation is to reduce operating costs, making the Scheme more profitable. It might also have the effect of increasing smallholder income. The rehabilitation plan may be both too little and too late. It would seem, however, that—had tenants participated more actively in managerial decisions from the inception of the New Halfa Agricultural Scheme—economic performance at all levels would have been far more attractive.

Glossary

afandiya	educated workers
ʿangarib	a knotted rope bed with a wooden frame
ardab	2 sacks of wheat; 366 lbs.
batn al-wadi	the bottom (belly) of the wadi
beit	house; tent; the people of the house; the kin group
birish	mat; a tent constructed from mats
damar	pastoral home area
darat	beginning of the rainy season
daris	educated
dura	sorghum
feddan	1.04 acres; 0.42 hectare
galabiyya	a loose white robe worn by Sudanese men
ghafir	guard
hadj	pilgrimage to Mecca
hafir	reservoir
hawasha	a government tenancy of 15 feddan; the three fields within
(pl. hawashat)	a tenancy are also referred to as hawashat
hillat	the neighborhood
husn dhiyafa	hospitality
imam	a man who leads prayer in Islam
iskan	Halfawi villages on the Scheme
jabana	coffee; also refers to the pot in which it is served
jalouth	a depression in a rock where rainwater collects
jamiʿi	university-educated
jiza	a variety of wheat
karam	generosity
khat	an administrative division within a nazirate
khawaja	foreigner, especially European or American
(pl. khawajat)	
lugma	a porridge made with sorghum flour, milk, and clarified butter
madina	city; New Halfa
majlis	council

malowd	a hoe made from a wooden stick with a horizontally attached metal blade
ma°rifa (pl. ma°arif)	connections
mit'alim	educated
mudhra	throwing sorghum high in the air to get rid of chaff
mullah	a sauce made with onions, tomato sauce, and sometimes meat
nafir	a work party based on labor exchange
namousa	a tractor attachment used for clearing field canals
nazir	the highest political rank in the Native Administration
nimra	a stretch of land with eighteen tenancies in Arab areas and thirty-six in Halfawi areas
nusab	genealogy experts
nushoug	transhumance
qantar	small qantar = 100 lbs.; big qantar = 315 lbs.
qash	hay
quttiya	a traditional conical hut
ribaa	interest; forbidden in Islam
rotl	1 lb. (0.373 kg); 12 fl. oz (0.35 liter)
rowb	a form of sour milk
sabbabah	animal traders
sallouka	a long wooden stick for sowing, at the bottom of which a piece of wood is attached horizontally
shaikh khat	a Native Administration position that falls between a nazir and an umda
sheil	a traditional credit system based on selling one's crop while it is still standing in the field
souq	market
tur°a	irrigation canal
umbaz	the remains of cottonseeds after they are pressed for oil
umda	a Native Administration position; see shaikh khat
umoudiya	the position of umda; the area under an umda's control
wadi	a riverbed or valley
wasta	connections
zakat	Islamic charity

Bibliography

Abdalla, Isma'il Hussein
    1970   The Choice of Khashm Al-Girba Area for the Resettlement of the
                Halfawis. *Sudan Notes and Records* 51:56–74.
Abou-Zeid, A. M.
    1959   The Sedentarization of Nomads in the Western Desert of Egypt.
                International Science Journal 11(4):550–558.
Abubaker, Gafar S.
    1979   Rural Participation in Program Phases: A Case Study of Resettle-
                ment and Rural Development of Khashm El Girba (New Halfa)
                Project. Ph.D. dissertation, State University of New York at Albany.
Adegboro, C.
    1983   The Process of Implementation in a Nigerian Bureaucracy: The Case
                of the Niger River Basin Development Authority. Ph.D. disserta-
                tion, University of Pennsylvania.
Agrar und Hydrotechnik
    1978   New Halfa Rehabilitation Project. Phase I. Main Report. Project
                Planning Unit, Ministry of Planning. Democratic Republic of the
                Sudan.
    1980   New Halfa Rehabilitation Project. Phase II. Main Report. Project
                Planning Unit, Ministry of Planning. Democratic Republic of the
                Sudan.
Ajouba, Mukhtar Ibrahim
    1979   Social Change in Rural Sudanese Communities: A Case Study of an
                Agricultural Development Scheme in the Sudan (Khashm el-Girba).
                Ph.D. dissertation, University of Khartoum.
Amiran, D. H. K., and Y. Ben-Arieh
    1963   Sedentarization of Bedouins in Israel. *Israel Exploration Journal*
                13(3):161–181.
Asad, T., I. Cunnison, and H. G. Hill
    1966   Settlement of Nomads in the Sudan: A Critique of Present Plans.
                In *Agricultural Development in the Sudan: Proceedings of the Thir-
                teenth Annual Conference of the Philosophical Society of the
                Sudan*, 1965, vol. 1, pp. 102–120. Khartoum: n.p.
Awad, Mohamed
    1954   The Assimilation of Nomads in Egypt. *Geographical Review*
                44:240–252.

Baker, Sir S. W.
 1868   *Explorations of the Nile Tributaries of Abyssinia.* Hartford: O. D.
             Case and Company.
Baldwin, K. D. S.
 1957   *The Niger Agricultural Project.* Cambridge, Mass.: Harvard Univer-
             sity Press.
Barbour, K. M.
 1961   *The Republic of the Sudan: A Regional Geography.* London: Uni-
             versity of London Press.
Barlett, Peggy F.
 1977   The Structure of Decision Making in Paso. *American Ethnologist*
             4(2):285–308.
 1980   Introduction: Development Issues and Economic Anthropology. In
             *Agricultural Decision Making: Anthropological Contributions to Rural
             Development*, ed. Peggy F. Barlett, pp. 1–16. New York: Academic
             Press.
 1982   *Agricultural Choice and Change: Decision Making in a Costa Rican
             Community.* New Brunswick: Rutgers University Press.
Barnett, Tony
 1975   The Gezira Scheme: Production of Cotton and the Reproduction of
             Underdevelopment. In *Beyond the Sociology of Development: Econ-
             omy and Society in Latin America and Africa*, ed. Ivar Oxaal, Tony
             Barnett, and David Booths, pp. 183–207. London: Routledge and
             Kegan Paul.
 1977   *The Gezira Scheme: An Illusion of Development.* London: Frank
             Cass and Company Limited.
Barth, F.
 1967   Social Spheres in Darfur. In *Themes in Economic Anthropology*,
             ed. R. Firth, pp. 149–174. London: Tavistock Publications Limited.
Bernstein, H., and B. K. Campbell, eds.
 1985   *Contradictions of Accumulation in Africa.* Beverly Hills: Sage Pub-
             lications.
Blanckenberg, P. von, and K. Hubert
 1969   The Khashm el Girba Settlement Scheme in the Sudan. *Zeitschrift
             für Ausländische Landwirtshaft* 8(4):328–365.
Blench, Roger
 1987   Livestock in the Gezira Scheme — 1986. Pastoral Development Net-
             work. Overseas Development Institute, March.
Bohannan, Paul
 1955   Some Principles of Exchange and Investment among the Tiv. *Amer-
             ican Anthropologist* 57:60–70.
Boserup, Ester
 1970   *Women's Role in Economic Development.* New York: St. Martin's
             Press.
Brokensha, David, Michael Horowitz, and Thayer Scudder
 1977   *The Anthropology of Rural Development in the Sahel.* Binghamton,
             N.Y.: Institute for Development Anthropology.
Cernea, Micheal
 1988   *Involutary Resettlement in Development Projects: Policy Guidelines
             in World Bank–Financed Projects.* Washington D.C.: World Bank.

Chambers, Robert
1969   *Settlement Schemes in Tropical Africa.* New York: Frederick A.
            Praeger.
Chibnik, Michael
1980   Working Out or Working In: The Choice between Wage Labor
            and Cash Cropping in Rural Belize. *American Ethnologist* 7(1):
            86–105.
Coward, Walter E.
1976   Indigenous Irrigation Institutions and Irrigation Development in the
            Southeast: Current Knowledge and Needed Research. Paper pre-
            pared for discussion at Symposium on Farm Water Management,
            Asian Productivity Organization, Tokyo, September 7–11.
1979   Principles of Social Organization in an Indigenous Irrigation Sys-
            tem. *Human Organization* 38(1):28–36.
1980   *Irrigation and Agricultural Development in Asia: Perspectives from
            the Social Sciences.* Ithaca, N.Y.: Cornell University Press.
1984   Improving Policies and Programs for the Development of Small-
            Scale Irrigation Systems. Paper prepared at Cornell University for
            the Water Management Synthesis II Project, USAID Contract
            DAN-1427-c-00–0086–00, to the Consortium for International Devel-
            opment.
Crowford, O. G. S.
1951   *The Funj Kingdom of Sennar.* Gloucester, England: n.p.
Dafalla, Hassan
1975   *The Nubian Exodus.* Khartoum: Khartoum University Press.
Dalton, George
1961   Economic Theory and Primitive Society. *American Anthropologist*
            63:1–25.
Deere, Carmen Diana, and A. de Janvry
1979   A Conceptual Framework for the Empirical Analysis of Peasants.
            American Journal of Agricultural Economics 61:601–611.
Dey, Jennie
1980   Women and Rice in the Gambia: The Impact of Irrigated Rice Devel-
            opment Projects on the Farming Systems. Ph.D. dissertation, Uni-
            versity of Reading, England.
Ebrahim, Mohammed H. S.
1983   Irrigation Projects in Sudan: The Promise and the Reality. *Journal
            of African Studies* 10(1):2–13.
Fahim, Hussein M.
1972   *Nubian Resettlement in the Sudan.* Coconut Grove, Miami, Fla.:
            Field Research Project.
1981   *Dams, People and Development.* New York: Pergamon Press.
Foster-Carter, Aiden
1978   The Modes of Production Controversy. *New Left Review* 107:47–77.
Frank, Andre Gunder
1969   *Latin America: Underdevelopment or Revolution.* London: Monthly
            Review Press.
Godelier, Maurice
1978   The Object and Method of Economic Anthropology. In *Relations of
            Production: Marxist Approaches to Economic Anthropology*, ed.

David Seddon, pp. 49–126. London: Frank Cass and Company Limited.

Hance, William Adams
1958   *African Economic Development.* New York: Harper.

Hasan, Yusuf Fadl
1973   *The Arabs and the Sudan: From the Seventh to the Early Sixteenth Century.* 3rd. rpt. Khartoum: Khartoum University Press.

Heinritz, Gunter
1978   Social Geographic Problems in the Khashm el Girba Project, Sudan. In *Land Reform, Land Settlement and Cooperatives*, vol. 2, pp. 25–35. Rome: Food and Agricultural Organization.

1980   The Rahad Scheme: A New Irrigation Project in the Sudan Republic. *Zeitschrift für Wirtschaftsgeographie* 24(3):81–87.

1982   The Migration of Westerners in the New Halfa and Rahad Schemes. In *Problems of Agricultural Development in the Sudan*, ed. Gunter Heinritz (selected papers of a seminar). Germany: Edition Herodot.

Hillelson, S.
1920   Historical Poems and Traditions of the Shukriya. *Sudan Notes and Records* 3:33–75.

Hitti, P.
1960   *History of the Arabs.* 7th ed. London: MacMillan and Company.

Holt, P. M.
1958   *The Mahdist State in the Sudan 1881–1898.* London: Clarendon Press.

1976   *A Modern History of the Sudan: From the Funj Sultanate to the Present Day.* 3rd ed., 4th rpt. London: Weidenfeld and Nicolson.

Horowitz, Michael M
1967   A Decision-making Model of Conjugal Patterns in Martinique. *Man* 2(3):445–453.

1972   Ethnic Boundary Maintenance among Pastoralists and Farmers in the Western Sudan (Niger). In *Perspectives on Nomadism*, ed. W. Irons and N. Dyson-Hudson, pp. 105–114. Leiden: E. J. Brill.

Hoyle, S.
1977   The Khashm el Girba Agricultural Scheme: An Example of an Attempt to Settle Nomads. In *Landuse and Development*, ed. Phil O'Keefe and Ben Wisner, pp. 116–131. London: International African Institute.

Idriss, Usman
1978   *mu'assasat halfa az-ziraaᶜya—ams wal-yawm* (The New Halfa Agricultural Corporation: Yesterday and Today). New Halfa: New Halfa Agricultural Production Corporation (in Arabic).

Keesing, Roger
1967   Statistical Models and Decision Making Models of Social Structure: A Kwaio Case. *Ethnology* 6(1):1–16.

Leach, E. R.
1961   *Pul Eliya: A Village in Ceylon.* Cambridge: Cambridge University Press.

Leclair, E., and H. K. Schneider, eds.
1968   *Economic Anthropology.* New York: Holt, Rinehart and Winston.

Little, P. D., and M. M Horowitz
1987   Subsistence Crops Are Cash Crops: Some Comments with Reference to Eastern Africa. *Human Organization* 46(3):254–258.

Little, Tom
  1965   *High Dam at Aswan: The Subjugation of the Nile.* New York: John
              Day Company.
Long, Norman
  1977   *An Introduction to the Sociology of Rural Development.* London:
              Tavistock Publications Limited.
MacMichael, H. A.
  1967   *A History of the Arabs in the Sudan.* 2 vols., rpt. London: Frank
              Cass and Company.
Meillassoux, Claude
  1972   From Reproduction to Production. *Economy and Society* 1(1):93–105.
  1978   Kinship Relations and Relations of Production. In *Relations of Pro-
              duction*, ed. David Seddon, pp. 127–158. London: Frank Cass and
              Company Limited.
  1981   *Maidens, Meal and Money: Capitalism and the Domestic Commu-
              nity.* Cambridge: Cambridge University Press.
Moris, J.
  1987   Irrigation as a Privileged Solution in African Development. *Devel-
              opment Policy Review* 15(2):99–123.
Moris, J., D. J. Thom, et al.
  1987   *African Irrigation Overview: Main Report.* WMS II Report 37. Logan:
              Utah University Press.
Moxon, James
  1969   *The Volta Resettlement Experience.* New York: Frederick A. Praeger.
Musham, H. V.
  1959   Sedentarization of the Bedouin in Israel. In Nomads and Nomad-
              ism in the Arid Zone. *International Social Science Journal*
              11(4):539–549.
New Halfa Agricultural Production Corporation (NHAPC)
  n.d.   Corporation Files. New Halfa.
New Halfa Farmers' Union
  n.d.   Farmers' Union Files. New Halfa.
Ortiz, Sutti
  1967   Decision Making among Indians of Colombia. In *Themes in Eco-
              nomic Anthropology*, ed. Raymond Firth, pp. 181–228. London:
              Tavistock Publications Limited.
  1973   *Uncertainties in Peasant Farming.* London: Athlone Press.
  1979   The Effects of Risk Aversion Strategies on Subsistence and Cash
              Crop Decisions. In *Risk, Uncertainty and Agricultural Develop-
              ment*, ed. J. A. Roumasset et al., pp. 231–246. New York: Agricul-
              tural Development Council.
Pearson, M.
  1980   *Settlement of Pastoral Nomads: A Case Study of the New Halfa
              Irrigation Scheme.* Development Studies Occasional Paper No. 5.
              Norwich, V. K.: University of East Anglia.
Polanyi, Karl
  1957   The Economy as Instituted Process. In *Trade and Markets in Early
              Empires*, ed. K. Polanyi, C. Arensberg, and H. Pearson, pp. 243–270.
              New York: Free Press.

Prattis, J. I.
1982   Synthesis, or a New Problematic in Economic Anthropology. *Theory and Society* 11(2):205–228.

Quinn, Naomi
1973   Do Mfantse Fish Sellers Estimate Probabilities in Their Heads?
American Ethnologist 5:206–226.

Reeves, Edward B., and Timothy Frankenberger
1981   *Socioeconomic Constraints to the Production, Distribution and Consumption of Sorghum, Millet and Cash Crops in North Kordofan,
Sudan: A Farming Systems Approach.* Report No. 1. Lexington:
University of Kentucky.

Reining, Conrad C.
1966   *The Zande Scheme: Anthropological Case Study of Economic Development in Africa.* Evanston, Ill.: Northwestern University Press.

Rondinelli, D. A.
1983   *Secondary Cities in Developing Countries: Policies for Diffusing
Urbanization.* Beverly Hills: Sage Publications.

Salem-Murdock, Muneera
1979   *The Impact of Agricultural Development on a Pastoral Society: The
Shukriya of Eastern Sudan.* IDA Working Paper No. 17. Binghamton,
N.Y.: Institute for Development Anthropology.

1984   Nubian Farmers and Arab Herders in Irrigated Agriculture in the
Sudan: From Domestic to Commodity Production. Ph.D. dissertation, State University of New York at Binghamton.

1987   Rehabilitation Efforts and Household Production Strategies: The
New Halfa Agricultural Scheme in Eastern Sudan. In *Lands at Risk*,
ed. Peter Little and Michael Horowitz, pp. 337–351. Binghamton,
N.Y.: Institute for Development Anthropology.

Salzman, P. C.
1972   Multi-Resource Nomadism in Iranian Baluchistan. *Journal of Asian
and African Studies* 7:60–68.

Scudder, Thayer
1973   The Human Ecology of Big Projects: River Basin Development and
Resettlement. In *Annual Review of Anthropology*, ed. B. Siegel,
pp. 45–55. Palo Alto: Annual Reviews.

1975   Resettlement. In *Man-Made Lakes and Human Health*, ed. F. Stanley
and M. P. Alpers, pp. 453–470. London: Academic Press for Institute of Biology.

1976   Social Impacts of River Basin Development on Local Populations. In
*River Basin Development: Politics and Planning: Proceedings of the
United Nation Inter-regional Basin and Inter-basin Development*,
pp. 45–52. Budapest: Institute for Hydraulic Documentation and
Education.

1981   *The Development Potential of New Lands Settlement in the Tropics
and Subtropics: A Global State-of-the-Art Evaluation with Specific
Emphasis on Policy Implications.* Binghamton, N.Y.: Institute for
Development Anthropology.

1988   The African Experience with River Basin Development: Achievements to Date, the Role of Institutions, and Strategies for the Future.
Cooperative Agreement in Human Settlements and Natural Resource
Systems Analysis. Unpublished ms., Clark University and the Institute for Development Anthropology.

Scudder, Thayer, and Elizabeth Colson
1979   *Long Term Field Research in Social Anthropology.* New York: Academic Press.
1981   From Welfare to Development: A Conceptual Framework for the Analysis of Dislocated People. In *Involuntary Migration and Resettlement: The Problems and Responses of Dislocated Peoples,* ed. Art Hansen and Anthony Oliver-Smith, pp. 267–288. Boulder, Colo.: Westview Press.
Smith, Carol A.
1976   Analyzing Regional Social Systems. In *Regional Analysis*, vol. 2, ed. Carol Smith, pp. 3–20. New York: Academic Press.
Sørbø, Gunnar
1973   Scheme-and of-Scheme Interests. Unpublished M.A. thesis, University of Bergen.
1977a   *How to Survive Development: The Story of New Halfa.* Monograph No. 6, Development Studies and Research Centre, Khartoum: University of Khartoum.
1977b   Nomads on the Scheme: A Study of Irrigation Agriculture and Pastoralism in Eastern Sudan. In *Landuse and Development*, ed. Phil O'Keefe and Ben Wisner, pp. 132–150. London: International African Institute.
1985   *Tenants and Nomads in Eastern Sudan: A Study in Economic Adaptation in the New Halfa Scheme.* Uppsala: Scandinavian Institute of African Studies.
Staudt, Kathleen A.
1982   Women Farmers and Inequalities in Agricultural Services. In *Women and Work in Africa*, ed. Edna G. Bay, pp. 207–224. Boulder, Colo.: Westview Press.
Sudan Agricultural Bank, New Halfa Branch
1980   *Annual Report.* New Halfa: Sudan Agricultural Bank.
UNESCO
1959   Nomads and Nomadism in the Arid Zone. *International Social Science Journal* 11(4):481–595.
Wingate, Major F. R.
n.d.   Ten Years' Captivity in the Mahdi's Camp 1882–1892. (From the original manuscript of Father Joseph Ohrwalder, late priest of the Austrian Mission Station at Delen, Kordofan.) 13th ed. revised and abridged. London: Sampson Low, Marston and Company Limited.
Wood, Charles
1981   Structural Changes and Household Strategies: A Conceptual Framework for the Study of Rural Migration. *Human Organization* 40:338–344.
Woodhouse, Philip
1988   *The Green Revolution and Food Security in Africa: Issues in Research and Technology Development.* Development Policy and Practice Research Group. Working Paper No. 10. Milton Keynes, U.K.: Open University.
Yousif, H. M.
1985   An Integrated Economic-Demographic Theoretical Framework for the Analysis of the Factors Related to the Rural Labour Force in the Gezira Scheme: A Micro Household Level Analysis. Ph.D. dissertation, University of Pennsylvania.

Index

199